44,50

Black politics
and urban crisis
in Britain

This book examines the race and immigration issues by considering the nature of the black 'constituency' and its political responses to issues related to the crisis of Britain's inner cities. It centrally examines black access to and integration into the public policy process and views public policy responses and how these affect black politics. American experience provides a 'model' against which the British approach is viewed.

The book looks at the background to the crisis, and its roots in economic decline. It also elaborates the historical development of government policy and legislation towards race and immigration, and the impact of community relations agencies, housing and education policy, and immigrant legislation. Black political action is considered, with particular emphasis on interest-group activity and community organization.

A concluding chapter looks at various policy options affecting blacks in Britain, comparing British and American approaches to community development and participation.

Black politics and urban crisis in Britain

Brian D. Jacobs

Senior Lecturer, Department of International Relations and Politics, North Staffordshire Polytechnic

The right of the
University of Cambridge
to print and sell
all manner of books
was granted by
Henry VIII in 1534.
The University has printed
and published continuously
since 1584.

CAMBRIDGE UNIVERSITY PRESS

Cambridge
London   New York   New Rochelle
Melbourne   Sydney

Published by the Press Syndicate of the University of Cambridge
The Pitt Building, Trumpington Street, Cambridge CB2 1RP
32 East 57th Street, New York, NY 10022, USA
10 Stamford Road, Oakleigh, Melbourne 3166, Australia

First published 1986

Printed in Great Britain at the University Press, Cambridge

British Library cataloguing in publication data

Jacobs, Brian D.
Black politics and urban crisis in Britain.
1. Great Britain – Social policy   2. City
planning – Great Britain   3. Blacks – Great
Britain – Political activity
I. Title
307'.12'0941   HT133

Library of Congress cataloguing in publication data

Jacobs, Brian D. (Brian David), 1950–
Black politics and urban crisis in Britain.

Bibliography: p.
Includes index.
1. Blacks – Great Britain – Politics and government.
2. Great Britain – Social policy.   3. Great Britain –
Politics and government – 1979–   .   4. Great Britain
– Race relations.   I. Title.
DA125.N4J33   1986   305.8'96042   85–26994

ISBN 0 521 30841 0

Contents

Acknowledgements

I wish to thank all those individuals and organizations who have co-operated with the research for this book between 1976 and 1985. Without their assistance the present study would not have been possible. I also wish to thank those who have helped in the preparation of the present text: Diane Aitkin, who assisted with the production of the early drafts and, in particular, Nicola Pike, who typed and proofread the entire text in its final form. Thanks also go to Christine Poile who helped me to conduct some of the interviews associated with the research in 1982 and also to the North Staffordshire Polytechnic and the British Association for American Studies for funding part of the research exercise.

The author and publisher wish to thank the following, who have kindly given permission for the use of copyright and other material: Birmingham Community Relations Council for data in Tables 8 and 9; the Commission for Racial Equality for reproduction of the Commission's structure chart in Table 4 and for the analysis of its annual expenditure in Table 5; the Greater London Council for the information in Table 6; the Controller of HM Stationery Office for reproduction of statistical data in Table 1 and the National Council for Civil Liberties for extensive quotations in Chapter 6.

Needless to say, the views presented in the book are entirely my own.

BRIAN D. JACOBS

Abbreviations

AFFOR	All Faiths for One Race
ANL	Anti-Nazi League
ARCAEL	Anti-Racist Committee of Asians in East London
BCRC	Birmingham Community Relations Council
BIC	Business in the Community
BNCA	Brixton Neighbourhood Community Association
CAA	Community Action Agency
CAF	Charities Aid Foundation
CALC	Community Advisory Liaison Committee
CARD	Campaign Against Racial Discrimination
CBI	Confederation of British Industry
CCRL	Council for Community Relations in Lambeth
CDC	Community Development Corporation
CP	British Communist Party
CPI	Communist Party of India
CPM	Communist Party of India (Marxist)
CPML	Communist Party of India (Marxist-Leninist)
CRC	Community Relations Council
CRE	Commission for Racial Equality
CRO	Community Relations Officer
DOE	Department of the Environment
EC	Executive Committee
EMLC	Ethnic-Minority Liaison Committee
FIG	Financial Institutions Group
GCE	General Certificate of Education
GDP	Gross Domestic Product
GLC	Greater London Council

GLEB	Greater London Enterprises Board
IAP	Inner Area Programme (Urban Programme)
IWA	Indian Workers' Association
IWA (GB)	Indian Workers' Association (Great Britain)
IWA (Southall)	Indian Workers' Association (Southall)
LARRIE	Local Authorities Race Relations Information Exchange
LEA	Local Education Authority
LEntA	London Enterprise Agency
LIS (UK)	Local Initiative Support (United Kingdom)
LISC	Local Initiatives Support Corporation (United States)
MDC	Merseyside Development Corporation
MRE	Multi-Racial Education Service (Wolverhampton)
MSC	Manpower Services Commission
MTF	Merseyside Task Force
NCCI	National Committee for Commonwealth Immigrants
NCCL	National Council for Civil Liberties
NCVO	National Council for Voluntary Organizations
NF	National Front
OSG	Official Steering Group (Urban Programme)
PEP	Political and Economic Planning
PSI	Policy Studies Institute
PWA	Pakistan Welfare Association
RRB	Race Relations Board
RSG	Rate Support Grant
SCRO	Senior Community Relations Officer
SPG	Police Special Patrol Group
SWP	Socialist Workers' Party
SYM	Southall Youth Movement
TUC	Trades Union Congress
UDG	Urban Development Grant
UP	Urban Programme
WARC	Wolverhampton Anti-Racism Committee
WCCR	Wolverhampton Council for Community Relations
WMCA	West Midlands Caribbean Association (Wolverhampton)
WVSC	Wolverhampton Voluntary Sector Council
YMCA	Young Men's Christian Association
YTS	Youth Training Scheme (Manpower Services Commission)

Introduction: Black politics and urban crisis

This introduction is in two sections. The first section provides a description of the scope and nature of this study set against recent literature on race and urban politics and the second section examines the general urban setting against which black politics can most effectively be understood and which defines the nature of the 'urban crisis' affecting black political action. The introduction as a whole, therefore, makes a case for examining black politics and race issues as part of the broader urban political environment.

The literature on race and urban politics

A comprehensive study of black political responses to public policy relating to race and community relations in Britain today presents the individual researcher with a mammoth task, made greater by the enormous diversity of organizations representing the various segments of the 'black community'. Patterns of political activity vary widely – what may hold as a reasonable statement about black politics in, say, Bradford may not necessarily hold true in Southall or Brixton. Britain's black minorities have tended to develop their own local varieties of political expression, producing a multiplicity of responses to issues relating to urban deprivation, unemployment, racial harassment and so on.

Despite this, it is important to begin to make generalizations about black politics in Britain. There are certain important commonly exhibited characteristics of black organizations in different cities which enable the researcher to study a number of selected situations which may produce worthwhile conclusions about the public policy and political setting affecting black access to government and attitudes to government initiatives. It is therefore important to look at political actions with a view to the broader context of black political action and the activities of black political organizations. Given such a brief, this study concentrates upon political motivations which are set within a broad public policy environment. It therefore differs from the more common sociological approach to the study of black communities by stressing the impact of a range of policy settings upon the nature and extent of black co-operation with the state and private bodies and upon the consequent degree of 'integration' of black political groups into the British political system. The predominance of sociological studies highlights the need for the kind of political study which is offered here as a contribution to filling the long-standing research gap in British writings on race.

Ben-Tovim and Gabriel have suggested that one aspect of the 'under-development' of the field of political research relating to race in Britain concerns the attitudes of researchers and black organizations. The argument is that there seems to have been a reluctance by social scientists to engage in policy-related research and in empirical and analytical research about black political movements. Many have regarded research into black politics as a form of surveillance of benefit only to the state, while others have tended to regard the whole area of study as generally too sensitive for close analysis (Ben-Tovim and Gabriel, 1979).

There is some substance to this argument and some black organizations and researchers have indeed harboured genuine suspicions about such inquiry. In the 1980s, however, there seems to be emerging a change in attitude, as social scientists have come to regard such research as having potential benefits for black political activists who are keen to understand underlying political trends or who see the value of research which may be of direct relevance to policy makers.

British race research

The sociological studies of the 1960s and 1970s should in no way be undervalued in respect of their contribution to race-related research. The large literature about black communities has produced a greater understanding of many aspects of racism, racial disadvantage and urban deprivation. Some of this literature has dealt with many of the political consequences of social phenomena (Lawrence, 1974; Rex and Moore, 1967; Rex and Tomlinson, 1979) and has contributed to a fuller understanding of the characteristics of community-based black organizations and political associations, while other studies have provided vivid descriptions and analyses of the black experience (Bains, 1984; Banton, 1972; Berger and Mohr, 1975; Miles, 1982; Hiro, 1973). The literature also represents research into the sociological theory of race and ethnicity which has extended our knowledge of social structure and opened important debates about the relationships between race, class, caste and social action (Banton, 1972; Pearson, 1981; Rex, 1970; Rex and Tomlinson, 1979).

There is actually little in this literature, however, which provides the framework for a coherent analysis of black politics and interest groups in Britain. The same may be said for the literature which has, to date, concentrated on party political and electoral factors affecting blacks. Electoral studies have provided evidence of the lack of representation of blacks in British political institutions and have drawn attention to some of the difficulties faced by black politicians seeking office at national and local levels (Community Relations Commission, 1975; Deakin, 1965; Le Lohe, 1984). Fitzgerald (1984) has provided an excellent and detailed account of black participation in Britain's four major political parties, while Layton-Henry (1980) and Behrens and Edmonds (1981) have studied the relationship between blacks and the Conservative Party. Again, these studies have produced valuable insights into some major political issues facing blacks, but they have, nevertheless, failed to provide any general analytical framework within which black politics may be understood. Indeed, such works do not specifically set out to achieve such an objective, implicitly remaining content with descriptive and historical explanations of black responses to government policies and changing electoral conditions.

Katznelson (1973) probably provides the most comprehensive attempt to place blacks in the context of a wider political and administrative setting. Much of Katznelson's analysis of black politics in a hostile environment is policy-orientated and set within an analytical perspective, identifying a black political 'elite' which is becoming integrated into white political institutions. Katznelson's comparative research of Britain and the United States regards these political institutions as crucial in integrating blacks into what he regards as white racist societies. In Britain community relations bodies are seen to be instrumental in this process, blunting militant black demands and hindering the development of an independent black politics (Katznelson, 1970).

Despite some useful insights, Katznelson tends to deal in generalities and does not explain adequately *why* black political groups are prepared to play along with this close identification with community relations bodies. His study fails to provide an explanation of the process of integration by straightjacketing the analysis with an essentially passive conception of black organizations seen as victims of political isolation in a white power structure. This kind of analysis represents a view of black political participation emanating from the black-power period in the United States of the 1960s and early 1970s. The logic behind this thinking is that black politics can be either passive (accommodated within white society) or militant in defence of black interests. As will be seen in this study, such an 'either/or' choice is not relevant when viewing the relationships between black groups and governments in Britain in the 1980s.

More recent British works which have touched upon some of the broader issues considered by Katznelson have failed to meet the challenge raised by the position developed in the 1970s relating to black power and black autonomy. In many respects the British attempt to research black politics in the 1980s has taken a step backwards either by maintaining the partial perspective characteristic of electoral studies or by manifesting a confusing theoretical eclecticism. Often such work is contained in edited compilations which adopt a variety of research methodologies and which, under one cover, present quite diverse perspectives and conclusions about black political currents, social developments and urban deprivation (Centre for Contemporary Cultural Studies, 1982; Husband, 1982). This is not to devalue individual contributions which are quoted elsewhere in this book, but it underlines the general lack of coherence and theoretical unity which still pervades British race-related political research. Only one compilation, edited by Miles and Phizacklea (1979), comes anywhere near to developing a coherent political perspective (see their Chapter 1 in particular), but success in this effort is limited, with contributions seeming to adopt both social-class and implicitly non-class frames of analysis. A much clearer class analysis does, however, emerge in Miles and Phizacklea's (1984) further attempt to link the race issue with a political analysis of the black experience under capitalism. Again, this approach fails to adequately examine the policy process and 'administration of race' within the urban context and leaves the reader with a rather generalized view of black politics.

Urban politics and race

In contrast to race-related literature, there is much to be gained, with respect to political analysis, from the large body of literature which has concentrated upon the urban context affecting city-based pressure groups and communities. Black politics in Britain is essentially the politics of urban-based minorities who express their political demands at national and local level in terms of issues which largely relate to urban problems. The 'atomization' of black politics and the lack of a single national black political pressure group underscores the localization of so much black political activity. As with white community groups representing the inner city, black organizations compete for resources within an urban environment and liaise with urban agencies and central government departments in the process.

Cockburn (1977), Newton (1976) and Saunders (1979) have all pointed to the significance of the urban context. Their research has tended to be broad in coverage, looking at the nature of government policies, characteristics of the state and the position of pressure groups in relation to policy processes at national and local levels. These studies have covered the difficulties faced by pressure groups in gaining access to political structures and have alluded to the ways in which groups attempt to gain access to political institutions (Dearlove, 1973; Saunders, 1979). Explicitly the search for various degrees of participation is an activity which involves the attempts of groups (taken here to refer to organized political and other interest groups) to achieve economic gains for their members and/or to achieve a degree of political representation or access to the policy-making process. While there are many manifest differences between writers in the urban politics field, there seems to be wide acceptance of this question of access (explicitly or implicitly) as being of importance in providing one focus for research into the nature of urban policy processes and group interactions with governments. This book, therefore, follows Newton, Saunders and Dearlove in treating these interactions as a point of reference for explaining the dynamics of urban politics. Such an approach, related to black group activity and taking account of the useful areas of race-related research, will hopefully contribute to the meeting between urban political research and the field of race.

This meeting is one which is based on a selective acknowledgement of the contributions made in the urban field. Dunleavy correctly points out that there is no single coherent body of urban political analysis as such, despite the evident 'inter-action and common ground between different perspectives' (Dunleavy, 1980, p.21). Indeed, for Dunleavy, there has been debate over the precise scope and focus of 'urban' research and he quotes Williams (1971) who pointed to the 'catch-all' adjective 'urban', with respect to a wide variety of studies which have little theoretical affinity and which do not really exhibit anything intrinsically urban. The geographical focus of such urban analysis has thus sought to identify distinct urban characteristics which affect political activity and has de-emphasized the wider socio-economic and political environment in which these areas exist. Dunleavy calls for a redefinition of the urban field and a new approach to urban analysis which would break away from spatial or institutional definitions of the urban field and concentrate on a more broadly defined focus concerned with the impact of 'collective consumption'. The patterns of policy change in 'urban aspects of social life' could be explored more effectively by adopting such an approach (Dunleavy, 1980, p.163). Collective consumption here relates to the provision of public services (housing and transport, for example) by the state and analysis of this area would centre upon questions relating to the nature of the state and its class characteristics. Dunleavy alludes to Castells who argues that the urban spatial dimension is 'scarcely important' when looking at the development of production activities in advanced capitalist societies. Such a view expands the scope of urban analysis by relating urban political processes to the very nature of capitalism and the state.

By concentrating upon policy and the access question this study, however, immediately assumes a limitation. This is a study about politics in urban settings rather than a widely orientated urban study which treats the study of urban politics in the way described by Dunleavy. It does not set out to develop a theoretical argument which addresses Dunleavy's call for a broader analysis of these questions. This work is primarily concerned with policy questions and policy processes and not with the debate in urban political and sociological theory about the relationship between, for example, urban-based social movements and industrial or class-based politics.

Such questions are, of course, of immense importance in developing urban analysis. Castells (1975), for instance, within his broad urban perspective, draws a distinction between an urban politics and industrial class politics. According to this view 'urban struggles' entered into by particular groups do not constitute class struggles (in the Marxist sense) but are characterized by a 'reformism' which, unless linked to class struggle, prevents the development of working-class consciousness and the political mobilization of class interests (see Saunders, 1979, for a full discussion of this view). Other writers on urban politics have disagreed with this line of argument (Clarke and Ginsburg, 1975; Mingione, 1977, cited by Saunders) and have suggested that there is a connection between urban and class struggles and that this provides a more accurate description of the nature of urban social movements. The evidence presented in this book would seem to favour the critics of Castells insofar as the analysis points to a black politics which involves groups in raising demands which cover both specifically 'urban' and 'class' issues, or more correctly perhaps, 'urban class issues'. The distinction between urban issues and class-related questions is thus impossible to draw (Rex, 1979), particularly when the questions of black leadership and representation are raised. An examination of black representation, electoral behaviour, participation, leadership interests and social characteristics could potentially contribute as much to the understanding of black politics in Britain as such research has done in America, since it could address the question of differing *class* accommodations in society (Coleman and McLemore, 1982; Preston, 1982, for example). Preston's Chicago research uncovered some very crucial class-related issues which affected black community attitudes and 'antimachine' votes in primary elections – the Reverend Jessie Jackson's support for the 1979 transit strike and minority views on the teachers' strike and firefighters' dispute are examples of such urban class issues.

Urban, black policy research

As stated above, there will, however, be no theoretical treatment of the debate on class in this present work. The analysis of the nature of the interests of the state and of black groups is beyond the scope of this book, which is concerned with mapping the pattern of black political activity, establishing the parameters of black political debate, viewing the nature and extent of black integration into public and private institutions and programmes and looking at the broad impact of black groups on public policy.

Recognition of the need for such urban-related *policy research* relating to race has long been evident in Britain, as policy studies are produced comparing public policy approaches towards blacks on both sides of the Atlantic (Glazer and Young, 1983; Jacobs, 1982, 1983). These studies have revealed important differences between Britain and the USA which have indicated both the potential for black representation and political influence (USA) and the relative under-development of black politics in representative and representational terms (Britain). Even so, American studies have continued to concentrate on the relative disadvantage experienced by blacks even within a comparatively pluralist setting (Gilliam, 1975; Hillson, 1977; Levitan, 1980; O'Brien, 1975; Palmer and Sawhill, 1984; Perkins, 1975), which suggests that representation and access to governments are no guarantee that the special problems of blacks will be easily overcome. As these studies point out, the deeper societal problems of racism and discrimination intervene in political life to work against the 'equal' treatment of black demands and the 'equal' consideration by politicians and government officials of black needs.

An urban dimension for black politics

By adopting an urban overview in relation to 'equity' and other issues it may, of course, be argued that the urban context is one which affects black and white communities in the same way and that the concentration of research here upon ethnic minorities serves only to conceal this. The answer lies in a consideration of the distinctiveness of black politics and the fact that blacks experience certain problems which are not faced by native white or even white ethnic-minority communities (such as the Poles and Ukrainians). Racial discrimination on the grounds of colour is the most obvious problem special to black people in Britain. It adds a harsher edge to the urban condition by affecting employment and educational prospects and the political attainments of blacks seeking entry into the mainstream of British public life. Racial antagonisms may be covert rather than clearly manifest in society. Local politicians and government officials may resent black leaders and political organizations simply because they are black or because they are thought of as 'immigrant' (Reeves, 1983). Indeed, the 'alien' aspect of black politics is reflected in the need for special race-relations bodies designed to adapt black people to a 'host' society and 'native' political institutions (Hill and Issacharoff, 1971).

Adaptation is difficult, not only because of racist attitudes, but also because there exists a great ethnic and cultural diversity between black communities. The term 'black community' must be used with reservation, because there is no single 'black community' as such which could be taken to encompass all Britain's Afro/Caribbean and Asian minorities. The coverall term when used here is applied as a shorthand for describing all non-white or non-oriental ethnic minorities within the broader 'native' society. The 'black community', therefore, includes individuals, groups and organizations which represent an enormously diverse range of class, religious and cultural, racial and caste affiliations. This consequently exacerbates the difficulties for blacks relative to whites in attempting to come to terms with political practices and institutions in an urbanized society.

To illustrate this we may point to the so-called 'second generation' blacks who have never been to their parents' 'homelands'. They may be of Afro/

Caribbean origin, but may have spent all their lives in Brixton or Lambeth acting and speaking as Londoners. Cockney blacks from London and 'Scouse' blacks from Liverpool have little sentimental affinity with sunbathed islands across the Atlantic and focus their aspirations towards making a living in an urban environment beset with racial disharmony and social decline.

There are those who have emigrated to Britain, perhaps from the Punjab in India or from Jamaica. Many will have waited for years to arrive in Britain, playing a waiting game with the immigration authorities before being allowed to unite with families and relatives. They bring with them their own mother tongue, their religious beliefs and their cultural traditions, which are catered for by British-based immigrant groups, religious temples and churches and political and community associations. These associations place demands upon local authorities in attempting to promote the interests of their members and followers, but they do so in a society which is ill-equipped to meet the challenge posed by ethnic and cultural/religious diversity.

Government officials and politicians are at the receiving end of demands from black representatives, and it is highly unlikely that these demands will always be judged by those in positions of authority in a rational and dispassionate way. With planning applications, social welfare claims, housing and educational problems, blacks have experienced discrimination and have often been frustrated by the inequities of an administrative system which is at best bureaucratic and at worst lacking proper comprehension of the particular needs of black people.

Government and race: a problem area

Race and immigration have become interlinked with such social problems. Immigration, in particular, has been regarded as a 'problem' which is related to numerous tensions within urban communities (Humphry and Ward, 1974). Government's perception of race as a problem therefore provides a further distinctive characteristic of black politics, since it is within a framework where blacks are regarded in a *special* way that black political organizations have to operate. Black groups tend to be viewed by politicians as requiring special attention with respect to their qualifications to participate in community-relations institutions and as being in need of special allocations of money. Community-relations bodies, to some degree, thus exist in an environment which tends to separate blacks from government, with their own administrative arrangements, policies and minority programmes. This marks community-relations agencies out so that they can easily be criticized by politicians who may be seeking popular acclaim in the white community by attacking provisions for minorities.

Under such circumstances, government policy has reflected an apparent contradiction which in practice manifests itself as a 'dual' approach to policy affecting race and immigration. Firstly, central government has adopted physical measures of control to reduce the number of immigrants coming to Britain. The immigrant 'problem' has usually been formulated in terms of a problem of numbers, concentrating upon the flow of black immigrants into the UK (Foot, 1965). Restrict numbers coming in, it is argued by the pro-immigration lobby, and thereby relieve internal problems associated with settlement and assimilation of black minorities. The support for such arguments effected a significant reduction in immigrant numbers by the late 1970s following, in particular, legislation designed to reduce the inflow of Asians expelled from African nations such as Uganda in 1972. About 35,000 East African Asians were admitted to Britain in that year and over the next five years around 7,000 a year came, reducing in 1982 to about 4,500. By 1979, the total number of so-called 'New Commonwealth' and Pakistani immigrants was about 30,000, or about half the level of the early 1970s (Brown, 1983).

The other side of government policy has been the more liberal 'assimilationist' approach applied to offset some of the consequences of immigration itself and also to reduce racial tensions, which tend to be worsened when blacks are treated as a 'problem' in the first place. It was perfectly consistent for governments to implement both immigration control ('physical control') and 'social control' measures simultaneously, since the accommodation of black leaders within government agencies was generally regarded as beneficial to governments (Mason, 1982). Black 'assimilation' legitimated community-relations bodies at 'grass roots' level and channelled black political demands into the confines of a relatively manageable and low-cost administrative framework. However, the increasing integration of leaders imperceptibly created its own problems. From the late 1960s a gulf began slowly to widen between an older generation of essentially middle-class black community leaders and a growing number of disaffected, young, working-class blacks. Leaders were generally articulate, well-educated and committed to the values traditionally associated with 'homeland' cultures. The young were more anglicized, with the experience of poor education, unemployment and social hardship which produced bitterness and hostility towards government agencies and programmes and even towards community leaders.

Co-operation with community-relations bodies, politicians and government appeared to many to have produced little in the way of economic returns for black communities and little which young blacks could readily identify with (Bridges, 1981). Community leaders had become ensconced in local authority committees, police liaison committees and in the Commission for Racial Equality. In London's Brixton, Liverpool's Toxteth and Manchester's Moss Side, the tangible results of such representation were often hard to distinguish as far as the young unemployed were concerned. Leaders perceived the benefits of participation differently because it afforded them an opportunity of access which led to the local town hall or to government departments in Whitehall. This may, indeed, have produced economic or welfare commitments from government, but that was a fine point to those at the lower end of the social scale, experiencing the blunt end of racial antagonism and economic adversity.

In this situation the 'generation gap' was transformed into a credibility gap in which the 'unorganized' came to be frustrated with the slow-moving procedures of local government and the Community Relations Councils and in which a feeling of cynicism and rejection of the 'usual channels' developed. The 1981 'riots', which involved both blacks and whites, seemed to stem partly from this growing mood of pent-up frustration rather than from any concerted organized political design. Despite allegations made by some politicians that the disturbances were instigated by 'outside' agitators there was no evidence to support this claim (Scarman Report, 1981). It may also be argued that there was no hard evidence to support the argument that the events were the result of a process of disaffection which began many years prior to the communal disturbances. There is, indeed, little in the way of substantial research which points to this, but it seems reasonable to assume that such dramatic events do not simply happen by accident or purely as the result of isolated local incidents and that social tensions develop within a broader political, social and economic environment which shapes the preconditions for urban violence and which generates foundations for social conflict.

Urban crisis

These problems are part of an 'urban crisis' which also involves a crisis of political leadership in the black community, since these are issues which black leaders are forced to contend with but in which success has not always been dramatically forthcoming. This is instanced by reference to the problem of unemployment and the position of young blacks. The black population is, on average, younger than the population as a whole, with the majority of older blacks having been born overseas (Brown, 1983). Consequently, black youth has to compete for educational resources and housing within an urban environment that restricts access to these provisions. Community leaders are involved in a political process which limits expectations as to what is obtainable from the economic system and what can reasonably be expected from pressure-group activity. The 'realities' of the situation have tended to produce a cautious attitude on social issues, which many black leaders prefer to be handled in such a way as not to impair their good relations with officials and decision-making politicians. This relatively low-key approach simply throws into relief the overall lack of impact which black demands have had with respect to the elimination of inner-city unemployment. Blacks in the United States, by contrast, have effected significant social and political changes through community agencies and through effective representation in national and local government (Preston, Henderson and Puryear, 1982). In Britain blacks are still waiting to attain the influence which may help them to meet Britain's pressing urban problems more effectively.

A recent House of Commons Environment Committee Report (HC, 18i–iii, 1983) illustrated the scale of these problems and, when looking at Merseyside, implied that inner-urban deprivation had a significant impact upon social tensions. A memorandum prepared by Dr K. Young indicated some of the problems which have contributed to urban stress, covered by the Department of the Environment's indicators used to assess local authorities under the Inner Urban Areas Act, 1978. The indicators were: mortality rate; unemployment; single-parent households; households lacking exclusive use of basic amenities; residents in New Commonwealth and Pakistani households; and population change between 1971 and 1981. The DOE makes calculations which facilitate comparisons under each of these headings and local authority 'profiles' are produced to assess levels of 'multiple deprivation'. Deprivation may be expressed by examining the frequency with which particular authorities appear in the 'worst fifty' and 'worst ten' on each indicator. The DOE calculates scores for each indicator which may be summed to provide a measure of 'the total level of deprivation' in an area.

Liverpool, scene of some of the most serious disturbances in 1981, featured six times out of eight in the 'worst fifty' and twice in the 'worst ten' with respect to population loss and unemployment. Liverpool's total deprivation score was exceeded only by Birmingham, Manchester and Lambeth (containing Brixton) in London. Unemployment showed up as a particularly pressing problem in all of Britain's other major cities. Among these, Merseyside's core (within the Department of the Environment's so-called Partnership Area designated in the City of Liverpool) had the highest unemployment rate, the highest youth unemployment rate, the highest proportion of chidren in households receiving supplementary benefit and the lowest proportion of households having a car. Young (HC, 18iii, 1983) showed that Liverpool's unemployment rate had been consistently high since the Second World War, but had worsened dramatically recently relative to other areas of other conurbations (see Table 1).

Table 1. *Percentage unemployment rates in the inner areas of the six major conurbations, 1951–81.*

Inner Area	1951	1961	1971	1981
London	2.5	3.1	5.9	11.8
West Midlands	1.2	1.4	4.8	15.2
Manchester	2.0	3.8	8.2	15.8
Merseyside	4.5	5.8	9.8	19.8
Tyneside	4.0	4.6	9.4	14.1*
Clydeside	4.5	6.0	9.0	19.2
Great Britain	2.1	2.8	5.2	10.9

*Owing to boundary changes, this figure is not comparable with those of earlier years.
Source: *Cambridge Economic Policy Review*, December 1982, reproduced for the House of Commons Environment Committee, May 1983.

Young's survey compared Merseyside's economy with other areas. Like them, Merseyside's inner areas had received substantial inputs of resources from expanding industries in the 1950s and 1960s, but by the 1980s economic expansion had given way to population decline and economic stagnation, transforming Merseyside from an area of great potential to an area of 'serious concern'. Young also pointed to the argument which saw the area as a 'branch-line economy' where employment was vulnerable to the disinvestment decisions of large multi-national companies able to shift investment from place to place on an international basis.[1]

Birmingham, in the West Midlands, may also be cited as a case of inner urban decline. Until the late 1970s, Birmingham was often held up as an example of rapid growth, urban prosperity and dynamic civic pride. In 1982 Birmingham's Inner City Partnership (bringing together representatives of central government, the City Council, the West Midlands County Council and Birmingham Health Authorities) produced its *Inner City Profile* (1982a) and its *Inner City Partnership Programme* for 1983–6 (1982b). The major characteristics of the inner area of Birmingham were summarized as follows:

(1)   Between 1979 and 1982 total employment in the Partnership Area fell by 20%. Between 1979 and 1982 there was a net loss of 46,000 manufacturing jobs in the Area.

(2)   Between 1979 and 1982 the number of registered unemployed in the Area rose by 145%, representing a 22.8% level of unemployment. In some inner-city wards the rate of unemployment was nearer 35%.

(3)   Youth unemployment over the two years to 1982 had risen by 67% in the Area (i.e. for those under 19 years old).

(4)   One in six of the city's unemployed belonged to ethnic minority groups. The proportion in the central Partnership Area was as high as 50% at some employment offices.

(5)   In the very core of the city one in eight households was reported to be overcrowded, compared with one in 22 for the rest of the city.

(6)   24.8% of Core Area residents were born in the New Commonwealth and Pakistan and 43.1% of residents belonged to households where the head of the household had been born in the New Commonwealth or Pakistan.

(7)   Young males under the age of 25 accounted for 36% of the unemployed ethnic minorities.

(8)   Between 1961 and 1981 the Core Area had lost 40% of its population.

(9)   The Core Area suffered from a high proportion of outdated and obsolescent industrial premises. Over 50% of stock was over 50 years old, 37% being pre-1914. It was estimated that 80% of firms operated on unsatisfactory sites. In addition, there was over half-a-million square metres of empty manufacturing space (Birmingham Inner City Partnership, 1982b, pp. 9–12).

The political responses of black and white urban communities are moulded by the intricate interlacing of these social and economic problems. The political economy of urban politics, seen in these terms, indicates an unfavourable climate within which political groups have to operate. Public expenditure restraints reduce the ability of local governments to provide funds for communities and this in turn affects the degree to which community leaders can obtain returns resulting from their co-operation with governments. The success or otherwise of leaders in this respect influences the attitudes of the broader community and the more politicized elements in the community (Walker, 1983). Under such circumstances even marginal changes in the economic fortunes of groups may come to assume great political significance. Tightly controlling the real returns to communities in economic terms poses a problem for governments and for 'moderate' community leaders who are keen to maintain broad consent for policies within the communities affected by particular resource decisions. In practical terms, the incrementalist pragmatism of local black leaders in times of economic adversity generally has the effect of heightening their desire simply to defend the resources which their groups currently possess rather than to extend their demands to achieve more than just potentially marginal benefits (see Chapter 5). Adversity may simultaneously invoke a more measured attitude towards resource-constraining governments which pose a threat to the prevailing commitments but in turn produce a 'militantly defensive' position on the part of moderate black organizations (a stand which was frequently adopted following the 1981 disturbances). Adversity also creates a defensiveness on resource commitments by governments which changes the terms of debate about resource allocations and leaves groups 'demanding' resources which in better times would probably have been met rather more readily. In this respect current urban political debate is essentially about issues of marginality rather than about fundamental changes in resource allocations or changes in political and economic structures, the 'legitimate' reference points of this debate being determined largely by the magnitude and pattern of deployment of available economic resources (see Chapter 5).

The impact of restraint

The public-expenditure problem facing the cities needs to be more clearly defined if these assertions are to take on a concrete meaning. The full impact of public expenditure constraint began to be felt as a really serious crisis around 1980, when central government further tightened its control over central and local expenditure. The decisive abandonment of the Keynesian demand management approach by the Conservative government demanded strict control of public spending and monetary expansion within the economy. In practice this objective was difficult to achieve, despite increasingly concerted efforts by the Treasury to bring spending under control. By 1984–5 the government seemed to be hoping for more or less 'no growth' in real government spending, implying a significant reduction in spending in certain important programme areas. The overall situation is illustrated in Table 2, which shows public expenditure variations between 1979–80 and (planned) 1985–6 (HM Treasury, 1984).

With regard to local-authority expenditure, it was estimated at the end of 1984 that there would be strict cash restrictions amounting to a cash slowdown in expenditure by 1985–6, with particularly severe restraints being imposed on capital spending. Programme expenditures, such as housing and transport, were expected to fall, while others, such as education, were expected actually to increase slightly in cash terms.

These government expectations, of course, tend always to be subject to change, as individual local-authority spending reflects a combination of central and local spending objectives. In general, however, particular local attempts to go beyond centrally set targets were facing increasing obstacles by 1985, which severely restricted local discretion. Travers (1984a) showed that many local authorities had actually managed to spend increasing sums on certain services between 1981 and 1983, in spite of central government penalties against 'over-spending' authorities. Even so, by 1984–5 the situation facing local authorities was one of a systematic attempt by the centre to reduce grant-related real expenditure, control local rates (property taxes) and even abolish high-spending Metropolitan authorities and the Greater London Council.

Travers (1984b) points to proposed reductions in expenditure financed by

Table 2. *Public expenditure planning totals, 1979–80 to 1985–6*

	Cash	Planning Total Cost terms, base year 1983–4	£ billion Public expenditure as 1% of gross domestic product
1979–80	76.9	111.7	39.5
1980–1	92.7	113.5	42.0
1981–2	104.7	116.5	43.5
1982–3	113.4	118.4	43.0
1983–4	120.3	120.3	42.5
1984–5	126.3	120.6	42.0
1985–6	132.0	120.6	41.0

Notes: 1.   Based on table reproduced in HM Treasury (1984).
2.   Cost-terms column indicates cash figures adjusted for inflation.
3.   Figures for 1984–5 and 1985–6 are estimates.
4.   Expenditure as a percentage of gross domestic product (GDP) relates to the planning total plus net debt interest, refunded payments of value added tax by local authorities and central government, and an allowance for non-trading government capital consumption, expressed as a percentage of GDP at market prices.
5.   Figures for 1979–80 to 1983–4 are actual or estimated expenditures; figures for 1984–5 and 1985–6 are planning figures.

central grants and the effects of capping the rates.[2] In looking at the 1984 Rate Support Grant (RSG) settlement, Travers indicated that for 1985–6 the grant percentage support was to be cut from 51.9% to 48.7%. His figures indicate a yearly reduction in support in terms of planned and outturn/budgeted spending each year since the introduction of the present block grant system in 1981–2. Travers also makes the point that central penalties against over-spenders would be increased under the terms of the 1984 settlement, with rate capping contributing further to their problems, although a number of rate-capped councils would actually experience small increases in their grants under the complex system in which grant calculations are made. Local authorities, such as Sheffield, would face real expenditure reductions and grant reductions, forcing the issue of large cuts in local services onto the political agenda.[3] If these factors are taken into account alongside reductions in the Urban Programme (see Chapter 7) and cuts in regional incentives to industry, then local authorities can be seen to be facing possibly the most testing time in the whole history of local government.

Perhaps the most dramatic illustration of this to date is the plight of Liverpool City Council. In 1984 the Council faced the prospect of insolvency as the Labour-controlled authority came into conflict with the Secretary of State for the Environment on the spending issue. At one stage the local authority was preparing to pass an illegal budget which would transgress central spending limits and prevent widespread public sector redundancies. Midwinter (1985), in an article in the *Local Government Chronicle*, suggests that the appalling problem was partly created by the city's former Liberal administration and by rapid population loss in the city reducing its rates base. In 1984 Labour were in the position of proposing a £262 million budget, involving a £161 million shortfall after grants had been taken into account and assuming a 9% rates increase.

Eventually a compromise was worked out between the Council and the Secretary of State. The Council revised its expenditure growth downwards from £22 million to just £1.6 million, with no major concessions being made by the government on grant or targets and penalties (Midwinter, 1982, p.19). The government did, however, increase Liverpool's Urban Programme allocation and announced the provision of £0.5 million expenditure on 'environmental works', plus a modest housing subsidy. All this was in return for a legal budget. By 1985, however, Liverpool was joined by the London Borough of Lambeth in passing budgets which were assumed to be illegal, and at the time of writing these local authorities were therefore heading for renewed confrontation with central government over the issue of local government finance.

This author has also examined other central/local conflicts over spending (Jacobs, 1984a), where Labour authorities have clashed with the Conservative government over spending controls. While such disputes have been contained so far, there is no guarantee that future clashes will not create serious constitutional and legal problems for the government and pose doubts as to whether the present local government financing system is to survive. City 'bankruptcies' would, for instance, raise questions about the whole viability of local autonomy during a period of economic stringency and about the efficacy of strengthened central control of local affairs.

The crisis defined

In the light of everything said so far, it is hardly surprising that there seems to be a general consensus (Lawless, 1981, p.13) amongst urban commentators that the main cause of the urban crisis is economic. Economic resources affect political debate about race relations, employment, housing, education, social services and community development. These areas are affected by national economic conditions and particularly by the decline in Britain's manufacturing industries and the inability of even strongly interventionist governments to halt inner-urban decline. In summary this provides a definition of urban crisis involving:

(1)   The general decline of urban and, in particular, inner-urban economies in terms of their industrial bases, producing unemployment and a range of other social and economic problems.

(2)   Under these circumstances, local authorities have experienced serious problems in maintaining local services and have been subjected to severe economic restraints and cut-backs affecting those services.

(3)   Resource scarcity in times of adversity has narrowed the conception of what is legitimate in terms of group demands and shifted group politics towards more marginal considerations, with groups seeking to maximize the political and economic benefits accruing from co-operation with public and private sectors (Chapters 7 and 8).

Social and economic conditions have produced communal tensions in the cities, which represent a problem for all community leaders (black and white), elected politicians and political institutions. This problem is a political one and involves moderate leaders in a quest to bridge the gulf between themselves and the 'unorganized', and an attempt to maintain social peace. For national and local governments the desire to maintain stability relates to the effective integration of groups (black and white) into legitimate political processes.

The urban-economics literature provides evidence of the structural determinants of the urban problem and of the sectoral differences within the urban economy which produce both areas of decline and areas of expansion in some industries. Watkins (1980) illustrates this differentiation very clearly within the context of a general urban problem. The urban crisis, therefore, should not be regarded simply as an absolute problem, but rather as one involving the *relative* decline of economic sectors which has produced *political* problems for urban areas (Cameron, 1980) and urban social groups with special race-related problems providing an overlay for the politics of black communities.

Black politics and urban crisis

This, then, is the backdrop against which black politics in Britain is viewed. The study begins with an examination of the race and immigration 'problem' area and then considers the nature of the black 'constituency' and its political responses to issues related to the urban crisis and black access to and integration into the public-policy process.

Chapter 1: Race and policy

Chapter 1 examines the historical development of government policy towards race and immigration and alludes to the nature of legislation in this area. Mention is made of the prevailing political movements and social situations affecting central policy initiatives and the way in which government policy has tended to adopt strict physical controls on immigration during periods of open conflict between the black and the white communities. The chapter outlines the development of the community-relations agencies and the urban pro-gramme, which formed the 'social control' and 'harmonization' aspect of government policy intended to counteract the more abrasive effects of immigration legislation. 'Harmony' effectively came to stand for policies and programmes which fostered the co-operation of black community groups and the identity of these groups, to greater or lesser degrees, with more formal administrative political structures at national and local levels.

Chapter 2: The black constituency

This chapter is concerned with the 'grass roots' nature of black organizations and their impact in black communities. A description of some of the more important political and 'non-political' black groups in Wolverhampton, in the West Midlands, is provided, showing that black political activity around the various agencies established by central and local government is influenced by the strategic implantation of organizations in localities, and by the traditions embodied in diverse cultural and religious beliefs and practices.

Traditionalism modifies the political orientation of groups, discouraging some from participating in 'white society' while more modernist community leaders tend to be more willing to take part in political activities and programmes which they feel will benefit their own organizations. Because of the differences between groupings it is necessary to distinguish between leaderships with respect to their attitudes and ideologies and in particular to analyse the reactions of 'politicized' leadership types to various communal conflicts and issues.

Chapter 3: Black political action

'Black political action' proposes a framework for understanding these leadership motivations. The argument presented is that leaders generally value their participation within local and national agencies because there are a number of important benefits to be obtained from participation which enhance the legitimacy of black politicians, increase their status and chances of social success and promise economic rewards in terms of government grants and subsidies. The 'costs' of participation are regarded by leaders as being of less importance set against these benefits, to the extent that the majority of black organizations seek access to government agencies and politicians.

While this spirit of co-operation in the 1960s and 1970s facilitated the drawing of black politics into legitimate channels of expression, it tended to increase the isolation of black leaders from their rank and file organizations and from the broader 'unorganized' black community. The gulf which separated leaders socially and sometimes politically from the 'black constituency' began to grow. In order to enjoy the benefits of participation and at the same time defend their groups and maintain their own positions, black leaders tended to 'balance' between the aspirations and demands of the community (sometimes expressed in militant terms by black political activists) and the expectations of white politicians concerned to preserve ordered policy processes and decision-making.

Chapter 4: The race industry

This chapter assesses the role of the Commission for Racial Equality as an agency promoting black participation. The Commission, a much criticized agency, acts as a focus of black opinion and as an agency which promotes and funds voluntary organizations and local Community Relations Councils. In the 1980s black organizations are likely to be increasingly involved in government programmes and the Commission for Racial Equality, at national level, will be forced to adapt to a situation in which local agencies increasingly come to be a central arena for black political activists.

The chapter discusses participation in local Community Relations Councils and outlines the nature of the local structures which are linked to the national Commission for Racial Equality. It will be seen that the local Community Relations Councils are heavily involved in youth, educational, housing and employment programmes and afford community leaders a valuable platform for their views on these important areas of public policy. Community Relations Councils are integrative agencies, in that they consolidate the leadership status of moderate representatives and enhance their prospects for making an impact on local policy processes.

Chapter 5: Housing and education: compromise and consent

Chapter 5 looks in detail at the role of the local Community Relations Council in Wolverhampton with regard to its attitude towards housing and education in the town. As in other towns and cities, the Community Relations Council, the local authority, central government departments and black organizations exist side by side within the context of the local administrative structure, affecting a broad range of issues. It is here that we can best identify an area of ordered consultation and decision-making which is governed by certain accepted 'rules of the game'. Black organizations attune their demands and their group strategies and objectives to the prevailing ordered processes and work with agencies to ensure a relatively stable political environment. This attitude does not always bring results and on occasion groups may adopt a more critical stance in the face of economic constraints which limit local government's ability to produce tangible benefits for community organizations.

Chapter 6: Riot and dissent

Having viewed a relatively ordered political environment, attention turns to a turbulent one. The disturbances of summer 1981 served to highlight the consequences of the divide which had grown up between the 'unorganized' and the community leaders. Events prior to 1981 saw street violence associated with politicized demonstrations and protests organized by the Anti-Nazi League and others. These protests themselves often went beyond the control of the organizers, threatening their ability to maintain order and effectively challenging the authority of community leaders. Subsequent riots arose from spontaneous actions taken mainly by youths against the police. Communal disturbance became divorced from politicized protest and challenged the viability and effectiveness of existing mechanisms created to handle black demands. The mainstream black leadership had a direct interest in re-establishing its authority and appealed for calm, while adopting a critical attitude towards government policy which would strike a popular chord in the community. The leaders responded by encouraging their members and supporters to abandon violence in exchange for seeking redress of grievances through established political structures. In this way community leaders played an important role in turning the black community back to their traditional political organizations.

Despite the seriousness of the 1981 events, the black leadership was *not* deposed. Once traditional leaders asserted their positions they were able to present themselves as the articulate and informed spokesmen for their communities. However, in the more politicized disturbances (Southall, 1979, and in the East End), active militant elements participating in the protests were potentially better placed to pose a challenge to traditional leaders. The demands of militants could be directed positively against 'moderates', who could be accused of compliance with the police and government representatives, and such demands galvanized dissenters organizationally around left groupings and left-orientated 'defence committees'.

In Britain the 1981 riots in Brixton were the subject of an inquiry conducted by Lord Scarman. The Scarman Report is examined in this chapter from two points of view. Firstly, the attitude of black organizations to Scarman is described with reference to the report itself. Consultation with black leaders again revealed their desire to return to ordered consultation. Secondly, attention is drawn to the concern of Scarman with police meaures designed to deal with any future disturbances. Scarman thus represented a reaction to the riots which combined emphasis upon the 'physical' side of public policy to communal problems and upon social policies intended to ease inner-city tensions.

Chapter 7: Urban renewal

Chapter 7 deals with the 'community development' side of public policy and responses to the riots. It is true that Scarman was, to some extent, concerned with community-relations management through social reform, but it is in the area of urban renewal initiatives that a more defined social and economic programme for reform and urban change emerges. The public and private initiatives described in this chapter were not all designed to cater specifically for the black community, but the policies adopted by the various agencies examined suggest that often ethnic minorities were central to strategies designed to create a greater identification of localities with the aims and objectives of government and the private sector and to achieve minority integration into programmes.

Chapter 8: Policies considered

This chapter presents some tentative conclusions about the role of blacks at a time of crisis in Britain's inner cities. The chapter is not intended as a final assessment, but as a general overview of some of the factors discussed in preceding chapters and as a consideration of a number of broad policy options open to governments seeking to come to terms with urban decline. New ways of bridging the gulf between community leaders and the 'unorganized' are discussed with reference to experience in the United States and there is some discussion of the effectiveness of British urban policy measured in terms of the degree of identity which blacks have with the political process.

The study, as a whole, is not attempting to explain the causes of urban distress, racial disadvantage or communal disorder. The intention is to describe the pattern of black political activity in the policy process and with regard to the structures of administration. It is hoped that objectivity will be maintained by revealing relationships between agencies and organizations, describing political processes, noting characteristics of groups, and providing a perspective and analytical framework free from partisan comment.

I Race and policy

In the field of race and immigration British governments have mainly responded to events pragmatically. There never has existed any grand design or strategy for handling race relations and never any conscious attempt to 'buy off' black organizations to gain their co-operation. The historic development of policy towards minorities has, however, produced a discernible tendency in the direction of an accommodation of increasingly large numbers of black organizations within 'the system'. This will be referred to as the 'integration' of black politics into the legitimate institutions of the state. To understand the development of public policy fully, this concept must be explained.

Integration should be regarded as a relative concept. Compared with the United States, Britain's black population is poorly represented in political institutions (Fitzgerald, 1984) and in community development agencies (Jacobs, 1982). Britain and the USA have different histories as far as their handling of race issues is concerned, with British approaches to minority problems tending to regard blacks as 'immigrants' rather than native participants in the political system. The British approach has also been one which has relied upon central government initiative, linked to the control of immigration and the handling of the immigration 'problem'. The way in which this approach developed will be examined in this chapter. British centralization of this kind inevitably acted as a disincentive for many black groups to co-ordinate their activities with government.

Despite this comparative difference, black groups in Britain have, particularly over the last twenty years, entered into a closer relationship with national and local governments. Integration has been of crucial importance to governments, since the stability of the political system may be enhanced if diverse racial groups are granted representation within it and in society in general (Piven and Cloward, 1972). In addition, many writers have stressed the importance of ethnic pluralism in assisting democratic societies to attain democratic goals more fully. Banton (1972) sees 'assimilation' as an important prerequisite for blacks to achieve political equality and Claiborne *et al.* (1983) argue that black democratic representation can be gained through legislative action to overcome the discrimination faced by blacks in political life.

Political rights, however, are not the sole condition for an ethnically plural society. Economic advancement and greater social equality are frequently cited as being of importance in liberating blacks from their general condition of comparative disadvantage. This would apply over issues such as education, housing, employment and income distribution (Freeman, 1983; Karn, 1983; Kirp, 1983; Ollerearnshaw, 1983; Parekh, 1983), although there seems to be general agreement in the literature that political equality must come first, so that blacks may actually be able to exert their political strength freely and raise demands for social justice. This has also often appeared to be the 'official' view of reforming legislators when dealing with anti-discriminatory race legislation and legislation affecting community relations (Brown, 1983; Liebman, 1983; McCrudden, 1983).

Pluralism and integration

Manley (1983) has pointed to the political manifestation of pluralism and the economic condition of plural society. For Manley, the whole notion of societies with democratic systems being classified as 'pluralist' has been severely tested in the light of social inequality and economic stagnation. He examines the pluralist view of American society which views political activity in terms of the competition between groups and their relatively extensive access to political institutions. Plurality thus implies a wide degree of group integration and significant group influence over government policies.

The modification to the 'classical' pluralist view usually associated with Dahl and Lindblom has, according to Manley, produced a reassessment of the pluralist position by these very pluralist advocates. The 'flaws and deficiencies' (Manley, 1983, p.369) in pluralist systems have been recognized and this for Manley has led Dahl and Lindblom to adopt a more radical and reforming attitude to pluralism in response to the maldistribution of wealth and income in society and to the shortcomings in the democratic process. Dahl and Lindblom have criticized the 'incapacities' and even 'perversities' of American pluralism (or rather their 'polyarchical' version of it), which they see as remaining even after government attempts to engineer social and economic reforms. The economic system:

remains both sluggish and feckless in advancing on problems on which it has the advantage of decades of experience in policy-making: poverty and maldistribution of wealth, racial inequality, health care, public education, inflation and unemployment, and industrial relations . . . (Dahl and Lindblom, 1976, p.21, quoted in Manley, 1983, p.372).

This view of pluralist democracy combines an analysis of political participation in government with a recognition that access by itself does not necessarily imply social and economic advancement. In this respect we may regard access as being linked to the problem of urban crisis, since political participation is regarded not so much as an element of social change but more as a way of obtaining consent for the implementation of programmes which themselves may not alleviate serious social inequalities.

Voluntarism versus corporatism

The various degrees of integration of black groups into a fairly open polity defines the historical nature of group accommodation within the political system in Britain. Accepting this implies a relatively 'free' kind of relationship between groups and governments, where groups liaise with governments as a result of their own voluntary decisions to do so. This implies that groups may become willing partners with governments and are not 'controlled' or 'manipulated' in the process. In this way the integrationist perspective differs from the corporatist view of group/government relations which in political science literature has emphasized governmental control of relations with groups and the manipulation of resulting 'agent' type relationships. Jordan (1981) alludes to Schmitter's (1974) definition of corporatism, which sees interest representation in terms of the centralized organization of political interests by government and the 'ordering' of political demand articulation through central political control and authority. As seen below, there is no evidence of this kind of relationship between groups and government in the field of race relations. On the contrary, governments have often been reluctant to identify their policies with the interests of ethnic minorities and even where they have established community-relations bodies there has rarely been any doubt as to the right of groups to enter voluntarily into co-operative arrangements with such agencies, despite centralized administration and funding. Corporatism lays stress upon hierarchical control, which disciplines groups and regularizes group activity and demands to satisfy governments' own relatively narrow criteria for admission to decision-making. As with the 'command' thesis, this would lead to an analysis of essentially passive groups, which were becoming little more than agents of government and enjoying little opportunity to formulate demands which challenged government policy commitments.[1] In fact the evidence suggests that one of the major concerns of black organizations is the preservation of their independence and their ability to act freely to pursue demands which frequently conflict with governments, particularly during periods of social tension or communal disorder. The corporatist position is therefore essentially an 'assimilationist' one, as opposed to an 'integrationist' position, since integration implies a firmer maintenance of individual group identities and policies rather than the gradual abandonment of group/government organizational and political differentiation.

Jordan (1981) regards the so-called 'issue network' description of group/ government relations as a more satisfactory characterization than corporatism. This is based upon Heclo's (1978) view, which concentrates upon administrative fragmentation of the political system allowing for access of diverse political interests. Jordan sees this as applicable to both the United States and Britain where the 'issue network' assumes that political alignments are relatively unstable, the number of political participants in the political process is unlimited, groups maintain their voluntary status and issues frequently remain unresolved due to the complex inter-play of interests (Jordan, 1981, p.98). In Britain race-related policy has involved elements of these kinds of interactions, although governments *do still exercise control over access* of groups in this context (see chapter 3).

These kinds of political relationship do not preclude a degree of sacrifice on the part of interest groups. Groups entering into a relationship with government or with the private sector *will compromise their full independence* to some degree by the very nature of mutual co-operation (Richardson and Jordan, 1979). The integrationist view, however, allows for considerable variation in the degrees of participation which groups may seek or achieve. The process of integration may begin with groups having a very informal relationship with government, possibly developing into a more formal association over a period of time. With black groups in Britain, for example, a period of group formation preceded the coming together of black leaderships willing to work with government. Blacks in this country had to go beyond the bounds of welfare associationism in the 1950s by forming political organizations (in the late 1950s and early 1960s) more suited to actively promoting black interests. It was not until then that community-relations committees could seek government aid more effectively and thereby assist the development of a recognizable 'black lobby' in British politics. Group/government relations today are the result of the development of a variety of group co-ordinations, some of which have produced new forms of linkage between public sector, private sector and voluntary groups (see Chapters 7 and 8). In recognizing the value of black participation, governments have devised administrative arrangements which are not always obviously hierarchical or narrowly centralized. They have often striven to de-emphasize their own direct involvement in local agencies and attempted to enhance agency autonomy so as to encourage groups to participate in 'community'-based initiatives. In Britain this 'arm's length' approach has not been particularly successful (in contrast to the United States), since governments have persisted in administering race relations through the centre. In addition, attention has focused on central government as the initiator of immigration controls and race-relations legislation which has frequently been the source of heated debate about the 'racism' contained in policy. Black organizations have thus become suspicious of central initiatives at crucial periods in the development of public policy, when government has been unable to reconcile successfully the problems of trying to integrate organizations on the one hand and legislating against black immigration on the other.

Policy and race: integration and control in practice

The recognition of this conflict in public policy is quite widely accepted, not only by those active in community work with black minorities, but also by a number of academic researchers (Ben-Tovim and Gabriel, 1979, for example). Immigration controls arguably place a stamp of approval on racist attitudes in society by giving credence to extreme political organizations such as the right-wing National Front and British Movement, which campaign in favour of repatriation of blacks and an end to immigration. If this is true, then discriminatory immigration legislation can serve to legitimate the arguments of the far right and racists in general, thereby undermining the social harmony aspect of government policy. This would suggest that legislation has been a significant source of inspiration to those wishing to perpetuate discrimination against blacks. Continued racial tensions in the cities therefore seem to underline the degree to which 'race harmony' and 'improved' community relations have not been sufficient to offset the wider political effects of physical immigration controls and officially manifested discrimination (Reeves, 1983).

With respect to integrative policies, race-relations initiatives have provided programmes designed to facilitate minority participation and social integration, which at times can be instrumental in calming potentially explosive racial tensions. There has therefore been an attempt to gain the support of black leaders and their followers by encouraging black groups to participate in the very political system that has produced immigration controls. Viewed this way, government policies may be seen in a radically different light: from one which sees them as promoting well-intentioned anti-discrimination measures, to one where governments are seen to implement physical controls which are legitimated through the co-operation of moderate black leaders.

This view suggests that there has been no straightforwardly socially 'enlightened' side to race policy, since both the physical control and the integrationist strategies come together with respect to the desire to 'manage' and 'control' rather than eliminate racialism (M. and A. Dummett, 1969). It is therefore important to consider the historical connection between alien control measures and social control which has been a characteristic of British policy towards minorities, and to explain how both Conservative and Labour governments have utilized the two planks of public policy to moderate racial conflict more effectively. The inter-connection between these strands of policy is thus characterized by governments' concern not to legislate progressive measures for their own sake or primarily for the good of blacks as such, but to alleviate some of the social consequences of racism, economic disadvantage and so on which create the conditions for social unrest. As John

Dearlove (1973) has suggested, politicians and government officials are keenly aware of the need to maintain stability and foster consent to policies by encouraging the co-operative attitudes of interest groups and politically active organizations. If groups can be persuaded to act in a 'helpful' manner, supporting government actions and assisting constructively with the formulation of policies, then governments will be able to reduce political disturbance and potentially serious threats to their ordered policy-making processes more effectively.

The handling of immigration legislation has, therefore, never been an easy task for governments. Britain has a long record of receiving minorities (e.g. the Jews and the Irish in the nineteenth century) who have themselves been keen to be integrated into the political system and have become used to working with and within British political institutions. Restriction of immigration has been accompanied by hostile reactions from minority leaders and those directly affected by a denial of entry into the country or threats to their democratic rights. On the other hand, the history of state restriction is one in which the anti-immigration lobby has been skilful in engendering moods of public hostility against the entry of minorities, facilitating, for example, the passing of the 1905 Aliens Restriction Act which was intended to control 'undesirable and destitute aliens'. The 1905 Act broke the principle applied over the previous 80 years, that Britain should be open to immigrants, particularly those seeking refuge from oppressive overseas governments (Rees, 1979). In circumstances where there is hostile opinion there generally exists an atmosphere which becomes increasingly charged with racist overtones and is frequently accompanied by outbursts of violence.

The 1919 Aliens Restriction Act, for instance, was a subject for heated debate when a series of serious race riots broke out in the summer of 1919 in Liverpool, Cardiff, Manchester, Barry, Hull and Newton. At a time of intense labour militancy, race riots and immigration restrictions provided a cue for the authorities to introduce more restrictive police measures in areas where black people were concentrated. Significantly, the police actions, taken in particular in Cardiff and Liverpool during the disturbances, served to illustrate the developing control aspect of the state's response to black minorities and communal violence, to the extent that the police acted to shield the blacks against attacking white racists, appealing for a restoration of order to reduce community tensions. Within the context of a legislative setting which, between 1914 and 1919, imposed stricter controls on immigration, a strengthening of the powers of immigration officers, a restriction on the numbers of work permits and a tightening up of the law on deportation, the 'community relations' policy of the authorities in Cardiff and Liverpool stood out more clearly as a tactical expedient produced by the pressure of events, but nevertheless setting the tone for the future.

Racism matured in areas, particularly in British ports, where black people had settled and had then come to experience unemployment alongside the indigenous working class. During the First World War, blacks from Britain's colonies had found their way into the services of the Empire and into many war industries where labour shortages existed. James Walvin (1973) has described the events surrounding early racial disturbances. The troubles were ignited in Liverpool when police raided an illegal black gaming house. The worst violence occurred in June 1919 when whites clashed with blacks in a series of bloody encounters resulting in houses belonging to the immigrants being wrecked and hundreds being forced to take shelter under police cover. A similar pattern of events emerged in Cardiff where, if anything, the situation produced even greater hostility against the black population. Walvin describes a four-day period in which whites fought blacks, with heavy injuries on both sides and three deaths.

Walvin and others (for example, Law and Henfrey, 1981) have examined the role of the police in these disturbances. Law and Henfrey allude to the protective role of the police in Liverpool, but claim that there was considerable racial prejudice amongst police responsible for dealing with black people seeking refuge. There were allegations of brutality and accusations that the number of blacks arrested was out of all proportion to the offences allegedly committed by them. Walvin, however, makes the point that in London at least 'legal discrimination seems to have been absent' (Walvin, 1973, p.208). This means that there was no official sanctioning of police racism at a time when the authorities were keen to maintain an increasingly characteristic aura of neutrality with respect to black/white relations.

The disturbances did not effect any significant change in the direction of black immigration into Britain, nor did they mark any particular endemic move towards white racist hostility to immigrants. The 1920s saw a brief period of economic upturn in Britain, which reduced the impact of unemployment and seemed to hold out a prospect of social advancement in an era of peace. Blacks were thus attracted to Britain and black communities slowly expanded as a result of fresh immigration and the settlement of a British-born 'second generation'.

Public order: prelude to 'community relations'

By the late 1920s, when the economy had again definitely taken a downturn, political changes had taken place which led racists to regard their main target as the Jews. The rise of the so-called continental 'Modern Movement' with its Fascist ideology became the inspiration of those seeking to place the blame for the problems of the world on a mythical conspiracy of Zion. The Jews were in many respects far easier prey for the Fascists than were the blacks, since they were to be found in positions of power and influence and were dispersed in identifiable, numerically large and cohesive communities. The Jews were better organized as a community than the blacks and thus appeared to pose a more clearly defined threat to the interests of a middle class feeling itself pressured by big business and an active labour movement, although this should not be taken to imply that the Fascists were simply indifferent towards blacks. Nazi ideology actually alluded to what were claimed to be racial connections between blacks and the Jews, which made both groups legitimate targets for attack. Walvin points to the activities of Oswald Mosley's Fascists in London who often campaigned vigorously against both Jews *and* blacks in the East End (Walvin, 1973, p.211).

In looking at the public policy response to these developments it is important to examine the attitude of government and the nature of police action during the 1930s, since there are similarities between the measures adopted in 1919 and measures adopted when handling situations involving conflicts between Fascists and anti-Fascists. The attacks against Jews took on a similar character to those instigated against blacks in Liverpool and Cardiff, although in the 1930s such incidents were positively political and led by organized Fascist groups.

For public authorities the major concern was again with the maintenance of stability and the eradication of disturbance (Cross, 1961). The Mosleyites, however, were able to slant their propaganda towards support for law and order and this frequently placed them at an advantage with respect to their relations with the authorities, who were accused by the left of defending the Fascists at various demonstrations. Many of the left, almost by definition, became associated with direct action and agitational politics and this put them in an essentially defensive position in their relations with the police, who had always been aware of the potential for conflict on labour demonstrations.

Mosley's activities came to a peak in 1936 when he planned to march with his supporters *en masse* through the Jewish areas of the East End. Preparations preceding the march led trade unions, left and Jewish organizations to mount a concerted campaign of opposition to the march and physically to stop it if possible. Mosley's Blackshirts, expecting trouble, paraded in Royal Mint Street near the Tower of London prior to the march, surrounded by a strong force of police.

In the East End itself street fighting was already under way. Thousands of anti-Fascists had come on to the streets amassing, in particular, around and in Cable Street, where barricades were erected to block Mosley's way. Colin Cross describes the situation graphically, detailing police attempts to clear a way for the Blackshirts (Cross, 1961, p.160) by charging the crowd on horseback with batons drawn. The Cable Street incident achieved the cancellation of the Fascist march and Mosley was ordered by the authorities to disperse his followers.

The anti-Fascists were jubilant at their victory, but Mosley was determined to avenge this setback. A week after Cable Street Fascists went on the rampage down the East End's Mile End Road, smashing windows of Jewish-owned shops and houses and perpetrating attacks on passers-by. As Cross (1961, p.161) states: 'it was the most violent anti-Semitic outbreak the East End had seen'.

These incidents led directly to government measures designed to reduce the level of disorder and a Public Order Bill was brought before Parliament. The legislation reflected the government's desire to extend the powers of the police and to introduce legal measures to deal with the effect of deeply ingrained social attitudes. The wearing of uniforms by members of the public at political meetings was banned (intended to prevent the Fascists wearing their blackshirt uniforms), the use of stewards at open-air gatherings was prohibited and police powers to ban political marches and processions were extended. The legislation also made it an offence to use insulting language likely to lead to a breach of the peace.

However limited this last provision was, it was seen by the left as a concession to those who had been calling for a curtailment of open Fascist abuse against Jews. In this respect the law embodied an element of the kind of reasoning that lay behind the Race Relations Acts after the Second World War, with its expectation that the law could be used to control racist expressions. However, the Public Order Act could also be used against the anti-Fascists and in this any parallel with race-relations legislation ends, since blacks are presently unlikely to be brought before the courts under race-relations law, although in theory there is probably nothing to stop this in certain circumstances. In a similar vein, the 1936 Act could be used to ban trade union rallies and restrict stewarding of peaceful labour demonstrations, thus enabling the authorities to point to 'even-handed' treatment of both left and right.

Embryonic community relations agencies

Organized Fascism declined dramatically after Cable Street and with the advent of a war which brought Britain into conflict with Hitler's Germany. Thus the problem of social unrest arising from anti-Semitism was removed from the political agenda. Of much greater importance to government was the question of implementing effective wartime measures to restrict and control the entry of aliens into the country. At the start of the war the black population was estimated to be only around ten thousand (Walvin, 1973, p.213) and had generally been integrated into the war effort. To some extent black people were 'hidden' from the majority of native white British and not only did racism no longer pose as an open political issue, but blacks themselves seemed to be content to remain politically passive and to rest content with being left to themselves.

There was continued immigration into Britain at this time. Substantial numbers of Poles entered the country, many having fought on the side of the Allied Forces in Italy and France. The Poles joined Jewish and other refugees who had been arriving before 1939 and who had formed part of the immigrant flow to Britain during the 1930s. To facilitate the influx of Poles after the war the Polish Resettlement Act of 1947 was passed, which established the so-called Polish Resettlement Corps, charged with handling a wide range of problems facing the newcomers (housing, education, social services, etc.).

Rees (1979) argues that the 1947 Resettlement Act created an important precedent, in that it recognized some of the broader social aspects of the immigration of relatively large numbers of foreign nationals. The Act was not simply intended as a means of controlling numbers coming to the UK, but was seen also as having to provide for the assimilation of migrants into the host community. The National Assistance Board helped with this task of integrating people into the British way of life, providing hostel accommodation and giving advice on employment, health and other matters. Rees (1979, p.80) argues that: 'the Act was one of the few constructive legislative initiatives in the field of immigration' because of this social approach – an approach which was also adopted, with less vigour, to aid Hungarian refugees in 1956 and Ugandan Asians in 1972.

There were also increasing numbers of immigrants coming into Britain from other parts of the world, actively encouraged by Clement Attlee's Labour government in a conscious attempt to alleviate labour shortages which were affecting key sectors of the economy. Many European workers entered Britain having obtained short-term work permits but, unlike the Poles, they were subject to far stricter entry restrictions and, because of the lack of welfare provisions on arrival, found it more difficult to make the necessary adjustment to British society. Consequently many of them left Britain in later years, either to seek greener pastures in the United States and Canada, or to return to their native lands.

The work-permit regulations, however, did not apply initially to citizens of the British Commonwealth. Under the British Nationality Act of 1948 this group was allowed entry to Britain to find employment and it was under this law that growing numbers of black Commonwealth immigrants entered the country, mainly from the Caribbean, India and Pakistan. Between 1951 and 1961 the official population of those from West Indian backgrounds rose from 15,300 to 171,800, those of Indian origin from 30,800 to 81,400 and those from Pakistan from 5,000 to 24,900 (Rees, 1979, p.83).

During a period of modest, but sustained economic growth, the flow of immigration was regarded as tolerable, if not positively advantageous. However, a combination of factors was to bring about a change of attitude in government and in the House of Commons. To some extent the change was prompted by a stagnating economy, but there also emerged distinct social pressures in Britain, connected with the whole issue of race relations, which prompted a reassessment of the post-war entry regulations.

Nottingham, Notting Hill and black awareness

The extent to which these social pressures had been simmering under the surface during the 1950s became clear in August 1958 when, to the surprise of politicians and community leaders, serious racial disturbances broke out in Nottingham and in London's Notting Hill area. The events of August 1958 were to spark off a debate on race which has lasted to this day and which prepared the way for further restrictions on immigration.

The troubles began in Nottingham on 23 August in the St Ann's Well Road district, when a group of West Indians launched a reprisal attack against a group of whites, following incidents over the previous two weeks when 'teddy boys' had assaulted blacks. This initial outburst was followed on 30 August when some 500 'teddy boys', reinforced by a gang from Leicester, roamed the area picking fights with black people.

More serious, however, were the Notting Hill disturbances, which started in the early hours of 24 August when a number of youths toured Shepherd's Bush and Notting Hill in a car, with the intention of harassing blacks. Five black people were attacked with iron bars and other assorted weapons. Inevitably news of the incidents spread through the area and on the night of 30/31 August fighting broke out in Notting Hill involving 200 people, both black and white. A petrol bomb was hurled into a house occupied by a black couple and other houses were stoned by white hooligans. Police intervened as the situation deteriorated and larger numbers of people came on to the streets. On 1 September a West African student was chased by a gang of white youths who were reported to have shouted: 'Lynch him'. This started off what could only be described as an anti-black rampage, when some 2,000 youths roamed the streets attacking black homes and insulting black people generally. (The next day banners appeared calling for the deportation of black people.) Although these events have subsequently been called the 'Notting Hill riots', the incidents in fact took place over a wider area of London. Trouble occurred in Bayswater, Paddington and in Shepherd's Bush; petrol bombs were thrown in Bayswater, and in Paddington the house of a black family was set alight by whites.

Considerable attention was given to the events in the press, where the general consensus of opinion seemed to be that the root cause of the disturbances in both Nottingham and London had been the serious shortage of houses and a growing competition for employment. There was also some evidence of the involvement of Oswald Mosley's Fascist Union Movement in Notting Hill, where Mosleyite propaganda material had been circulating during the period of the racial clashes and where the Union Movement had organized open-air political meetings. Also active in Notting Hill had been the so-called National Labour Party, which was in fact a National Socialist or Nazi formation which had recently broken away from the far-right League of Empire Loyalists.

Despite the eventual calming of the situation in the streets, the events of August and September sent a shock wave to the Conservative government. The Home Secretary reported to the Prime Minister that the disturbances had both 'an immediate and a long-term importance'. The 'immediate' implications referred to the maintenance of law and order, but perhaps more importantly the longer-term implications related to the whole question of black immigration. In a statement from Downing Street, the Home Secretary said:

As regards the wider aspects of policy, H.M. Government have for some little time been examining the result of this country's time-honoured practice to allow free entry of immigrants from Commonwealth and colonial countries. While this study of major policy and its implications and effects on employment will continue, H.M. Government do not think it right to take long-term decisions except after careful consideration of the problem as a whole.

If anything, the tone of the Labour opposition was much more strident in seeking for something to be done to avert future troubles. Hugh Gaitskell, Labour Leader, called for the suppression of street riots with what he called 'the utmost firmness'. The combination of Government and Opposition in focusing attention on the 'immigration problem' tended to take attention away from the problems raised in some sections of the press relating to housing and unemployment. The argument, not only in 1958 but for the following period, became focused upon the 'immigrant' and upon 'numbers', either in the country or about to enter the country. The conditions were ideal for legislation which would concentrate, not on the need to bring about some kind of community 'harmony', but simply on the restriction of black immigration. Although there were those in all political parties who were keen to promote social changes to alleviate the problems of deprived areas like Notting Hill, their voices were drowned by those who wished to control entry first and then, perhaps, think about measures to improve race relations.

The response of the black minorities to the emerging 'immigration issue' took the form of a spawning of organizations within the black community dedicated to defending immigrant rights and black interests in general. These were voluntary interest groups, which often combined a welfare-orientated approach to community problems with a political profile which strove to mobilize a broad range of black opinions. The formation in 1959 of the Standing Conference of Leaders of Organizations Concerned with West Indians in Britain and the continued growth of the Indian Workers' Association marked an important stage in the development of an identifiable black leadership, which was to assume a central position when it came to implementing race-relations legislation in the mid 1960s and early 1970s.

Many of these growing black-interest groups were faced with the task of countering what they regarded as racist propaganda circulated by various candidates in the 1959 General Election. Hiro (1973, p.46) makes the point that the election was not about the race issue, despite the Notting Hill events, but that there was an underlying current of debate about race in certain local campaigns, especially in areas where Labour candidates were associated with 'open' immigration policies. After the election the anti-immigration and restrictionist attitudes amongst politicians seemed to harden as rumours abounded that the government was preparing new immigration legislation against a background of concern over the issue within the Conservative Party (Hiro, 1973, p.47).

The 1962 Act and its aftermath

The speculation ended with the publication in 1961 of the Commonwealth Immigrants Bill, which was allegedly intended to immediately stem black, as opposed to other, immigration. As Hiro states, the Bill was opposed by what amounted to a broad 'coalition' of organizations representing West Indians and Asians. In Birmingham, some 450 people marched under the banner of the Co-ordinating Committee Against Racial Discrimination, which acted as an umbrella body co-ordinating the campaign activities of a number of moderate, leftist and liberal organizations. In London the Committee of Afro-Asian/Caribbean Organizations was established, which backed the Labour Party's opposition to the Bill, but black organizations soon became disappointed with Labour's attitude towards the proposed legislation. Labour appeared to be falling far short of total opposition to the apparently discriminatory aspects of the Bill and to be reluctant to identify with policies which could undermine their national electoral support.

Seriously weakened by Labour's stance, black organizations had no chance of preventing the Bill from going through Parliament with its perceived discriminatory clauses. In 1962 the Commonwealth Immigrants Act was passed. It laid down conditions of entry which required Commonwealth citizens either to be in possession of a valid work voucher issued by the Ministry of Labour, or to be a dependant accompanying an entrant or joining somebody already resident in Great Britain. Entrants could also claim student status or enter for limited-period stays (holidays and so on).

It was the voucher system which was particularly contentious. The number of vouchers to be issued was controlled by the Ministry of Labour subject to Cabinet decision, but not to be ratified by the House of Commons. The vouchers were valid for six months and if entry were not effected within that time they became invalid, although Immigration Officers were allowed a degree of discretion with respect to this. Even those having jobs assured to them prior to entry had difficulties in obtaining vouchers, since the so-called Type A vouchers for this category had to be applied for by the prospective employers. In the application to the Ministry of Labour the employer was required to name the person offered employment in Britain, whereupon the Ministry ordered a detailed investigation into the applicant's background. If the application was accepted the voucher would be forwarded to the hopeful would-be migrant via the employer. Type B vouchers, mainly for professional people and nurses, were much easier to obtain; but Type C vouchers for the unskilled and those without job offers were exceptionally difficult to get and were phased out altogether in 1964.

Public debate about the voucher system and about the Act in general in the period immediately following its enactment ensured that the immigration issue remained firmly in the minds of politicians. Discussion of the issue was not, of course, always conducted within the confines of what may be called the 'liberal consensus'. This point was brought home very forcibly in 1964 with the election to Parliament of Peter Griffiths in a by-election in Smethwick near Birmingham.

Griffiths managed to defeat Patrick Gordon-Walker, standing for the Labour Party and backed by Harold Wilson, Labour's recently elected Prime Minister. While there was an electoral swing nationally in favour of Labour at that time, in Smethwick Griffiths managed to reverse the trend in favour of the Conservatives by standing on an openly anti-immigration platform. Indeed, the campaign was not simply anti-immigration but thoroughly racist, Griffiths at one point condoning the slogan: 'If you want a nigger neighbour, vote Liberal or Labour' (Foot, 1965, p.44). Many people at that time who opposed Griffiths and who were becoming increasingly concerned about the manifestation of racist sentiments, pointed to the 1962 Act as having opened the door to a tide of anti-immigrant sentiment.

Anti-racists could argue that the public debate around the 1962 Act had legitimated racism in discussions about law and immigration. The Act had made the cause of the racists 'respectable' and had created the conditions for further restrictions to be made at the expense of the so-called 'open door' policy of the 1950s. Typical of those taking up these arguments was CARD (Campaign Against Racial Discrimination), which was a grouping formally inaugurated in February 1965. CARD in fact marked an important step in the history of black politics in Britain, in that for the first time in this country there appeared a national organization representing a wide variety of black political groups with what appeared at the time to be a real potential for influencing central government's attitude towards immigration.

CARD was committed to an essentially liberal conception of political action, despite the rhetoric often exhibited by some of its members. It attracted the Indian Workers' Association (Great Britain), the National Federation of Pakistani Organizations and the West Indian Standing Conference to its ranks, in addition to a number of more militant advocates of black nationalism. However, as Hiro (1973, p.52) has pointed out, CARD remained wedded to an approach which was implicitly that of Martin Luther King in the USA – moderation; 'legitimate' pressure on the government; and an overriding sense of moral justification for its cause.

Integration and community relations

CARD had an opportunity to implement its moderate approach upon publication in 1965 of the Labour government's White Paper, *Immigration from the Commonwealth*. The White Paper proposed further restrictions on entry by imposing controls on the total number of voucher holders, abolishing

Type C vouchers and imposing a limit of 8,500 per year on remaining vouchers (of which 1,000 were allocated temporarily to Maltese citizens). In addition, the White Paper redefined the 'dependant' status which affected the rights of families to come together in Britain and recommended certain restrictions on visitors and students from black Commonwealth states.

There was, however, another aspect to government policy at this time. This was the 'social control' element which paraded, in the mid 1960s, as the liberal plank of the Labour government's race-relations strategy. The increasingly evident overt racism in society, highlighted during the campaigns mentioned above and in localized racist incidents in major cities, became a definite concern of the Home Office. The 1965 White Paper, despite its restrictionist content, also dealt with the question of community relations and indicated the future strategy to be adopted in bringing about more harmonious relations between blacks and whites. Edwards and Batley have identified the connection between social tensions, discussion about immigration and moves to establish community-relations machinery. They point to the centrality of the Home Office as the department traditionally concerned with race issues, although in the mid 1960s there was apparently some government uncertainty as to precisely which department was to handle the wider responsibility associated with community relations (Edwards and Batley, 1978, p.37). While the Home Office drafted the anti-discriminatory 1965 Race Relations Bill which followed the White Paper, the responsibility for co-ordinating race-relations matters in Whitehall was somewhat surprisingly allocated to the Department of Economic Affairs, although with the demise of this department responsibility was then clearly located at the Home Office.

In September 1965, the Home Office promoted the establishment of the National Committee for Commonwealth Immigrants (NCCI), which replaced the old Commonwealth Immigrants Advisory Council which had operated since 1962 as an advisory body sanctioned by the Home Secretary. The NCCI was seen to be an independent committee under the Chairmanship of the Archbishop of Canterbury and charged with the objective of co-ordinating efforts to bring about harmony and racial integration. The NCCI, together with local authorities, provided funding for the local Community Relations Councils (CRCs), together with central government grant aid. The 1968 Race Relations Act established the Community Relations Commission to replace the NCCI. This was an important development since, unlike the NCCI, the new Commission had statutory recognition and was assigned with the task of promoting good community relations through the funding and encouragement of the activities of local CRCs. This provision for what was essentially a centralized funding of community relations involved a line of responsibility starting in the Home Office, running through the Commission and ending with the CRCs and local black organizations. Many organizations consequently became highly suspicious of this lineage and distanced themselves from the community-relations agencies, remaining critical of their government connection. On the other hand, organizations were beginning to see their interests as generally being enhanced within such a formal participatory structure, since it appeared to provide funding which would promote the activities of some organizations and, perhaps even more importantly, appeared to legitimate the position of black leaders in relation to government. Instead of being the objects of abuse in election campaigns, black organizations clustering around the Commission and the CRCs could go on the offensive more effectively with the official backing of a statutory agency.

In addition to the Commission, in 1968 the Labour government embarked upon its 'Urban Aid' programme which, as Edwards and Batley (1978) point out, was linked to the question of alleviating racial tensions in the inner cities despite its general application to urban regeneration. The programme concentrated financial resources on designated areas, initially giving help mainly to schools in educational-priority areas and to diverse community projects. The Urban Programme is discussed in more detail in Chapter 7, but it should be regarded here as one of a number of important measures designed specifically to reduce urban instability and to improve the economic position of blacks.

The Community Relations Council and black interest groups

The 1968 Commonwealth Immigrants Act, restricting African/Asian inflow, led to the national CRC being pressured by black organizations to become more effective as a campaigning body representing community opinion. Hopes were dashed, however, as it became increasingly evident that the Commission, partly because of its London-based centralization, was not only often out of touch with local communities, but also ineffective as a body charged with promoting the improvement of race relations. This last point became a particular issue of contention for black groups when the Conservative government passed the 1971 Immigration Act, which tightened entry restrictions for immigrants even further. The Community Relations Commission was accused of failing to provide an adequate forum for debate about the Act and remained largely isolated from the criticisms of the more militant black groups, which at that time had not focused their political demands on official bodies.

The statutory status of the Commission was retained in Sections 44 and 45 of the 1976 Race Relations Act, which empowered the new Commission for Racial Equality (CRE) – a fusion of the old Commission with the Race Relations Board (responsible for bringing cases under the anti-discrimination clauses of the 1968 legislation) – to render assistance to any organizations appearing to be concerned with the promotion of racial equality and good relations between different races. During the late 1970s the CRE and local CRCs came under attack again, but this time the most vociferous criticisms tended to come from politicians in the Conservative Party who, from their own standpoint, pointed to the ineffectiveness of the CRE. They, like the militant left organizations, claimed that the CRE and the 'race relations industry' were doing little to improve community relations (see Chapter 4). Unlike the left, however, this line of argument was linked to calls for a reduction in CRE funding, and, in more extreme cases, for the abolition of the CRE and the abandonment of attempts to improve race relations through legislative measures. In some ways, therefore, the left's concentration on the CRE's 'ineffectiveness' actually provided the right with an opportunity to extend the logic of the argument which claimed that the CRE was not really earning its living.

The arguments of the Conservative right and of the left's 'ineffective' lobby both missed the significance of the CRE's role in community relations. The rationale, recognized by successive governments, lay less in its impact upon racialism than in its encouragement of black organizations to co-operate in various degrees with centrally funded agencies. Race bodies at national and local level provided black leaders with at least 'something' which they could take back to their supporters as evidence of the benefits of working within the system. The CRCs in particular provided a channel into which demands could be directed and through which black leaders could liaise with politicians and government officials. The degree to which black groups were eager to work through such channels was indicative of the importance of the CRCs in bringing organizations together within a relatively ordered and formal setting.

For government, this kind of forum for black community organizations was particularly useful at times of communal disturbance. The late 1970s saw an unprecedented occurrence of civil disorder connected with racial conflicts and the mobilizations of extreme right-wing groups. The CRCs remained an effective means of co-ordinating diverse organizations with government. However limited many CRCs proved to be as platforms for the expression of 'grass-roots' opinion, they nevertheless provided a reasonably structured way of getting local authorities, central government, black groups, white groups and the police around the same table. Indeed, the role of the CRCs in promoting police/community liaison committees became crucial at times when the re-establishment of civil order was of prime concern for local authorities (see Chapter 6).

The CRE itself has also performed a valuable role, as far as governments are concerned, with respect to implementing the anti-discrimination aspects of race-relations legislation and engendering a degree of support for immigration legislation and government policy on race in general. The CRE is in a unique position with regard to this, since it integrates the debate about race and immigration into 'acceptable' channels and effectively limits the degree to which black, and white, organizations participating in CRE programmes dissent from central government policies.

It is hardly surprising, therefore, that in 1979 the newly elected Conservative government under Margaret Thatcher ignored right-wing criticisms and maintained its commitment to the CRE and the CRCs. David Lane, the CRE

Chairman, was himself a Conservative who had managed to steer the Commission down the road of moderation and co-operation with the Home Office. Indeed, a memorandum submitted by the staff side of the CRE to the Home Affairs Committee of the House of Commons in 1981 implicitly criticized the CRE for having aligned itself too closely with central government (see Chapter 4). One result of this, according to the memorandum, was the effect which certain aspects of government policy had in restricting the role of the CRE as an active campaigning body. The memo pointed to the CRE's lack of resources, which had tended to mute the agency's criticism of legislation affecting race. An example of this was the guarded response to the government's legislation on nationality.

Black immigrants; black British

The British Nationality Bill was introduced in the House of Commons in January 1981 and enacted in October of the same year. It introduced three citizenship categories: British citizenship; citizenship of British dependent territories; and British overseas citizenship. The Act replaced the 1948 Nationality Act and revoked the right of *jus soli*, which previously gave British citizenship to anyone born in the UK; a child born in the UK would be British at birth only if one of his parents was a British citizen or was legally settled in the UK. In addition the 1971 Immigration Act was amended by the new legislation, so that the right of abode was redefined in terms of British citizens and certain Commonwealth citizens who would keep their present right of abode for their lifetime.

One reason for enacting this legislation was that the citizenship created by the 1948 British Nationality Act no longer gave any clearly defined guidance as to who had the right to enter the UK. The Conservative government argued that the 1981 Act would not adversely affect lawfully settled immigrants and would generally update current legislation. The Home Secretary, William Whitelaw, was also keen to underline the point that the Act was not racially discriminatory, since the racial factor was not to be applied when examining, for example, the parentage of a child born in the UK.

Roy Hattersley, chief Opposition spokesman on Home Affairs, criticized the Bill for being racist. According to Hattersley, the Bill was essentially an immigration-control measure rather than a measure dealing with nationality. Despite the repeated allegations of racism, the Opposition proposed to amend the law by introducing its own Bill which would effectively be a 'real' nationality law; it was to contain a much more precise definition of what 'British' actually meant, which would include everyone born or adopted in the UK, and in addition wives and husbands, upon marriage to British citizens, would gain citizenship rights.

The debate over the Bill pinpointed not so much the areas of disagreement between Government and Opposition, but the shared desire by both sides to redefine the concept of nationality for purposes of clarifying immigration legislation. The Labour Party stood for a better definition of nationality rather than for a removal of immigration laws which were arguably already discriminatory. A more precise definition of the meaning of UK citizenship would do nothing to change such controls on immigration even under Labour's proposals.

The debate over nationality took place at a time of most severe distress in Britain's inner-city and black communities. The communal disturbances of summer 1981 threw into relief the delicate balance between community stability and disorder. Combined with calls for tougher police action against rioters and also for more effective 'community policing', the nationality legislation provided a strong reinforcement of the 'physical' methods of dealing with race.

The defensiveness of black groups under such circumstances was consistent with their defensiveness during the whole period since the 1950s, but in the 1980s their relationship with government was quite different. The Conservative government, local authorities and development agencies were more concerned to enlist black support for urban initiatives. The numerical size of the black population had created a new 'black constituency' which governments had to take into account when framing policies for the inner cities. The role of black leaders was of importance, since it was they who could command the support of their 'constituents' and persuade blacks to work through community relations agencies. For some moderate black leaders the nationality legislation could be seen as positively beneficial to their communities, since the black constituency was now able to assert its Britishness and its legitimacy within the mainstream of British politics and this could best be done by adopting a 'low profile' on nationality. The evidence of opinion polls seemed to justify this line, as black voters themselves were now ranking non-race-related issues as more important than the issues of immigration and nationality (Fitzgerald, 1984, pp.56–7); basic concerns such as inflation and unemployment were those which affected black voters immediately. Conditions were therefore right for moderate black leaders to use these issues to court the major political parties, which were becoming increasingly aware of the potential of the black vote.

The next chapter examines the nature of the 'black constituency' against this emerging political background and identifies some of the strategic advances made by Britain's growing black community. The chapter stresses the now centrally important quest by blacks to gain political influence and access to the political system under conditions which continue to militate against the full acceptance of black politics into the British political system and which continue to stress the question of 'immigration' and the 'alien' status of black ethnic minorities.

2 The black constituency

It has already been indicated that the problems faced by black minorities are apparent throughout the range of provisions involving black people. In housing, education, employment and in government there are permanent tensions brought about by racial animosities and the consequent attempts to exclude blacks from certain opportunities afforded by society to whites. Black politics has therefore been about overcoming exclusion from the political system, about the gaining of greater access to the institutions and decision-making processes of the state and about taking advantage of the community-orientated aspects of central government policy described in Chapter 1. It was suggested that integration into these agencies differed by degrees, with some groups being less well integrated than others. It is very important to remember this point, since black politics in Britain is characterized by a multiplicity of very 'localized' organizations of various sizes and dispositions. For some groups the process of integration is a non-issue, insofar as these organizations may be reluctant to participate in activities which bring them into contact with government (although virtually all groups have *some* contact in practice). Alternatively, some formations are simply too small to be significant 'group' entities at all – one- or two-man committees, or 'national' organizations with only half a dozen or so members. For these, integration is more of an abstraction than a practical political issue. This chapter is therefore concerned with groups within the black community which do actually represent more than just individuals, which do exhibit various degrees of willingness to work with governments and local agencies and which relate to the national and local black 'constituencies' in some significant respect. It is for these organizations that integrationist public policies hold important implications.

The term 'constituency' is used here to indicate the political aspect of the black community. Blacks affect public policies most effectively when they realize their identities and organize to achieve political influence or power, but they may become a political factor in spite of their disunity and in spite of their desire to maintain autonomy within the political system (Strange, 1973). A black community assumes political importance for governments and local politicians when it becomes numerically large enough, when it gives rise to a degree of political organization and when it independently begins to make demands in defence of community interests. These three factors define the nature of a black political constituency in this chapter, which forms a contrast to situations where, historically, blacks have *not* always attained this political position. In the USA, for example, blacks moving into the big cities in the nineteenth century were initially in a small minority, deprived of basic civil rights (and often the right to vote), without an independent political organization and with their interests subordinated within the city political machines (Clark, 1973). In many cases it was not until the 1920s and 1930s that local black 'constituencies' emerged in the USA, independent and numerically large enough to capitalize on their strategic political potential.

The size of the 'constituency'

The structure and size of the black community in Britain similarly have an impact upon its political influence and chances of access. Size becomes a factor in politics when the pressure of a distinguishable community begins to be felt. Immigrants begin to defend their democratic rights when they sense the resentment of the native community to their presence. Organizational networks spring into being when there is a felt need and where there is a numerical weight in the community which provides sufficient support to black leaderships seeking to establish themselves as representative of identifiable collective interests.

It has been shown in Chapter 1 how the growth of the wider black community and the level of immigration prompted governments to pass legislation to control the number of blacks in Britain. In the 1970s, however, the size of the community as a whole was determined not by immigration so much as by the 'natural' birth rate of black people. Today the vast majority of black children in Britain were born and educated here (that relates to children up to the age of 15). Of Britain's 54-million population it is estimated that 2.2 million, or 4.1%, were of New Commonwealth origin in 1981 (New Commonwealth refers broadly to Britain's ex-colonies which have achieved independence since the Second World War, plus Pakistan). Over four-fifths of those of New Commonwealth origin can be traced back to the Caribbean, the Indian sub-continent and Africa, which means that Britain's black population, on this definition, is estimated to be about 3.4% of the total population (not counting black minorities from other countries, but including British-born blacks of New Commonwealth origin). It should be noted, however, that this estimate is likely to be inadequate as a precise measure of the number of blacks in Britain. The 'New Commonwealth origin' count records the origins of blacks in households headed by persons actually born in the New Commonwealth. There is thus at present no detailed information about the ethnic composition of localities, since the 1981 national census omitted an ethnic-origin question which could have directly asked individuals about their racial background. Increasing numbers of ethnic-minority households are now headed by blacks born in the United Kingdom (Gutch, 1985, p.47) which implies a significant undercount of blacks in the official statistics. As a result, local authorities and other agencies are forced to make their own assessments of the size of their ethnic-minority populations in order to effectively plan their local service provisions and minority-related programmes.

The geographical distribution of the black population has been largely influenced by employment opportunities (Brown, 1983), immigrants being attracted to areas with a buoyant labour market. Brown points to the consequent concentration of minorities in the major conurbations of London and the West Midlands and in towns in Lancashire, Yorkshire and the East Midlands (in 1971, 72% of blacks lived in cities with over 250,000 inhabitants). Brown also indicates that there is a 'bewildering variety of local situations' with respect to settlement patterns. People of Indian and Pakistani origin are widely distributed, but those of West Indian origin are mainly concentrated in London and the West Midlands. In addition, there is frequently a high level of local residential segregation between Asians and West Indians where general patterns of joint settlement do exist (Brown, 1983, p.38).

Brown makes the point that although black settlement is essentially urban, it is not exclusively *inner* urban settlement. Black people have, for example, settled in Britain's satellite new towns and in smaller towns (such as Burnley in Lancashire) and in isolated black communities in cities such as Stoke-on-Trent. The implication of such a pattern of settlement for black political life is important, since it has led to the dispersal of blacks, which has been of fundamental importance in 'atomizing' the pattern of political organization. Localization of black politics is a consequence of such geographical patterns, while the diversity of black groups relates to this and to the ethnic differences and political rivalries within and between ethnic-minority communities.

Despite the fact that generalization about black politics is made difficult by these factors, the present research has been forced to make a choice about the selection of empirical material and cases which throw light upon the pattern of political activity and the nature of group/government interactions. Recognizing the incompleteness of the present study (by not, for example, looking at black groups in a new town), the case studies have been selected in order to illustrate political processes in circumstances where there are numbers of blacks able to make a significant impact on local politics, or where blacks make a real difference to public policy, or where communal tensions have assumed the status of a crisis in urban management. In approaching black politics in this way, research will generally adopt a big-city focus and tend to concentrate on the inner-city core areas.

Representing the black constituency

If the black constituency is then, in reality, a coverall term for differing local black sub-constituencies it is hardly surprising that it has been difficult for black politicians to gain extensive representation in British politics. There is no single national black political party or political interest group which can claim to speak for black people, let alone for all Asians or West Indians. The Indian Workers' Association (Great Britain) is a nationally organized group, but its sphere of influence is limited by being concentrated in particular localities. Attempts to launch a national organization for blacks of both Asian and Caribbean origin failed in the mid 1970s, despite the efforts of the Gulbenkian Foundation and others to promote such a project.

There are no black Members of Parliament, partly as a result of the lack of an effective national grouping and partly as a result of local constituency conditions and party-political factors. In 1983 the number of black parliamentary candidates from the four main political parties rose from five in 1979 to 22, four of these being Conservatives, six from the Labour Party and six each from the Liberal and Social Democratic Parties. Only one, however (Paul Boateng in West Hertfordshire), stood for a seat which was likely to be gained by his party (Fitzgerald, 1984, p.87). While the situation is rather more favourable when it comes to the election of local black councillors, there is still under-representation of blacks in local government in proportional terms, despite the fact that local political-party branches do seem to be adopting more black candidates (Fitzgerald, 1984, pp.100–1). It has already been indicated that this representational situation stands in stark contrast to the United States, but this is a point worth stressing. Britain's black community has less political impact in both representational and non-representational political terms because it is proportionately smaller, more differentiated, less well organized, financially worse off (in terms of the funding of political and other interest groups) and less committed to the idea of a politically highly skilled professional community leadership (Jacobs, 1983).

The population factor alone underscores the different political potential of American blacks. Between 1970 and 1980 the black population in the USA increased by 17.3% from 22.6 to 26.5 million. In 1980 blacks represented about 12% of the total population. In seven states blacks constituted more than 20% of the population and twelve states had black populations of one million or more. New York had the largest black population (1,784,337) and Washington DC's population was 70% black (Matney and Johnson, 1983).

The Afro-Caribbean/American black population is far more homogeneous than Britain's diverse black sub-constituencies. Jessie Jackson's Presidential campaign in 1984 showed the strength of American black identity in electoral terms, but blacks have also supported the formation of large national-interest groups to lobby in Washington on policy questions affecting both urban issues and matters of national concern. The National Association for the Advancement of Coloured People and the Urban League are well respected national groups which have become deeply involved in national politics and in programmes sponsored by national and local agencies. In the USA, therefore, the integration of black politics has been accompanied by the professionalization and expansion of major 'peak' political organizations and the increasing penetration of blacks into positions within the political parties and government agencies.

America's large black population achieved this identity under historical circumstances which were quite different to Britain's. These circumstances have produced an Afro-Caribbean/American black identity, strong, '*independent*', and politically differentiated from the political expressions of American Asian, Hispanic and other ethnic minorities (Gosnell, 1967, p.2). In Britain, however, black politics may be characterized by a public-policy view which collectively associates groups of different identities; but their very differences actually maintain sharp demarcations between groups. These demarcations are strengthened by the geographical concentration of minorities in particular areas and they become politically important insofar as none of the minorities, taken separately, represents such a cohesive, influential or politically 'independent' constituency as the Afro-Caribbean/American black community in the USA.

Where blacks in Britain identify with each other on a multi-ethnic basis, they would appear to be in a better position to increase the potential influence of the black constituency as a whole. Britain's ethnic minorities *do* represent a significant collective strength in particular localities – especially where a black identity has emerged. In some Parliamentary constituencies blacks make up nearly half of the constituency population – Brent South in London (46%), Southall in London (44%), Ladywood in Birmingham (42%), for example – and although these individual Parliamentary jurisdictions still fall short of the city counts of black minorities in the USA, the numbers have evoked responses from governments which themselves have effected a degree of inter-ethnic identity between black organizations.

Diverse backgrounds

In public policy, therefore, Britain's black minorities are generally treated collectively. Community Relations Councils impose a form of collectivism on participating groups which produces a more identifiable arena for black political activity. This partially draws the black sub-constituencies together, particularly at local level. A study of black politics in this country is therefore also about the 'collectivized' efforts of black groups attempting to benefit from the political system through community relations and other agencies designed by governments and the private sector to relate to *blacks in general.*

Black interests are, in this context, represented through a vast number of political and non-political, religious, cultural and welfare organizations. Some of these align themselves with white-interest groups or with labour and trade union groups or with local political parties. A distinction should be made, however, between those organizations which adapt quite successfully to British political life by taking advantage of the opportunities available to them, and those which remain isolated because of their inability to break away from religious and cultural traditions. The larger black associations have been able to expand their influence because they have broken with restrictive traditions and have realized their potential power within the community. Stress is placed here upon *potential,* because the ability to mobilize support, the opportunities to work effectively through community-relations bodies and the chances available to groups of utilizing various channels of access can occasionally be sacrificed, due to inexperienced or ineffective leadership (Katznelson, 1970, p.433; Lawrence, 1974, p.166). Moreover, groups are often reluctant to take initiatives in policy areas where they fear that upsetting the *status quo* would lead to dissent within their own communities and between different black groups represented on various government bodies.

Underlying these motivations are the cultural and ethnic histories of Britain's black minorities stemming from the immigrant experience. About four-fifths of the Indians in Britain originate from the Jullundar and Hosiapur districts of the Eastern Punjab (Banton, 1972, p.135). The majority of these people are Sikhs, most of them belonging to the Jat or farmer caste. The largest group in the remaining one-fifth are the Gujeratis, who are Hindus. Sikhs adhere to what is a comparatively young religion in terms of Indian cultural and religious history. They remain devoutly religious while in Britain and attend religious services in homes, rented halls and in their own temples or gurdwaras. The temples represent a focal point for Sikhs and some become involved in political activity designed to promote temple interests, although, in general, temple life tends to strengthen the resistance to involvement of members in the politics of the broader white community through an often rigid defence of Sikh culture and religion against the influence of the native culture.

The minority Gujeratis come from the districts of Surat and Charottar which lie to the north of Bombay in Western India. The most important aspect of life for people from these areas is their religion, which is a caste-based Hinduism. The caste religious system sees differences between higher and lower orders of people. Hindus are divided into four 'varnas' or colours which are inclusive national categories. From 'higher' to 'lower' these varnas are: Brahmin (priest); Kshatriya (warrior); Vaishya (trader); and Sudra (cultivator or artisan). Below the lowest of these come the untouchables, who are considered to be outside the caste system and inferior to those covered by it.

In Britain caste distinctions still exert an influence on attitudes, although nominally there are no castes among Sikhs and Pakistani Muslims; but all three – Sikhs, Muslims and Hindus – in practice tend to maintain forms of hierarchical status differences between people within their communities which reflect caste differences but which have become adapted to the British class system of social categorization. The form of caste discrimination, where it exists in Britain, is thus based upon occupation. Land-owning castes will tend to discriminate against those who were farmers in the homelands and will tend to affiliate to organizations which defend and maintain such distinctions (the more conservative temples, for instance). The lower castes may adhere to more militant groups and, as a result of discrimination by 'higher' castes, will identify more easily with trade unions and Indian Workers' Associations.

While religious and caste differences inevitably tend to reinforce the political differences between Asian political groups, such disunity is not so evident within the West Indian community. The reason for this lies in the fact that West Indians, with their Christian religion and their relatively weak community affiliations, have been able to adapt more easily to British cultural life. There are, of course, animosities between West Indians and Asians as well as between Asians themselves and these differences hinder the effectiveness of groups which have managed to overcome their distrust of British political institutions.

Many organizations, particularly the less 'political' ones (some of the temples), adopt traditional political styles and strategies which tend to be directly carried over from the homeland and are applied to British political situations in a quite inappropriate manner. Organizations will either adopt an uncooperative attitude (resistance to British influence by isolation of the minority community), or will display militant religious fervour characteristic of Hindu/Muslim conflict between Indians and Pakistanis after the Second World War. A clear example of this 'homeland' orientation is given by Beetham when he describes the activities of the Akali Dal organization between 1967 and 1969 in Wolverhampton:

the Akali Dal was an organisation of those whose main commitment lay to the Punjab rather than to Britain, and this was to have important consequences for the way they handled the turban issue (an attempt to persuade Wolverhampton Corporation to allow the wearing of turbans by Corporation bus drivers and conductors). It means that they were not primarily concerned with, or alive to its effect on race relations in Wolverhampton (Beetham, 1970, p.39).

In response to the Council's refusal of its demands, the Akali Dal threatened that its leaders would commit suicide unless the local authority granted its demands (which in fact the local authority eventually did).

Such political styles and strategies are often accompanied by campaigns related to homeland political issues. The conflicts beween different factions within the Indian Workers' Associations, for instance, often involve disagreements about issues relevant to the Indian political situation rather than about differences relating to British politics. Central to such conflicts are questions concerning the political programme of the Indian Congress Party factions, differences between the Indian Communist Parties, and policies to be adopted in relation to the Indian peasantry.

Despite the factors inhibiting integration into native political processes, there are a number of factors working in favour of a closer association. Indeed, such factors can place the less traditionalist black organizations in a reasonably favourable position, even relative to native British pressure groups, *vis à vis* the gaining of access to government and government-funded agencies. To illustrate this point it may be contended that the more politically active black organizations often tend to be much more ideologically and politically committed than 'white' pressure groups. In many areas of Britain black groups are influenced by left-orientated politics and ideology and pledge their support to Labour Party candidates at national and local elections. Frequently such groups campaign through the broader Labour Movement and trade unions on a multiplicity of issues affecting their members. Their ideological and relatively politicized approach often stands in sharp contrast to the 'single-issue' pressure groups which make up the constituency of native British local politics. The multi-issue slant of the more political ethnic-minority groups thus impels them to participate in political debate and in institutions which appear to afford them the opportunity to maximize their impact within the community.

Ideological integration

Given the differing dispositions of black groups towards political institutions and the attitude by which some see themselves as confronting the 'white power structure', there is nevertheless a general tendency for ethnic-minority or-ganizations to favour co-operation with government or government-initiated programmes. Recognition of this challenges the view which holds that traditional cultural factors will remain of primary importance in preventing black participation. Desai (1963), for example, concluded that traditionalist pressures lead to the almost complete rejection by black people of British culture and institutions. This, however, over-stresses the degree to which black leaders wish to isolate themselves politically and it neglects the role of the local community-relations agencies as institutions which facilitate group/government co-ordination by breaking down group suspicions.

Katznelson (1973) argues that black organizations become increasingly 'political' as they adapt themselves to the institutional and political environ-ment in which they find themselves, and that when race became a major political issue in Britain in the 1960s the black community was compelled to defend its own interests through the formation of its own political organiza-tions. He contends that at that time British political institutions reflected decisions made by white political elites, which inevitably tended to neglect the needs of the immigrant community. By relating to the highly political issues surrounding the question of race relations and immigration, and while confronting the white political parties, the black organizations themselves assumed ideological and political standpoints suited to their immediate interests and expectations. The precise nature of these ideological commitments was itself, according to Katznelson, a reflection of the various strands of political ideology (socialism, liberalism, etc.) found in the 'host' society. Thus groups in Britain adapted to the political environment and in the 'mother-country' society adopted liberal democratic forms, rhetoric and processes which accommodated them to the institutional expression of racism' (Katznelson, 1973, p.157). The strong implication here is of an integration of groups, both *ideologically and institutionally*, into the native or host political system. While Katznelson sometimes over-emphasizes the extent of this integration, his contention that black groups take on some of the forms of native British political groups is valid. The adherence, for example, of some groups to both militant and moderate varieties of socialist ideology in domestic politics reflects the influence of British Labour politics and the co-operation of black groups with other leftist groupings and trade union bodies.

It has been argued that the majority of politically active and ideologically committed groups generally adopts a moderate attitude towards co-operation with government bodies and seeks to maintain and develop a consensus in order to benefit from participation in local political institutions (Lawrence, 1974; Miles and Phizacklea, 1977). Such observations will be seen to be highly relevant in connection with the public agencies mentioned later in this book, since, although many groups display militant ideological commitments in a formal programmatic sense, they frequently adapt their positions and ways of presenting themselves in order to legitimate their demands more effectively before politicians and government officials. This would seem to be a very clear indication of political adaptation to native political practice.

Black mobilization

If the disposition of black groups points to an often active intervention in political institutions, then their position is further enhanced by the fact that the larger politically active groups have managed to use their political capabilities and the existence of local black constituencies to their advantage. Black leaders often regard themselves, with some justification, as being especially representative of their communities. This is a common enough claim by interest groups, but it is a claim which means rather more for black organizations than having an ill-defined popular local sympathy support and more even than the ability to gain electoral support. The significance of the relation between black groups and their 'constituents' lies in the degree to which groups have managed to build up political networks which penetrate the community and which by their existence engender support which can be very effectively mobilized. It is a relationship which few white interest groups, apart from the trade unions, can hope to match.

It is not only the leaders of the black community who perceive the existence of such a relationship. It is a view to which both politicians and government officials often subscribe. Research suggests (Jacobs, 1978) that councillors and officials at local level tend not to be concerned with the actual size of groups' paid-up memberships when assessing group representativeness – they are more concerned with the way in which groups articulate community demands and the degree to which the black community responds to group leadership initiatives, the ability of groups to mount large public demonstrations being one indication of this. Councillors are generally concerned with the extent to which groups are looked to by members of the black population (particularly for the expression of political discontent) as bodies capable of solving various social problems in the fields of housing, education, health and law. The apparatus involved in mobilization of support for groups is such that they become adept at organizing well-attended social events, political meetings and conferences. In this respect black people generally appear to be rather more disposed to attending political gatherings in large numbers than supporters of native British groups. In the Asian community in particular, such mobilizations are achieved through the contacting of individuals and groups of people in the temples and through trade union branches. The temples, with their large congregations, act as one focus of community activity and assume important social and political functions which facilitate mobilization for particular campaigns (Jacobs, 1978).

To illustrate more effectively the ways in which black organizations operate, it is useful to examine the situation in one British town. Wolverhampton, in the West Midlands, provided this author with a research base between 1978 and 1981 when a comprehensive survey of black organizations was carried out (Jacobs, 1978, 1980, 1982).

With a population of 252,000, the town has around 15% of its population belonging to black ethnic minorities. This gives Wolverhampton one of the largest black populations by percentage of its total population in Britain, behind only Leicester and some London Boroughs. Such a large black 'constituency' inevitably has given rise to a proliferation of organizations. Research covered all Wolverhampton's voluntary organizations. Black organizations could therefore be viewed in relation to other groups. Altogether 35 black organizations were identified, accounting for nearly 7% of all the non-trade-union voluntary organizations in Wolverhampton – this given that black people are able to join white organizations as well as their own community-based associations.

Table 3 illustrates the relative weight of the various categories of voluntary organization in Wolverhampton and indicates that black organizations, in terms of their distinctive presence, were strategically well placed to influence local politics. Moreover, because of their relatively high memberships and

Table 3. *Organizations based in Wolverhampton (May 1978)*

Type of organization	Number in town	% of total
Black ethnic minority	35	6.84
White ethnic minority	10	1.95
Tenants	32	6.25
Ratepayers	2	0.39
Youth groups	79	15.43
Senior citizens	38	7.42
Forces/ex-services	15	2.93
Professional	41	8.01
Civic	5	0.98
Religious	13	2.54
Social/welfare	47	9.18
Sports	42	8.20
Educational	6	1.17
Cultural	48	9.38
Others	99	19.33
Total	512	100.00

Source: B. Jacobs (1978), *Public Policy and Local Interest Groups in Britain: Three Case-Studies*, University of Keele Ph.D. thesis, p.67.

ability to mobilize support, many could be regarded as potentially more 'active' than the majority of white organizations compared, for example, to youth groups and senior citizens' groups (Jacobs, 1978).

The potential of black organizations was not, of course, always realized or developed. The proliferation of organizations as a factor taken by itself was not, therefore, an accurate indication of their influence. The maximum use of an organization's resources depended upon its desire to liaise with native political structures, to co-operate with other local groups and to establish links with organizations at national level. The following group profiles of a selection of Wolverhampton organizations therefore examine the different approaches adopted with respect to these factors and to methods of community penetration by different groups.

The profiles indicate how organizations implant themselves in the black community and the degree to which they may be regarded as being 'representative'. In addition, the nature of some of the inter-group rivalries and conflicts which often seriously affect the effectiveness of their political activities is mentioned. These differences are frequently played out within the official community-relations bodies, but also impact upon inter-community and intra-community relations on a much broader front.

In making this analysis it will be helpful to provide an account of the general aims, objectives and political/ideological characteristics of the organizations, drawing upon available literature and upon information provided through numerous interviews with representatives of the organizations studied (Jacobs, 1978). Because of the large number of organizations in the town, interviews were conducted with the larger and more active groups and with those which tended to be active nationally, but a number of interviews were also conducted with smaller localized groups and community-relations officials and workers. Together, these local contacts most commonly pointed to the so-called 'self-help' organizations, the Indian Workers' Associations and Asian religious and welfare groups, as being of central importance for community activists and for black people placing demands on local institutions.

'Self-help' groups

'Self-help' organizations were particularly common in the West Indian community. The largest of these was the Harambee Association affiliated to the National Harambee movement. The Association's constitution reflected the general objectives of the self-help organizations in general:

(1)   to promote the welfare, social and cultural well-being of unemployed, homeless and other under-privileged persons of Afro/Caribbean descent;

(2)   to provide a service whereby the Afro/Caribbean people of the (Wolverhampton) Borough can communicate their experiences to members of their own community and to the community as a whole;

(3)   to provide an opportunity for its members to gain respect through various self-help projects.

These objectives were a clear expression of the general orientation of self-help groups seeking to influence councillors and officials in order to obtain definite returns for black people. Harambee also involved a relatively high degree of political campaigning in the cause of 'black liberation and socialism' and the promotion of practical community projects such as the running of the 'Harambee Project', providing hostel accommodation to homeless West Indian youths in Wolverhampton. This project had the backing of the Wolverhampton Council for Community Relations (WCCR) and the local authority. A further activity of Harambee was the administration of the Marcus Garvey Advice Centre which, as the name suggests, provided an advisory service for black citizens, mainly relating to legal matters. The Advice Centre was jointly run with the Commonwealth Citizens' Association, which adhered to similar general objectives as Harambee.

The Commonwealth Citizens' Association was one of the more politically militant of the self-help groups surveyed, combining its leftist political campaigning with some rather 'mundane' grass-roots community work. Again, this tended to be mainly concerned with legal and social welfare advice for West Indians and some work involving prison welfare and defence of youths charged with various offences; but despite the routine welfare activities pursued, it should be remembered that organizations such as this regarded community work as a potentially politicizing activity. Involvement in the locality was seen as a way of promoting the cause of black liberation and socialism through the involvement of the community in self-help and 'defence' activities. Indeed, this view was shared by many left organizations, which to greater or lesser extents attuned their programmes to accommodate community politics within their spheres of activity. The cross-fertilization of ideas between the West Indian self-help groups and left groups and Labour Party branches tended to reinforce this approach as a practical political strategy.

Another self-help group surveyed was the West Indian Family Agency, which tended to have a more pragmatic concern for welfare rights and matters concerning the ability of individuals to obtain benefits from the social security system. Despite this concentration, the Agency had been involved with broader political campaigns. Such self-help activity had, in these campaigns, produced a perception of political rights within the context of making claims upon government agencies, and for the Family Agency and the other self-help organizations this expressed itself in terms of campaigning around the essential 'bread and butter' interests of the community. Community activists thus regarded themselves as providing assistance which would not otherwise exist and which was crucial in enhancing the social standing of blacks in what was regarded as a hostile environment. However, in practice this approach often led to ideological diffusion or dilution through the focusing of black demands upon a fairly narrow band of issues which did not have a particularly political content. Individual 'case-work' tended towards the de-emphasis of ideological questions and an emphasis upon legal, administrative and technical questions.

One important aspect of this was the facilitating of compromise in the political strategies of West Indian groups. Legal, administrative and technical matters were the central concern of local politicians who were generally keen to dissociate themselves from the overtly militant ideological commitments of some organizations. Community self-help was ideally suited to the objectives of community-relations bodies and agencies such as the Manpower Services Commission, which were keen to professionalize community organizations and gain their co-operation (Jacobs, 1978, 1980, 1982).

The Indian Workers' Associations

The political atmosphere in the Asian community could often be more highly charged and consequently somewhat less conducive to co-operation and compromise, although in general most Asian organizations had, to differing degrees, come to accept liaison with government agencies as being a distinct advantage to them.

The most important of the specifically political groups in this context was the Indian Workers' Association (GB). The first Indian Workers' Association (IWA) was founded in Coventry in 1928 and shortly afterwards a similar group was formed in London, consisting mainly of middle-class Indians who were prepared to co-operate with intellectuals and students to promote the cause of Indian independence. Associations of Indians in Britain spread, but only to decline after the granting of Indian independence in 1947. With the increase in post-war immigration, the IWAs were gradually revitalized and adapted to British domestic politics by way of their attempts to defend the interests of the growing Indian community.

The 1970s and 1980s reflected the serious divisions within the Asian community, which arose as a result of disagreements about developments on the political scene in the Indian homeland and resulted in the splitting of IWAs throughout Britain into three separate organizations, two of which existed in Wolverhampton at the time of the survey. The IWA (Great Britain) was the largest, reflecting the broad position of the Communist Party of India (Marxist) or CPM. There was also the IWA (without GB), sympathetic to the more militant political line of the Communist Party of India (Marxist–Leninist) or CPML. The third was the IWA (Southall) which was a moderate formation based in London's Southall and supportive of traditional cultural values in the Indian community.

The association of the majority of IWAs with Communism began in the 1950s when British Communist Party (CP) members campaigned on a programme of 'unity' for the Indian community in Britain which would cut across class lines and encourage traditional community and religious leaders to enter CP-led campaigns. DeWitt has described the nature of this unity perspective:

Unity was thus satisfying and reasonable. Also, there was an organized group of leaders in every Punjabi community which tried to achieve unity. This group was composed of Indian members of the Communist Party of Great Britain. Few immigrants had been Party members in India. According to the immigrants it is very difficult to join the Communist Party in India. One must do a great deal of work for the Party and remain on probation for a couple of years before being admitted. Joining the CP is an easy matter in comparison (DeWitt, 1969, p.66).

In areas where the British CP members had penetrated the IWAs there were separate branches established for the Indians:

the Indian branches had a great deal of freedom to direct their own activities. By and large they ignored British politics. The Communists were no more interested than the rest of the immigrants in the central issues of domestic British politics (DeWitt, 1969, p.67).

The CP generally co-operated with non-Communist leaders in the IWAs and even with those who they considered to be 'reactionaries' (DeWitt, 1969 p.67). Neither were there attempts to get the IWAs to adopt Communist slogans, since they were regarded as broad mass organizations which would provide the CP with a recruiting base rather than producing an ideologically 'pure' movement. This 'broad-front' approach persisted throughout the IWA movement right into the 1980s, but while the broad front failed to produce a clear class-orientated political programme for the IWAs, it did prove to be effective in expanding the social class base of the IWAs by attracting numerous intellectuals, professionals and students who were keen to obtain the backing of working-class Indians (DeWitt, 1969, p.71). Despite the eventual numerical superiority of the various brands of 'Marxists' within the IWAs, local branches were able to admit non-Communists who were simply keen to work on behalf of Indians over a range of localized community-welfare issues.

Divisions in the early 1960s had made many Indian Communists and the majority of the IWAs break away from the British CP, which supported the reformist, Parliamentarian Communist Party of India (CPI). The leftists formed their own organizations, abandoning the notion of one single united Indian movement, but retaining the broad front as a strategy for individual IWAs. Superficially these splits had little relevance to the community work of the IWAs in Britain, but closer examination reveals that the divisions did reflect differences in domestic British political orientations and group attitudes towards participation in British institutions. The more militant but 'constitutional' stance of the Indian CPM was consistent with the desire of the IWA (GB) leaders to seek a compromise with local British politicians, whereas the leftist CPML line in India was reflected in the IWAs marked suspicion of participation in community-relations agencies and hostility towards UK immigration policies. However, *strict* adherence to Indian party lines was less important as far as co-operation with British politicians was concerned. In Wolverhampton the two IWAs were prepared to participate in community-relations bodies and were keen to gain access to local authority decision-makers. Both groups came to regard access in terms of pragmatic politics rather than in terms of ideology or party orthodoxy. To this extent the IWAs were regarded as 'moderates' by local councillors (Jacobs, 1978).

The question of 'moderation' deserves closer attention, since there were essentially two sides to the political strategies of the IWAs. In its straight-forwardly 'moderate' guise the IWA (GB), for instance, maintained its 'broad front' approach – an approach orientated towards gaining the support of councillors and local government officials. The aims of the IWA (GB), contained in its national constitution, illustrated the general lack of ideological content of the broad-front strategy:

(1)   to safeguard and improve their [IWA] members' conditions of life and work;

(2)   seek co-operation and unity with the Commission in UK [Indian High Commission] towards fulfilment of its aims and objects;

(3)   promote co-operation and unity with the Trade Union and Labour Movement in Great Britain;

(4)   strengthen friendship with the British and all other peoples in Great Britain and co-operate with their organizations to this end;

(5) fight against all forms of discrimination based on race, colour, creed or sex, for equal human rights and social and economic opportunities, and co-operate with other organizations for the same;

(6) promote the cause of friendship, peace and freedom of all countries and co-operate with other organizations national and international, striving for the same;

(7) keep its [IWA's] members in particular, and people in Great Britain generally, informed of political, economic and social developments in India; and to

(8) undertake social, welfare and cultural activities towards the fulfilment of the above aims and objectives.[1]

These objectives enabled the IWA (GB) to continue to attract non-Communists to its ranks and to claim to be representative of a broader cross-section of the Asian community than would have been the case if the organization were seen simply to be Communist- or CPM-inspired. The infusion of non-Communists meant that they would be exposed to the CPM line at meetings and at the IWA (GB) conference, thereby being attracted to a stronger ideological commitment. Both the IWA (GB) and the smaller CPML IWA shared this approach to mobilization and recruitment.[2]

In Wolverhampton the focus of the IWA (GB) upon the moderate political strategy was highlighted in practical terms, not only by a willingness to participate in the local Community Relations Council, but also by a desire to widen the IWA's membership base through co-operation with conservative temple members and religious leaders. This moderation also required the IWA (GB) to abandon its one-time practice of running candidates against the Labour Party, by moving into a closer relationship with Labour councillors and Labour Party branches, and by encouraging IWA (GB) members to actually join the Party.

The other face of the IWA (GB) was that designed to meet internal party needs within the organization itself. The moderate programme did not mean that the more strongly ideological militants within the organization had to abandon their 'Marxist' commitments, but it did require them to tailor their 'maximum' programme to facilitate implementation of the 'broad-front' unity approach. Internally the use of leftist phrases was interlinked with a Labourist-style politics which satisfied militants and non-militants alike. While left-sounding rhetoric could be employed 'where appropriate', IWA (GB) leaders were keen to maintain a respectable distance from groups such as the Socialist Workers' Party (although there were organizational links with the SWP mainly through the local Anti-Racism Committee) and to level criticisms against far-left organizations in terms characteristic of the Indian CPM and the British CP.

The actual impact which this broad-front strategy had on membership was very difficult to assess accurately, in view of the inaccessibility of membership figures. The Wolverhampton IWA (GB) membership appeared to be in the

25–50 category in 1978, but according to the Commission for Racial Equality's 'Directory of Ethnic Minority Organizations' for the Midlands (1982), the IWA (GB) claimed over 3,000 members and supporters.

The IWA (GB)'s implantation in the community relied upon its links with other groups and the ability of the Association to mobilize electoral support for the Labour Party and to mount, with the assistance of the Anti-Racism Committee, large anti-racist demonstrations. The IWA (GB) (far more than the IWA) in Wolverhampton also had significant support in the temples, which provided a focus for political expression unmatched by other Asian political groupings. Aurora makes this point about IWA influence nationally and locally:

The response to the organizers of the Indian Workers' Association (IWA) was, therefore, tremendous and it very soon emerged as an organization with great authority over the Indians and influence with the host society.

According to Aurora this influence was partly responsible for IWA 'moderation' because:

leaders have a direct interest in the maintenance of the cohesion of the community. Even when two instrumental leaders oppose each other they do so within the framework of the communal life and its ethics of conflict (Aurora, 1967, pp. 101–3).

This particularly applied in situations where different factions were important and factional politics (often based upon caste differences) provided another reason why the IWA (GB) was keen to get involved in temple politics and elections of the temple committees. By courting members of particular factions, the IWA (GB) could obtain the support of faction leaders and thus the support of members of temple congregations which adhered to those leaders.

Generally the majority of temple committees in Wolverhampton, as opposed to temple members, were suspicious of British politicians and of formal involvement with community-relations activities except on issues which were of direct relevance to them (such as the search for suitable temple premises and the obtaining of planning permission for new temple buildings). This caution was related to the cultural and religious factors outlined above and it was because of the desire for non-involvement in debates about domestic British political issues and because of the distrust by Sikhs of Marxism, that the IWA (GB) nationally often found it difficult to work with the temples. The notable success which the IWA (GB) in Wolverhampton had in this respect related largely to its involvement with the large Cannock Road temple. As one member of the Sikh community stated in a 1978 interview with the author:

The Indian Workers' Association is totally political. The temple committee shouldn't have been political in my opinion. Noor [President of IWA (GB)] is now involved at Cannock Road and some executive committee [EC] members at the temple are members of the IWA/GB. Yes, IWA/GB has influence. [The EC was not, however, IWA(GB)-dominated.]

The 'success' at Cannock Road was offset to a great extent by the resistance of the other temples to penetration. There were deep-rooted differences between the IWA (GB) and the other temples and this general divide could be seen in terms of the competition which the IWA (GB) posed to temple leaders. Like the temples, the IWA (GB) leadership tended to claim to be the main legitimate political representative of the Indian community and, like the temples, the IWA (GB) provided assistance with social, welfare and educational matters. For the temple leaders, therefore, the aim was to provide a religious focus for cultural and welfare activity which could not be matched by the IWA (GB).

Other Asian groups

The temple committees in Wolverhampton were, therefore, perfectly adept in resisting the leftist political orientation of IWA (GB) and other political groupings seeking support in the Asian community. This situation prevailed into the 1980s, despite attempts by leftist groups to capitalize upon political issues which related to religious and 'homeland' affairs.

The Indian Government's 1984 siege of the holy Sikh Temple at Amritsar provides a good example of a 'homeland' religious issue which became highly charged politically. It was an issue on which many Sikhs in Britain committed themselves to a strong anti-Government line, opposing Indian Prime Minister Indira Gandhi and expressing a desire to join political demonstrations against the taking of the Temple from the hands of a group of Sikh fundamentalists. The Indian Army's forceful removal of the armed fundamentalists and the subsequent assassination of Indira Gandhi created tensions within British black communities between Sikhs and Hindus which were exacerbated by communal disorders between these religious groups in India itself.

Large public demonstrations were organized by Sikh organizations in Britain and a so-called Sikh Government in Exile was established in London. Leftist political groupings, however, adopted a position which sought to maintain peace in Britain's black communities, to overcome communal and religious animosities. Temple leaders, both Sikh and Hindu, also generally sought to moderate their responses, particularly in the period immediately following the assassination, because they, like the non-religious organizations, recognized the potential threat of disorder to the prevailing ordered political environment. Temple leaders were well aware of the serious implications of violence and many seem to have regarded lending too much support to militant Sikh sentiments as counter-productive in a setting in which co-operative relations with local authorities were seen to be more appropriate to their good relations with British politicians and government agencies.[3] These responses were consistent with the author's 1978–81 Wolverhampton survey responses and clearly in line with the gradual adaptation of black politics to the native political environment.

Apart from the IWAs and larger temples, the 1978–81 Wolverhampton research identified other, less active Asian groups, such as the Sant Nirarkari Madal (Universal Brotherhood), which was a minority 'sect', unlike the larger Krishna and Hindu temples. The Young Singh Missionary Society was, similarly, a relatively politically inactive group specializing in the promotion of the Sikh religious message. The Sikh fundamentalist Akali Dal Party, the Indian Republican Party and the Sikh Association of Great Britain also fell under the heading of essentially exclusive groupings which, because of their isolation from British political institutions and because of their consequent exclusion from local community-relations activities, were numerically small and unable to offer tangible welfare benefits which would attract significant support. All these groups were hostile to the IWA's socialism, although they were often sympathetic to Labour Party councillors.

The Pakistan Cultural Centre (incorporating the UK Islamic Mission and the Muslim Education Trust) acted as the focus of religious activity for the small Pakistani community in Wolverhampton. Like the Indian temples, the Cultural Centre occasionally entered the political arena to impress demands upon the local authority, particularly for the extension of Muslim religious and cultural education in Wolverhampton schools, and sought to be a representative community organization. Pakistan Welfare or Cultural Associations (PWAs) are now a common feature of the Muslim community in British towns and cities. The Associations concern themselves with numerous problems arising within their community, ranging from worship to advice and assistance on housing and educational matters. To some degree the PWAs are beginning to assume a role similar to the IWAs, but remaining devoid of the leftist political commitment and, in Wolverhampton, being less effective in pursuance of their aims and demands. In fact, the PWA in Wolverhampton remained a fairly insular organization: having been affiliated to the local Community Relations Council between 1967 and 1972, the PWA then withdrew, dissatisfied with its political emphasis and disappointed with the lack of apparent benefits arising from affiliation of direct advantage to the Pakistani community. The withdrawal was marked by bitter recriminations on both sides, which led to a complete breakdown of communication between the PWA and community-relations officials, although by 1977 informal contacts were re-established with individual officers. The break did not leave the PWA completely without access to councillors and local authority officials: the PWA's Muslim Education Trust remained as a participant in the local authority educational programme for multi-cultural education which was the result of co-operation which had been built up through the early 1970s.

Anti-racist activity

Finally there was the Wolverhampton Anti-Racism Committee (WARC). The Anti-Racism Committee, formed in the summer of 1976 on the initiative of the Wolverhampton branch of the IWA (GB), provided an important link between the ethnic minority communities and militant leftist groupings in the town. WARC was originally formed as an organization committed to opposing the National Front and, to this end, had been active in lobbying local councillors and the Community Relations Council. The preoccupation of WARC with an almost entirely negative 'anti-National Front' position is illustrated in the following extracts from a WARC leaflet issued in 1977:

The recent racial disturbances are caused by [Enoch] Powell's inflammatory speeches, and by racialist organizations such as the National Front and the National Party. Racialist organizations, taking advantage of the economic crisis, put forward the idea that blacks cause the crisis.

Further, the leaflet implores: 'fight racialism, repeal immigration laws, ban the National front'. This kind of 'anti' position was shared by the various factions represented on the WARC committee, but divisions within the committee were manifest, which affected WARC's orientation towards the WCCR and the local authority. The far left were in favour of non-cooperation with the WCCR, while the more 'moderate' elements (IWA(GB), Labour Party) favoured a closer relationship with councillors and community-relations officers. For a short period after WARC's formation the committee came under the control of the combined forces of the International Marxist Group and the Socialist Workers' Party. By the end of 1976 this leadership lost control as the result of the mobilization of support within the Wolverhampton Labour Party and, in particular, the active intervention of the Labour Party Young Socialists, the Wolverhampton Polytechnic Labour Club, the Communist Party and members of the 'Militant' grouping within the Labour Party. These forces combined to elect a more 'co-operative' leadership which drew WARC away from its former 'direct action' policy towards closer relations with councillors, the WCCR and the Labour Party, and enabled WARC to make a much broader appeal to the more moderate black community leaders.

The anti-racist campaign activity of WARC did much to encourage the participation of youth in political activity. WARC's committee presided as a co-ordinating group for the town's anti-racist events, which drew the support of many Asian and Caribbean organizations, with energetic young black members impressed by the national campaigns of the Anti-Nazi League (ANL) and its 'Rock Against Racism' offshoot. During the 1980s support for these campaigns lessened, but many of the young blacks brought into politics at that time maintained their interest in community action and became involved in local 'self-help' projects and welfare causes. Wolverhampton's Asian Youth Project, the YMCA and the Black Arrow Group provide examples of youth organizations which became actively involved with community work and which gained the respect of community-relations officials and local councillors. At national level, the Leicester-based National Youth Bureau became an important voluntary agency intent upon extending such community voluntarism amongst young people in general and also to young blacks keen to involve themselves in local schemes. The Bureau's work contains a strong anti-racist element which, to some extent, echoes the anti-racist objectives of the large campaigns of the late 1970s, but without the same definite commitment to a leftist political programme.

The voluntary sector

Wolverhampton's black ethnic groups, therefore, adapted to a variety of political situations in such a manner and on such a scale as to suggest a gradual but increasingly pronounced degree of 'anglicization' in terms of their relationships with British institutions. The black constituency, or, more precisely, individual ethnic groups, presently appear to be in a situation in which they are developing their interests much more extensively beyond their own communities and beyond traditional community-relations agencies. Some of the ways in which this is happening in the field of community development and urban renewal are dealt with in Chapters 7 and 8, and it is worth noting this point here too, by referring to black involvement in Wolverhampton's Voluntary Sector Council (WVSC). The WVSC enabled black groups to involve themselves in an 'umbrella' agency, backed by a local authority and not adhering to objectives or policies largely intended to benefit black people (as with Community Relations Councils). The WVSC case indicates the attraction of tangible resource benefits to groups seeking to operate effectively at community level and marks an early stage in the group professionalization process as evidenced in the USA.

Wolverhampton's VSC experienced really significant growth from about 1980 onwards. By 1982 the WVSC included 150 voluntary organizations, both black and white, in its membership and could boast of WVSC's involvement in a range of local-authority-supported programmes. WVSC's budget totalled just under £29,000 for 1981–2.

Ethnic-minority affiliates represented a wide diversity of interests. For example, the Asian Community Resources Project, the Afro-Caribbean Cultural Centre, the Bangladesh Association, the West Midlands Caribbean Association and the Commonwealth Citizens' Association, came together in the WVSC with an equally diverse range of groups, such as tenants' associations, Christian organizations and even marching display bands.[4] The WVSC's executive committee included representatives of affiliate organizations and WVSC officers. Participating black groups were therefore exhibiting a desire to take advantage of the WVSC's professional services and to bid for grants from Wolverhampton's Inner Areas Programme Committee, to which the WVSC was co-opted. Therefore, the question arises as to whether the benefits of participation in a non-ethnic organization such as the WVSC outweighed the apparent advantages to some groups of independence or ideological 'purity'. The WVSC directly involved groups in the Urban Programme and brought them into contact with the wider non-ethnic voluntary sector, local authority officials and local councillors. It is a pattern which could mark the direction of many black groups into the late 1980s.

Costs and benefits

The survey of groups in Wolverhampton reveals a pattern of black activity and integration which seems to be common in other urban black communities in Britain. An examination of the Commission for Racial Equality's regional minority directories gives a very clear indication of the types of ethnic, religious and political organizations in the major towns and cities. Localization is evident, insofar as most groups direct their energies inwards towards their own localities or towns, and the group *types* found show a similarity from city to city. There is generally an Indian Workers' Association, religious temples, cultural groups and self-help organizations. Some (such as Harambee Associations) will be linked to national organizations or federations, or will liaise with the Commission for Racial Equality or with the Indian High Commission (in the case of Indian groups). This does not, however, constitute a national black politics (as already mentioned), but it does enable the researcher to point to a national commonality in the pattern of black group clusters and group types between different localities. It is possible that the move towards greater integration will effect a drawing together of black organizations as they consolidate their national linkages and extend their politics into non-ethnic institutions and agencies and as they become more active in the political parties. The campaign for special black sections in the Labour Party in 1984 tended to galvanize blacks from different ethnic backgrounds, for instance. If that process were to continue, then Britain's black constituency would move much closer to the American model of 'black politics' proper.

3 Black political action

Access to agencies established to facilitate participation implies certain important costs and benefits which are taken into account by black group leaders. Costs and benefits, however, are calculated differently between black organizations and rank-and-file members and followers can have their own views about participation, which may be at variance with those of their leaders.

The wide diversity of organizations described in the last chapter would inevitably lead to such differences of subjective assessments relating to co-operation with government and other agencies. Religious and cultural differences produce a variety of attitudes, and it was seen that these determined responses to political questions. In this context it may be that group leaders perceive some very real benefits which they see as being gained from a more formal relationship with national or local government. Rank-and-file members may regard such a relationship with suspicion or even open hostility, either because they wish to adhere to traditional cultural or religious values or because they support militant political ideologies. Group leaders thus often play a bridge-building role which involves the drawing of the wider group membership over to a position where they will consent to closer liaison with politicians and permanent government officials. This moves followers over from relative political isolation into a closer relationship with 'external' agencies and political processes.

Many leaders will not face such tasks, since their followers will follow their general approach to such questions. Temple leaderships will frequently be in the position of bringing their followers behind them, without having to worry about the kind of bargaining and compromising involved in heading a more political organization, such as the Indian Workers' Association. In black organizations such as those mentioned in Chapter 2, leadership bestows not only authority within an organization but also a status which closely identifies the group with a prominent leader or leaders. This is evident, of course, in most groups and political organizations, but it seems to be especially import-ant in black minority political formations, where the most articulate tend to be the better-educated middle-class representatives of communities. These will be people who have managed to enter professional occupations and who hold 'respectable positions', perhaps in business or education and who may no longer even live in the areas inhabited by poor working-class blacks.

Perkins talks of black leaders in the United States as developing perspec-tives about their communities which begin to isolate them from the majority of black people. He argues that many black professionals and even full-time community workers display disdain for the plight of the ghetto poor which may be more intense than many illiberal whites. Although this situation has not developed to quite such an obvious degree in Britain, it is interesting to quote Perkins on this subject, while noting the development in Britain of a politically sophisticated black leadership which is developing similar appetites. Perkins states:

The self-imposed alienation of the black middle class from the black lower class has, unfortunately, developed a schism between them which finds the former group often identifying with and supporting the white racist values which oppress the latter group. Many black professionals seek employment outside the black ghetto colony because jobs in the 'downtown' area are more lucrative and many don't care to be associated with 'those niggers anyway'. Also many skilled blacks are diverted from working in the ghetto colony by large corporations which are seeking 'token niggers' to showcase their professed liberalism (Perkins, 1975, p.91).

We may disagree with the precise formulations used here, but Perkins makes the important point that there is a growing gulf developing at community level between the 'unorganized' blacks at local level and professionalizing representatives. While this situation may be 'unfortunate', it is, however, also appropriate and more analytically useful to see the social demarcation between the mass of blacks and their leaders as an inevitable consequence of the integration of black leaders into the institutions of the state and as an expression of the identification of the black aspiring social leaders with the state. The basis of this is the ability of the state to provide leaders with certain tangible returns which encourage them to co-operate with politicians, officials and private-sector interests.[1]

In Britain, black leaders tend not to be as socially isolated from their 'constituents' as in the United States, although the process of integration does produce the same kind of political collaboration with the state and corporate bodies. Many leaders in Britain still live in the inner urban areas and have originated from lower-middle- and working-class backgrounds. Indian Workers' Associations are, for instance, generally in contact with 'grass roots' opinions and keen to maintain leadership contacts with rank-and-file sup-porters. In Britain, government agencies have been unable to supply sufficient financial resources to enable leaders to improve their lifestyles to such marked degrees as is often the case in America. Despite this relative financial 'impoverishment' of British community agencies, the important point is that the process of professionalism, of integration and political co-operation in general, has produced favourable conditions for some leaders to pursue strategies in terms conducive to their own interests and objectives rather than by reference to the immediate concerns of the mass of urban blacks. The physical presence or otherwise of leaders in a particular area is thus in itself relatively unimportant, since their absence may be symptomatic of a process of integration but not one of its pre-conditions. Similarly, the class origins of leaders may be of little direct significance when what is crucial is the *response* of leaders to agency initiatives. It is thus useful to examine leadership *aspirations* to become 'respected' in the eyes of government and to eventually distinguish themselves by taking up positions within community or national agencies (rather as Perkins describes) where they may become career activists or community officials.

The leadership role

Consistent with the desire for legitimacy within the political system is the search for order. Black leaders have a vested interest in maintaining a degree of stability within the system in order to preserve and enhance the strength of their relationships with governments and local agencies and politicians more effectively. Stability also tends to facilitate the consolidation of their own leadership position and to facilitate upward social mobility or promotion within agency career structures. Leaders, in this attempt to maintain order, necessarily relate their policies and actions to 'system supportive' objectives which are generally acceptable to decision-makers in government.

Politically 'moderate' leaders following this approach also have to take account of their constituencies. Policies and actions have to satisfy rank-and-file supporters and, under certain circumstances, need to relate to the demands expressed by *unorganized* interests within the black community. Dissent amongst these groups threatens ordered relationships and requires leaders to persuade their constituents more concertedly that their interests are best served through support of legitimate institutions. This is not always a straightforward task, given the ever-present tensions which exist between different groups within the black community. For leaders in the more politicized organizations the task is particularly difficult in circumstances which often throw into sharp relief the differences between co-operative leadership objectives and militant demands of followers. Conservative religious leaders may face less of a problem, as their followers adhere themselves to philosophies which are inherently less radical. The pressures felt from 'below' were clearly illustrated by the recent communal 'riots' which affected Britain in 1981.

These disturbances were initially generally *leaderless* and spontaneous in nature, having only a very ill-defined political character. The outbreaks of street violence did not fit the neat category of 'race riots', despite the racial overtones of some of the disturbances, particularly in the London area.[2] The random looting and fire-bombing took place in a haphazard and confused way and, most importantly, without reference (in the early phases) to the 'usual channels' of liaison between black leaders, politicians and government officials or to the Community Relations Councils.

Such a situation posed a challenge to the ordered network of participation represented by the local government and community-relations agencies. This was a challenge but *not a threat* to those institutions, since following the disturbances the more traditional process of consultation and bargaining reasserted itself, as prominent community leaders came to the fore as representatives speaking *on behalf* of the black community. The assumption within the community that the existing organizations and leaders *did* in fact stand for the community was never seriously challenged either by the majority of black people or by those who had participated in the riots. Unorganized groups either had to become organized themselves or had to rely upon the established leaders who could take advantage more effectively of their extensive contacts with the authorities and with the police. The immediate necessity of having to express demands organizationally favoured established leaders by enabling them to extol the virtues of moderation while at the same time effectively channelling protest into less violent outlets.

It is useful, at this point, to allude to American experience. The pattern of the reassertion of traditional leadership roles was evident after the 1960s disturbances of the United States (Sears and McConahay, 1973). Perhaps the most serious incidents took place in Newark, New Jersey, in 1967. Like Liverpool, Toxteth, and Brixton in London, scenes of recent British street violence, Newark suffered from serious inner-urban deprivation, unemployment and latent racial tensions between blacks and whites. The July 1967 events were sparked off by a relatively small incident, the arrest of a black taxi driver, which led to an attack by large 'spontaneous' crowds, hurling bottles and rocks at the police (Boutelle, 1969). Similarly, Nashville, Detroit, Jackson, Houston, and Boston all experienced large 'unorganized' disturbances, accounts of which read very like some of the British 'riots', but reaching a far greater intensity. Again, as in the case of Britain, traditional community leaders managed to reassert their authority in the immediate aftermath. During the early 1960s in America, however, there was a significant politicized radical opposition to those leaders, which to some extent undermined the moderate civil rights leaders and threatened to seriously disrupt the order of 'legitimate' participation and consultation within government-funded agencies, even though many of the radicals themselves later came to terms with 'the system' and abandoned their militancy (Jacobs, 1982, 1983). Over a period leading to the mid 1970s the United States witnessed the integration of radical opposition into 'safer' channels of group/government co-ordination and many radical leaders began to identify politically with Democratic politics and to take advantage of the 'benefits' of participation offered to them by governments (see Chapter 8).

Such benefits can attract leaders and activists. In Britain, however, the magnitude of benefits has been less than in America. Governments have tended to underfund agencies in Britain and have achieved a greater degree of centralization than across the Atlantic. Consequently, blacks have tended to harbour suspicions about government agencies and, in particular, about community relations bodies, despite their common willingness to co-operate with them. In Britain the integration of black leaders and organizations has thus been rather less complete than in the United States and black leaders have frequently maintained a verbally hostile attitude to governments. In this setting it is important for governments, nationally and locally, to encourage greater political and organizational identification with the institutions receiving the demands of black people.

Access to the system: the view of government

If governments encourage the active participation of black and other organizations in the institutions of community control they do so within certain agreeable limits or by adhering to certain values which define the nature and extent of group access and which, most importantly, maintain or enhance the interests of the political and economic system as a whole.

In examining the question of access of groups to decision-making processes and to permanent officials and politicians, Dearlove (1973) stresses the importance of analysing the actions not only of groups but also of decision-makers in terms of their expressed attitudes under particular policy settings. He examines these with reference to the significance of the distinction between policy-making and policy maintenance.

Dearlove uses the term 'public policy' to refer to the 'substance of what government does; to the pattern of resources which government actually commits as a response to what it sees as public problems or challenges warranting public actions for their solution or attainment' (Dearlove, 1973, p.4). Not all governments are permanently involved in actually *making* policies, but all governments, when they assume office, face a whole range of previously worked out commitments and in many cases these are neither changed nor abandoned. Dearlove sees a public policy partly as the particular process of decision-making which may have established any particular pattern of resource commitments, although the actual maintenance or continuance of public policy will itself require decisions which involve decision-makers in a relatively routine defence of policies. Consequently, even when governments do embark on policy revision they tend to see change in terms of the maintenance of *continuity* with previous policy commitments. Thus change tends to take place within the bounds of a relatively restricted view of the scope of reform. Policy change, however, because of its controversial nature and because of the disturbance of previous commitments, does imply that governments will have to extend their operations in the search for information and advice which will assist them in formulating new policies or objectives. Decision-makers will try to reduce the degree of uncertainty involved in this activity by making the most effective use of information sources available to them. Governments will adopt either 'extended' or 'contracted' searches for assistance which imply greater or lesser degrees of reliance upon outside sources, such as voluntary organizations or pressure groups (Scott, 1967, p.219; Downs, 1967, p.185). In doing this governments attempt to reduce the level of uncertainty by encouraging interest-group co-operation and the establishment of formal contacts between groups and state agencies. Governments benefit, for example, from using reliable information which would not normally be available from internal government sources – this may relate to information about the state of tension within black communities or the attitudes of blacks in 'ghetto' areas.

Liaison with groups may thus offset the expenses involved in establishing costly research facilities or in employing external suppliers of information through, for example, consultancy arrangements. Communication with groups also facilitates the fostering of supportive attitudes within community organizations which are conducive to the defence of government policy objectives. Such considerations, seen in relation to the question of group access, help to explain the attitudes of decision-makers and their general desire to encourage what Dearlove describes as the 'helpfulness' of groups.

As far as black participation is concerned, governments on both sides of the Atlantic have benefited from group representation and have extended their 'search' to embrace many organizations which have provided valuable information about problems at local level. Many organizations have provided welfare, educational, legal and other services which have either supplemented those offered by government or have entirely substituted for non-existent and potentially costly government provisions (for example, where voluntary groups provide youth hostels, accommodation for the homeless and so on). Under such circumstances, groups can be perceived by governments as being 'helpful'. The costs and benefits which accrue to public authorities relate to the credibility of groups (benefits associated with admitted 'helpful' groups), the cost-effectiveness of search activity itself (the benefits of a reasonably short duration of search in terms of financial economies), the acquisition of technical information (as mentioned above) and benefits which relate to the control of disturbance (the admission of certain groups often implies their co-operation rather than their potential opposition). Groups which appear to pose cost-increasing policy strategies to governments will, not surprisingly, tend to be regarded as 'unhelpful' by decision-makers. Much will depend upon how far groups and governments can agree upon at least the broad objectives which should be contained in any policy goals and to what extent group and governmental perceptions converge about what should be done.

The notion of 'helpfulness' in this respect is central to assessing the ability of groups to gain admission to the decision-making processes of public authorities. If it is argued that this may be relevant to *both* policy change and policy maintenance situations, then the notion goes beyond Dearlove's concentration simply upon policy maintenance and enables the analysis to be extended to situations where governments are actively involved in search activity and policy change (Jacobs, 1979). However, the stress upon policy maintenance seems particularly appropriate to situations in which governments are defending prevailing institutions against communal disturbances and where moderate black leaders actively seek the same objectives by themselves seeing the advantages of an ordered political environment.

'Helpfulness' and black leadership

The emphasis upon continuity, stability and ordered change suggests that local groups which are considered as 'helpful':

either do not make claims on the council, or else make claims that do not conflict with the councillor's own views as to the proper scope of council activity (Dearlove, 1973, p.168).

Conceptions of how groups should behave and what policies should be adopted, according to Dearlove, lead policy-makers to view groups in terms of three criteria which are important to their assessments concerning the worthiness of groups. These three criteria concern:

(1) The source of the demand: the group itself.
(2) The policy content of the group and its implications for council activity and resource commitment: the demand itself.
(3) The method of articulation adopted by the demanding group: the communication method (Dearlove, 1973, p.157).

In the first of these it is argued that decision-makers make evaluations of the worthiness, reliability and overall helpfulness of groups. In the second category preferences as to policies which decision-makers hold are related to the conceptualizations which they adhere to with regard to policy commitment. In the third category the style in which groups express their demands to government is seen to be a crucial element in influencing opinions about group worthiness for access.

Groups which adopt 'improper' styles are, according to Dearlove, those which are less likely to gain access, whereas those which frame their demands in 'moderate' or 'reasonable' tones stand a better chance of access (Dearlove, 1973, p.169). Taken together with the other criteria for 'good behaviour', it will be seen that a composite picture of 'helpful' and 'unhelpful' aspects of group demands and activities can be built up. Thus, if groups behave 'badly' in the eyes of councillors and officials they are faced either with amending their strategies in order to obtain a more favourable response from government, or maintaining or intensifying their prevailing strategy and tactics in order to make an impact other than through 'accepted' channels. Dearlove summarizes such strategic choices in terms of the following combinations of styles and demands (using Dearlove's phrases):

(1)   The combination of unhelpful group with unacceptable demand and a proper communication style is unlikely, according to Dearlove, and this would certainly seem to be the case when viewing black organizations.

(2)   There may be a change to the combination: unhelpful group with acceptable demands and a proper communication style. This may be true of black organizations wishing to gain access to government but keen to maintain a militant profile to placate rank-and-file militancy (see Chapter 6).

(3)   For Dearlove, however, there is no necessity for unhelpful groups with acceptable demands to adopt improper communication styles (i.e. an unhelpful group might sometimes adopt an acceptable style in order to gain access for a limited period of time).

(4)   A helpful group with acceptable demands does not need to rely on improper communication styles, since it will be more likely to be well regarded by decision-makers (although black organizations may act in this way to preserve an aura of militancy (see Chapter 6).

(5)   Helpful groups will be reluctant to take up unacceptable demands, since they may be able to gain effective access for those demands by using proper communication styles. This is because they will be keen to preserve their good reputations.

The analysis so far presented describes the rules applied by decision-makers who are faced by differing group demands and methods of presenting those demands. Clearly the success of any demanding group in actually getting its policies accepted by governments in whole or in part is seen here to depend upon how responsive decision-makers are to them and to what degree groups are afforded access to the policy-making process. It is arguable, however, that demands can be accepted, under certain circumstances, which have been raised *without* groups having previously been afforded direct *access* to government, but while it is possible to envisage such situations where demands are 'imported' without access, in the main there is a correlation between access, group effectiveness, and the kinds of strategies which groups thereby adopt (Jacobs, 1979).

It is possible also for governments to respond to black demands expressed through the electoral system. In the United States, the advance of blacks in the electoral arena was preceded, however, by an upsurge of militancy and protest through the American Civil Rights Movement, which used 'direct action' as a tactic designed to overcome discrimination and racial segregation and to open up the political system to the demands of black Americans. In this way the Civil Rights Movement forced the question of black access onto the political agenda and successfully changed the terms of reference about black political participation to favour minority interests. Urban unrest, too, provided moderate blacks with an opportunity to join with white politicians, particularly through the Democratic Party, to resolve community tensions.

In Britain black political movements have been far less successful in directly impacting upon government responses to minorities in this way. The threat of general communal disturbance *has* been a factor in framing government responses, but there has never been a British equivalent of the American Civil Rights Movement, effecting changes of direction in government policy. In Britain access has been granted through a process involving the gradual integration of black organizations into agencies, following a series of related policy problems connected to the immigration issue and the need to foster racial harmony (as discussed in Chapter 1). Dearlove's criteria for group access thus remain valid with respect to the development of group/government relations in Britain and also with respect to the activity of black organizations within Community Relations Councils and other local bodies.

Access and the interests of governments

The above analysis implies that governments assess the helpfulness or otherwise of groups because they have certain interests to defend. Restricting access is of importance only if governments and politicians perceive a reason for distancing groups from the political system. It has been seen that control of disturbance is one such reason, but *why* control disturbance; to defend what? It seems reasonable to see the 'rules of the game', and especially those governing access, as existing to defend the interests of government, and ultimately the state, through a degree of regulation of participation in agencies and to provide a set of guidelines relating to the effective functioning of the political and administrative system.

This conception of 'rules' of access requires an examination of the broader interests of the state and the very nature of democratic politics. As stated in the Introduction, a detailed examination lies beyond the scope of this book, which essentially remains content with a consideration of the nature and extent of access within the capitalist state. Dearlove's criteria similarly limit the study of broader interests, suggesting that the political system, given the context of a capitalist society, reacts in a defensive manner to exclude unhelpful groups and demands in the majority of circumstances. In this context access does not necessarily mean *influence*. Black organizations gain access to participatory institutions, but they may not significantly affect decision-making by governments because of the defensive attitude of officials and politicians. It is thus difficult to find examples which point to *major* policy changes or initiatives having been affected as the result of pressures from Community Relations Councils, or to identify major changes in the balance of political power in favour of black ethnic minorities at local level. Blacks in Britain have at times been able to modify public policy, but this has been achieved through a compromise between blacks and policy-makers, largely based upon adaptation of black organizations to prevailing administrative and political practices.

If this is the 'highpoint' of the integration of blacks into institutions, it should not be seen as the sole form of co-operation to which blacks give consent. The gradations of integration (Chapter 1) relate to the willingness of governments to work with voluntary groups and also to the willingness of groups themselves to co-operate. Saunders lays stress upon the disposition of governments to work with business-orientated organizations and with 'middle-class groups'. Black groups would, in this setting, appear to be rather less favourably placed *vis à vis* government and, indeed, their relationships with decision-makers are sometimes rather less well founded when compared to organizations enjoying a strategic economic position in a locality. There are, however, quite wide local variations and it would seem inadvisable to identify the economic position of groups as the single decisive factor in gaining access. Much depends upon group strategies and political attitudes and upon the desire of lcoal politicians to court organizations for electoral purposes. Approaches by groups may be formal or relatively informal, giving groups different opportunities for influencing local policy-making. Saunders is clear on this point (my italics):

The strategies which may be available to different local groups for pursuing their interests in relation to the local state may therefore be understood to vary along a continuum between conciliatory action (which in most cases will come to be defined as 'responsible') and coercive action (i.e. attempts to force concessions – a strategy which in most cases will come to be defined as 'irresponsible'). *These strategies can only be explained with reference to the interests of the different groups in question,* and here it is necessary to distinguish whose interests are broadly consistent with current state policies and those whose interests run counter to them (Saunders, 1979, p.223).

This seems to fit well with Dearlove's view of helpfulness, although Saunders is much clearer in defining group/government relations in terms of a definite state interest. He talks of a political partnership between groups and government which involves an identity between groups and the objectives pursued by government (Saunders, 1979, p.234). At the other end of the scale is political exclusion, where groups and government have no common ground.

It is important to add that the 'partnership' between governments and black organizations is to some extent mediated by the agencies which cater for the special interests of blacks. The Community Relations Councils act as intermediaries between politicians and black leaders. The consequence is a frequent divergence between the objectives of the community bodies and the local authorities which fund them. This may produce situations where groups are deeply involved in the community relations bodies, but they do not necessarily enjoy the support of local political leaders for their demands. This complicates the Dearlove and Saunders versions of access by building in a delayed reaction between groups making often militant demands and politicians reacting directly to them. To some extent community-relations bodies can be left to themselves, producing their own policy initiatives and administrative practices. Local politicians and the Commission for Racial Equality nationally will tend to react unfavourably to those initiatives which seriously transgress the 'rules of the game', but this will only take place by recourse to often time-consuming institutional procedures. Ultimately, there-fore, the Commission for Racial Equality *does* act to preserve 'helpful' local CRCs and to promote moderate black political organizations. This will be illustrated in Chapter 4.

Costs and benefits: leadership motivations

It is appropriate now to view group leadership motivations in such a general environment in more detail. It has been suggested that the attitudes of black leaders towards a relatively centralized administrative framework such as this implies are tempered by their calculation of the costs and benefits of participation in agencies and in liaison with government. Contrary to the general assumption of pluralist studies (particularly in the United States), Olsen (1976) has suggested that groups are often reluctant to enter into close relationships with governments because of the costs to them incurred by participatory arrangements which adversely affect group commitments. Olsen deals with situations where 'formal' group/government co-ordination exists. However, in view of the blurred distinction between informal access and formal participation it is assumed here that groups will incur costs and benefits over the whole range of relationships with government. These relationships, which describe the process of integration, may be summarized as follows:

(1) Informal contact with politicians or government officials at local or national levels, possibly over issues of 'immediate' concern to groups (e.g. planning permission or housing allocations or education).

(2) Groups may develop more regular informal contacts, possibly seeking contacts with a wider range of decision-makers or public agencies.

(3) Groups may participate in local or national agencies (e.g. Community Relations Councils) and regularize their contacts with those agencies and with politicians and government officials.

(4) Groups may, once having made this entry into agencies, gain represen-tation on agency committees or executive committees and thereby formalize their relationships with those agencies and with decision-makers.

(5) Co-option to local authority committees or sub-committees could precede or follow this formalization, depending upon circumstances. This may also, in the case of black groups and others, be accompanied by more regular contacts with local authority race-relations officers or race-relations committees.

(6) Again at local level, groups may become involved in projects funded by the Urban Programme or the Manpower Services Commission, or

receive funding from other local and national public or private agencies which promote closer relations between groups and fund providers.

(7)   Groups may gain representation on elected local councils by running their own candidates or by working through the major political parties.

(8)   In some cases groups begin to supplement certain local-authority services (social services, advice services, provision of hostel accommodation) with public fund assistance. This implies a degree of functional integration.

Distinctions between formal and other forms of access are more important insofar as some groups may wish to maintain contacts with politicians which imply the virtual identification of the groups with government. Such 'formality' comes close to the concept of 'corporatism' covered in Chapter 1, but it is untypical of the majority of situations in which black organizations in Britain find themselves. They generally attempt to maintain a certain 'informality' which enables them to assist governments and agencies, but which also preserves a degree of group identity and independence.

This 'informality' enables black leaders to maintain their critical stance in relation to the policy commitments of public authorities. Leaders see themselves as expressing the dissatisfaction, within the black community, with methods of handling community relations and with certain actions taken by the police. This compels group leaderships to emphasize their independence and freedom of action as a way of distancing themselves from government and police authorities. Leaders are, however, also keen to maintain contacts with these authorities in order to further the advantages accruing to their organizations arising from co-operation. Groups remain 'helpful' despite the fact that many of them may, for a time, adopt 'improper' styles of communication.

In deciding just how far to go in seeking admission to agencies and to institutions which make public-policy decisions, groups will assess the potential advantages inherent in different degrees of co-ordination with government. Representatives may be co-opted to local authority committees, gain representation on local CRC executive committees, or take part in special local-authority consultative committees. The decision to co-operate, in each case, involves a subjective assessment by the groups of the most important costs and benefits. Subjectivity, however, makes a precise analysis of the *objective* magnitude of such factors difficult. Olsen makes this point:

it is not possible to measure costs and benefits in a way that permits a precise calculation of net return. Nor is it possible to compare the magnitude of one kind of cost or benefit with another cost or benefit. For the most part, the terms are used in a much more general way to suggest aspects of a particular policy area, organisation, or context, that tend to make an organisation more or less receptive to formal participation in a governmental institution (Olsen, 1976, p.2).

The different valuations involved produce a measure of variability between groups as to their attitudes towards governments and public agencies. Group calculations of costs and benefits may alter under changing conditions, reflecting changes in the attitudes of community leaders towards government in response to developments in the political environment. During the 1981 riots, for example, many black leaders moved ground between outright condemnation of government and quite enthusiastic acclaim of initiatives announced by the Department of the Environment, especially as it became clear that the disturbances had not produced a coherent political opposition to 'traditional' leaders.

As a modification to Olsen's view that groups are commonly disposed to remaining outside participatory arrangements, it would seem that the benefits perceived by leaders in the above circumstances generally attract them towards gaining access to politicians and officials. Interviews conducted with black leaders in Wolverhampton and the West Midlands suggested that leaders and group members took a very practical and pragmatic view of co-operation, seeing government and community programmes as means whereby groups could achieve at least some of their social and economic ends. Often government was regarded as a provider of resources and as a producer of services which black people could claim as a right. Organizations in the self-help category were particularly prone to regard local authorities in this way (Jacobs, 1979). Co-operation thus appears to be the rule rather than the exception and perhaps rather more evident as a characteristic of more informal non-corporatist participation in particular.

This observation possibly relates to the nature of black politics itself. Black leaders sense their distinctiveness within a 'white' political environment and attempt to overcome their feelings of isolation in order to legitimize their claims to economic resources and political advancement. As one black community worker in Wolverhampton stated:

We have to be assertive to get what we want. We have to fight discrimination – unlike white organisations. We need to have our voice heard above the rest (1979 interview).

Incentives to participate

By looking at Olsen's costs and benefits in specific terms it is possible to view group motivations in terms of their subjective assessments of participation and to relate these to the strategies adopted by groups in gaining admission to politicians and officials. Richardson and Jordan (1979) have used Olsen's analysis to explain group strategies at national level, set within the context of what they regard to be a very 'open' group political setting. The cost/benefit approach, however, seems to be appropriate where groups find entry to the political system set within the bounds of a more exclusive political framework. As seen above, the 'rules' applied by governments which influence access tend to create barriers for groups wishing to influence public policy. The incentives to participate must thus be sufficient for groups to make an effort to overcome the disadvantages of sacrificing some of their freedom of activity. This effort is important since it strengthens the validity of the cost side of the cost/benefit analysis. If access was as 'open' as Richardson and Jordan argue (1979, p.41), then the costs of participation would tend to decrease in importance. Governments would not, for instance, place such high barriers before organizations prior to admission. The decision-making process would be more accessible as a result and generally more conducive to blacks actually making an impact on public policy. Groups would enter into the policy process much more as equal partners with government.

While access may look like this for certain groups at national level (the Confederation of British Industry, for example), the picture is different for black organizations. Political advancement for black groups is often viewed in terms of their influence or otherwise over policy. Olsen sees influence as a major benefit and an incentive to participate, since one of the most significant opportunities provided by access is that which enables group leaders to take part in the formulation of policies or, at least, in tendering advice to politicians which may eventually have an impact on policy. Clearly, the more limited the access to government, the more difficult it will be for groups to have a direct influence upon the framing of policies or to have a say in their implementation.

The *potential* to influence policies would thus seem to be crucial as an incentive to black groups. In asserting their claim to legitimacy the *promise* of influence is often enough to persuade groups to participate (Jacobs, 1979). Their expectations will be met according to local circumstances. The degree to which access actually enables black groups to influence policy directly varies, being limited at national level but fairly extensive in some local authorities. Of interest in this connection is the role afforded to voluntary organizations through the Greater London Council (GLC). The GLC states that:

The Council has involved voluntary organisations in its decision-making process through standing committees and through a series of borough-based consultations. This openness in policy formation and this willingness to take account of the views of voluntary and community groups is evident throughout the Council, and is an initiative that has been applauded by voluntary organisations (GLC, 1984, Section 27, p.4).

The GLC's Ethnic Minorities Committee established an Ethnic Minorities Unit to help implement its aims to secure racial equality and to assist ethnic minorities in general. Thus, 'the Council has incorporated a racial dimension explicitly into all its policy making and implementation' (GLC, 1984, Sections 24/5, p.27). This involvement holds economic advantages for groups which receive funding from the authority and for the black community, which benefits from a number of programmes and projects supported by the Ethnic Minorities Committee.[3]

The GLC approach is relatively 'open' and *superficially* fits the Richardson and Jordan conception of group involvement in policy-making. Under such circumstances the 'rules of the game' seem less important to local politicians, who actually make a point of encouraging black organizations to participate in council policy-making. The Labour GLC appears to be less concerned about 'proper' communication styles than about group commitment to the council's own community-orientated approach. This does not automatically ensure the co-operation of those groups which still wish to preserve their identities, but it does reduce the exclusiveness of government to some extent, thereby increasing the attraction of groups to co-operation and reducing the apparent costs or disadvantages.

The resemblance of this pattern of group/government co-ordination to Richardson and Jordan's 'open' system is of character rather than of substance, since with the GLC example black organizations are set within a policy process which involves a different range of policy commitments by local politicians to those more commonly met in, say, Conservative or right-of-centre Labour authorities. The 'rules of the game' have been re-defined so that council policy commitments and black group objectives more commonly coincide. This is consistent with Dearlove's view that access opens up as group/council policy commitments converge and it implies that groups opposing the GLC's approach will tend to be regarded as 'unhelpful' and possibly disruptive.

In areas where local authorities are rather less enthusiastic about involving black groups in actual policy-making, voluntary organizations tend to rely either on their own efforts or more upon co-ordinated activities through the Community Relations Councils. In Wolverhampton the local authority was less ideologically committed to open access than the GLC. This will be illustrated in Chapter 5, since local-authority resistance to black group demands on education was a feature of the local political scene in the late 1970s. Black-group/local-authority relations have often been strained, despite the political control of the Labour Party in the town. Controversy over the appointment of the town's Chief Community Relations Officer in 1980 further underscored the barriers to black demands and the more important place of 'proper' styles of communication and more traditionally defined evaluations of 'helpfulness'.

This environment produced a strong Community Relations Council in Wolverhampton, which facilitated group co-operation. Olsen refers to benefits of 'cartelization', where groups came together as part of a process in which governmental institutions bring various groups together to facilitate their more effective operation, thereby assisting government. This may be in line with groups' own efforts to co-ordinate their activities. A number of organizations, by coming together, are afforded the opportunity of exchanging information and linking their activities in the pursuance of common objectives, thereby enjoying economies with regard to the utilization of their resources.

Cartelization enables politicians to identify group representatives, to consult with them formally and to enhance the authority of cartelized organizations. Formal participation confers legitimacy upon groups and this will often be highly valued by leaders ranging from the conservative to the militant. Legitimacy is valued, for Olsen, particularly in terms of leaders claiming a share of the credit and praise for public policy successes with which they have been associated.

Benefits may also be gained for groups through greater organizational efficiency and division of labour. By creating positions of responsibility in government or government-backed programmes, leaders may develop expertise, technical competence and specialized knowledge in particular policy areas. Again, government stands to gain, since a more professional community leadership invariably develops a co-operative attitude which can contribute to the encouragement of moderation within quite militant organizations.

In short, participation in private-sector and government-supported programmes implies certain assurances that groups will observe a compromise, ensuring that there will be a satisfactory level of consent to policies. This relates to the analysis of the perceptions adopted by decision-makers which favourably dispose them to 'helpful' organizations. Groups which are prepared to accept constraints upon their 'freedom' and independence will tend to be more easily adaptable to a policy process which itself requires compromise and political restraint in presenting demands.

Access, centralization and loss of independence

The question of independence in relation to the participation of groups is of central political importance, since it marks the major dividing line between co-operators with government and non-co-operators. Black organizations which regard complete independence highly will tend to stay isolated from the public policy process. Those which regard some loss as an inevitable cost of participation will eventually increasingly ignore this 'cost' as a factor influencing their attitude to participation. The Indian Workers' Association (GB) provided an example of this kind of organizational perspective in Wolverhampton, and even the militant Anti-Racism Committee moderated its view and drew closer to local councillors (see Chapter 2).

Implicit in the 'loss of freedom' is 'loss of purity'. Entry into a bargaining, co-ordinating, compromising relationship with government usually implies a watering-down of doctrine or of pure ideological positions that might be held by a non-participating organization. The most commonly quoted example of this kind of cost relates to trade unions or socialist parties which abandon their original ideals once they confront the 'realities of power'. However, not all groups adhere to well-defined ideas or objectives – a factor which makes it easier for them to overcome suspicions which might otherwise be present. The less religious, less ideological or less traditionalist black organizations generally find it easier to make compromises and to adapt their attitudes and practices in entering into political activity.

It has been indicated that Britain's relatively centralized administration of race relations has been an important factor in affecting the attitudes of black leaders. In the United States ethnic minorities were encouraged to enter community-development agencies which were run at 'arm's length' from federal government (Dettmar, 1981). This enabled black leaders to enter local institutions which appeared to provide them with the opportunity of maintaining considerable freedom and independence over the making of decisions relating to community-based project implementation (Jacobs, 1982). This effectively reduced the importance of the cost of 'loss of freedom' to black organizations and opened the way for the integration of former black nationalists and leftist activists into local programmes. However, suspicions still tend to linger as groups concerned about this cost of access fail to improve their relationships with agencies associated with centralized funding. Centralization thus affects the attitudes of the broader black community. Many of the 'unorganized' find it difficult to relate satisfactorily to programmes provided 'from above', whereas an 'arm's-length' community development facilitates significant autonomous control and development of programmes at community level (see Chapter 8).

Loss of freedom may involve a further cost for groups. By accepting a position within the governmental apparatus, groups and their leaderships may become associated with the unsuccessful or unpopular policies of government. For black organizations this has frequently led to leaders becoming associated with the 'physical' side of government policy described in Chapter 1. Militants have been able to point to moderate leadership complicity with governments implementing allegedly discriminatory race legislation to control immigration and have characterized this sanctioning of policy as a support for the 'racist state'. Becoming so entwined in the political web of government may serve to isolate group leaders from their supporters or potential supporters and to reinforce the gap created by upward mobility of leaders in community agencies.

Olsen finally points to costs associated with 'loss of control'. Specialized group representatives with technical or managerial competence may undermine the control of members and even elected group leaders. Usually it is difficult to delegate responsibility without giving up some degree of 'democratic accountability' within an organization. It has been indicated above that black leaders in the USA often became integrated into government agencies as they developed a professional perspective towards their community activities. This may further compound the isolation of leaders who move closer to the more influential centres of local and national government.

Summary

The significance of Olsen's cost/benefit analysis lies in the notion that groups as well as governments tend to maximize benefits and minimize the costs and uncertainty arising from their actions. Participation operates most effectively where both sides have an interest in co-ordinating their activities and where there is, by implication, a closer identification between the interests of the parties involved. This identification is not always easy to achieve, since groups and governments may enter into participatory arrangements each for their own reasons, although compromise implies that those involved will have achieved a degree of consensus which is a necessary condition for a working relationship.

To summarize the nature of group/government relations as analysed in this chapter, the following points are presented:

(1)   Black leaders generally find it to their advantage to co-operate with public and private programmes or to seek access to agencies designed to cater for ethnic minorities. This enables leaders to co-ordinate their activities with those agencies and possibly to integrate more fully into them.

(2)   Integration can create a gap between leaders and rank-and-file group members and the 'unorganized' in the wider black community. Leaders attempt to placate the demands of their followers while attempting to gain access to politicians and government officials, and this often creates a two-sided aspect to their political demands, particularly in the more politicized organizations.

(3)   Many group leaderships 'balance' their demands between those of their rank-and-file members and militants and the requirements of decision-makers in public authorities and agencies. This produces a verbal 'militancy' tempered by a practical concern for moderation and consensus.

(4)   In examining the motivations of group leaders it was shown that black organizations adopt different postures. The more political and militant an organization, the less likely it is to be regarded as 'helpful' by decision-makers and the less disposed to come to terms with integrative community agencies. The evaluation of group helpfulness requires an examination of the divergence of interests between groups and government – the underlying factor defining the degree of 'helpfulness' perceived by politicians and officials.

(5)   It is possible for black groups to impact upon public policy by adopting 'unhelpful' styles and demands, by direct actions, for example; but in Britain this strategy has historically been used rarely, although in the USA such actions did force certain concessions from the state with respect to electoral and civil rights.

(6)   In the more 'normal' and ordered political environment blacks are prepared to express their demands within the confines of the legitimate political process, but the *degree* to which they are willing to integrate into the political system varies according to the political, religious and cultural backgrounds of different organizations. In assessing their

attitude to access, groups will take account of the advantages and disadvantages to themselves of closer co-ordination with governmental bodies and programmes based upon their subjective expectations and commitments.

(7)   The majority of groups appear to regard the benefits of access or participation as outweighing the costs, despite the loss of freedom associated with entry into participatory and consultative arrangements and despite the common tendency for politicized leaders to be suspicious of too close an identification with the 'physical' side of government policy and the centralization of funding in the race-relations area.

4　The race industry

There is no clear definition of the 'race industry' in Britain. The term has, however, frequently been applied to the activities and programmes initiated by government and private community-relations agencies at national and local levels. There is, of course, a great variety of initiatives which constitute central government strategy in the inner cities and these have, to various degrees, had the effect of enhancing minority-group community opportunities with respect to the maximizing of their resources. The benefits of co-operation and the general economic returns gained from the programmes, although limited by financial stringency, represent the available 'benefits' to groups. The 'race industry' – government and other agencies involved in funding the black community – directly contributes to this general pattern. Groups which choose not to take part in community-relations programmes will often stand to lose economically, although they may feel that their political independence has been preserved by their standing aside from government-funded projects.

Co-operation with the Commission for Racial Equality (CRE) and the local Community Relations Councils (CRCs) – the pillars of the 'race industry' – may be regarded as the traditional avenue through which groups work with and contact community-relations officials, central government agencies and local authorities. Perhaps in the 1970s the CRE and CRCs would have been the primary focus of attention in a study of race and politics in Britain, but today the situation has changed and black politics and black community action find expression through a broader range of bodies. Attention has shifted from the 'race industry' towards the kind of initiatives described in Chapter 7. Nevertheless, the 'race industry' still plays a major political role in providing an outlet for a sizeable body of black opinion and remains a major source of funds for ethnic-minority social, welfare and educational programmes.

In many ways the national setting is less important than the local when the politics and administration of race in Britain are being considered. This is because the local CRCs are the central focus of attention for black pressure groups. It is at the local level that groups affiliate to CRCs, participate in CRC decision-making, take part in CRC campaigns and generally attempt to influence community affairs. The CRE in London provides much less of an 'exciting' prospect, appearing to be remote, often bureaucratic and ill-equipped to facilitate pressure-group representations. The national level is, however, of importance politically, because it provides the local bodies with the financial lifeline which ensures their continued existence. From this it follows that black organizations often develop an interest in keeping good relations with CRE officials. This became abundantly clear following the 1981 'disorders' which prompted many groups to pay more attention to demands for action at the centre to tackle inner-city deprivation and social unrest.

The CRE thus assumed an important role in assisting with the solution to such problems, but just how effective it was in responding to the demands of black organizations remained open to heated debate. The 1981 events raised serious questions about the CRE's general performance as a body supposedly committed to alleviating racial tensions and social instability. A study of the CRE and its associated CRCs should not, therefore, simply concentrate on the financial incentives on offer to groups, but should also say something about how effective or otherwise community-relations bodies have been in promoting a co-operative black leadership and how they have acted as mechanisms for the maintenance of a reasonably stable political environment.

A commission for racial equality

The Commission for Racial Equality was established by the Labour government under the 1976 Race Relations Act. The Act gave the CRE powers which went beyond those performed by the CRE's predecessors, the Community Relations Commission and the Race Relations Board. Common to all these bodies was, first and foremost, the objective to promote good race relations upon the basis of a three-tier administrative structure involving the Home Office, the Commission and the CRCs. Chapter 1 showed that this objective could be traced back to the mid 1960s when race relations was rapidly becoming a key area of specific governmental responsibility. Chapter 1 also indicated the connection between an increasing concern by government to control political events relating to race and community relations and the introduction of programmes designed to aid black communities. This led to a succession of events between 1958 and 1961 which 'transformed the situation' (Edwards and Batley, 1978, p.26) from one in which government saw its role largely in non-interventionist terms to one in which conciliation and co-operation with black community leaders were the order of the day.

John Rex has described the mid 1960s' institutions as 'paternalist in nature'

(Rex, 1979, p.87). The National Committee for Commonwealth Immigrants (NCCI), for instance, had been 'conceived partly as providing a political lobby for the immigrants'. Rex alludes to the compromising of immigrant leaders who were invited to join the NCCI 'backed by prestigious non-party political figures'. Following the publication of a White Paper in 1965, the government set up a newly constituted NCCI, while increased finances enabled it to provide more staff to develop the services provided by the CRCs. To assist the CRCs the Home Office made grants available to the NCCI which could be distributed to the local bodies. The NCCI could also ensure that the CRCs employed competent personnel to look after these funds and to assist in the training of community-based officers.

Hill and Issacharoff (1971) provide the most detailed account of this early period and describe the development of the relationship beween the NCCI and the CRCs. What is important in their account of the NCCI's funding of local bodies is the constant desire by the centre and by the CRCs to maintain a voluntaristic element in the relationship. This was, and still is, central insofar as interest groups seek to maintain their 'independence' as pressure groups. Convincing groups that they were not to be simply appendages of the NCCI or the government took time to achieve and, as Hill and Issacharoff themselves point out, this created tensions concerning the precise supervisory relationship between the NCCI and the CRCs and over constitutional points such as the balance to be achieved between individuals, organizations and local authorities in the membership of the CRCs.

Many of these tensions were actually sharpened when the Community Relations Commission replaced the NCCI under the provisions of the 1968 Race Relations Act. The new Commission, unlike the NCCI, possessed statutory recognition under the Act and was charged with the task not only of encouraging harmonious community relations but also of co-ordinating voluntary organizations nationally to achieve this. The Commission was also to advise the Secretary of State on matters referred to the Commission by him and to consult him on matters relevant to its brief (Hill and Issacharoff, 1971, p.27). The Act enabled the Commission to assist not only CRCs but also other organizations concerned with community relations. In addition, the Commission co-operated with the Race Relations Board, originally set up in 1965 and empowered by the 1968 Act to investigate and where necessary bring charges against parties guilty of breaching the provisions of the non-discrimination sections of the Race Relations Act. The Board did not, however, assume judicial powers itself and was therefore restricted in its attempts to counter discrimination (Rex, 1979, p.89).

The Race Relations Act of 1976 entirely replaced the 1968 Act and what remained of the 1965 Act. The new Act dealt with discrimination on the grounds of colour, nationality and race and made discrimination unlawful in employment, education, the provision of goods, facilities or services to the public and in transactions in property, including housing. Under the 1968 Act claims of discrimination could only be made to the Race Relations Board, but under the new Act victims of alleged discrimination could take their case to industrial tribunals (in employment) or to the courts. The Race Relations Board and the Commission were replaced by the present CRE, which had greater powers of investigation and enforcement of anti-discrimination legislation since it could initiate investigations and use full subpoena powers in the process.

It is not the purpose of this chapter to detail the provisions of the 1976 Act as far as racial discrimination is concerned, but it is important to note that the Act did imply a rather stronger political role for the CRE, which inevitably held attractions for voluntary groups both locally and nationally. For example, the Act allowed the CRE to become more closely involved with local authorities. In housing, for example, promotional work with local authorities was covered under Section 71 of the Act and this led to the publication of CRE guidance papers and discussions with authorities on ethnic record-keeping, monitoring and research and dealing with complaints. Discussions were held with local education authorities, with bodies concerned with youth and adult employment, and with Chief Executives and councillors about inner-urban problems. Of course many of these contacts existed prior to the 1976 Act, but the Act literally involved *more* legislation to monitor and handle a greater degree of inter-authority and CRE/local-authority activity.

CRE's role

Chapter 2 indicated how the CRE emerged from legislation which was essentially designed to offset some of the effects of discriminatory immigration legislation and how the former Race Relations Board and Community Relations Commission provided the foundations upon which the CRE was able to build. More specifically, the 1976 Act empowered the Commission:

(1) to conduct formal investigations and to issue non-discrimination notices;
(2) to give assistance to individuals wishing to seek redress against unlawful discrimination;
(3) to provide financial and other forms of assistance to organizations appearing to promote equality of opportunity and good race relations;
(4) to influence policy and to promote and encourage research in the field of race relations.

The Act made both direct and indirect discrimination unlawful and, in so doing, went further than previous race-relations legislation in defining areas of activity which were to be regarded as illegal. Indirect discrimination was regarded as arising from the general imposition of conditions or requirements detrimental to a person on racial grounds. Subject to certain exceptions the Act covered the following areas:

(1) employment;

(2) trade unions and employers' associations, qualifying and vocational training bodies, and the Manpower Services Commission and employment agencies;

(3) most educational services;

(4) the provision of goods, facilities and services;

(5) housing, subject to certain extensive exceptions;

(6) clubs, apart from small clubs and certain clubs which may discriminate on grounds other than race;

(7) discriminatory advertisements;

(8) instructing others to discriminate, pressure to discriminate and knowingly aiding discrimination;

(9) charities, apart from those which may discriminate on grounds other than race.

The CRE was established with an initial staff of 221 and was organized in three London-based divisions and four regional offices. The staff were appointed on identical grades to the home Civil Service and Civil Service financial control and establishment rules and procedures were applied in the Commission's administration (although the staff were not actually 'civil servants'). Responsibility for major areas of the CRE's work was divided between three divisions: the Equal Opportunities Division; the Community Affairs and Liaison Division; and the General Services Division. The Equal Opportunities Division was responsible for the investigations initiated under the 1976 Act and performed a function similar to the old Race Relations Board. The Community Affairs and Liaison Division was in charge of the promotion of 'equality of opportunity' and good race relations through the administration of grant aid to assist voluntary organizations and local CRCs. The General Services Division was responsible for providing administrative back-up and research for the other divisions and it was also concerned with personnel, organization and finance and the CRE's public relations work.

This structure appeared to be adequate in the CRE's early years, but in its 1981 Annual Report the Commission admitted that 1981 'was in some respects our hardest year yet'. The Report pointed to what were described as 'strains in race relations' aggravated by economic recession and high unemployment and underlined by the 1981 urban disturbances. To some extent this could be taken as an admission that the CRE could not be expected to contribute much to the elimination of racial tensions in society, although the CRE did believe that the situation would have been worse if local CRCs had not acted as moderating influences. The Report seemed to equate racial harmony with a lack of open conflict rather than with a broader conception of racism seen in terms of societal attitudes reflecting deep-rooted racist ideologies and social sentiments. In this respect, the CRE continued to regard its interventions in community relations as positively affecting the race issue but the implication remained that legal prescriptions combined with broader participation in government-backed agencies could reduce racial prejudice and ultimately reduce the incidence of racial discrimination. Not surprisingly, therefore, the CRE called for a 'clear determination' (using Lord Scarman's term) to enforce the law and to encourage 'responsible' community leaders to take a lead in bringing about reconciliation.

In one sense, therefore, the CRE laboured under an illusion. That illusion, widely criticized, assumed that legal measures could effect deep social changes with respect to attitudes about race. Of course, the CRE's enforcement role *did* serve to protect some blacks from the harsher manifestations of racial discrimination, but it did not ensure the tranquillity of Brixton, Toxteth or Moss Side.

In view of the CRE's position, some Conservative politicians pointed to the resources devoted to community relations and called for the CRE to be made more accountable for its activities. Many Conservatives criticized the CRE and race-relations legislation for being ineffective in eliminating social tensions. This was criticism from the political right, some of whom wished to undermine the CRE and eventually repeal race legislation, which was claimed to be ineffective against the 'inevitable' existence of racial animosities.

The debate about the CRE's role and functions thus came to focus upon the question of its effectiveness and this involved discussion, within and outside the CRE, of the general impact of the agency's activities, its political role, its managerial competence and its organization. Conservative and Labour politicians were keen to improve the CRE's management, either to obtain 'value for money' or to ensure that the Commission made a positive contribution to the promotion of racial harmony. With these objectives in mind, the Home Affairs Committee of the House of Commons conducted an inquiry in 1981 into the operation and effectiveness of the Commission. Criticisms were concentrated on three main areas: the CRE's operational efficiency; grant-making arrangements; and its overall role in the field of community and race relations.

Costs and disincentives?

The Committee's report highlighted a number of important aspects of the CRE's work, which may be taken here to constitute significant disincentives for black groups to co-operate with the body. The Committee pointed out that the CRE had been established with a set of 'loosely defined and difficult tasks; tasks which required great administrative ability, political imagination, sensitivity, energy and skill' (HC 46-1, para. 5). This deliberately wide conception of the CRE's role was seen to have given rise to a number of problems affecting the CRE's ability to develop its own policy initiatives and impacting upon its general style of operation.

There was, according to the Committee, 'no doubt' that central government did not always respond to the Commission in a very favourable or positive way (HC 46-1, para. 6). This applied particularly to equal employ ment policies within the Civil Service and to the CRE's own draft Code of

Practice on Employment, but Commission witnesses to the Committee accused the government of lacking the will to take more positive action to back measures promoting good race relations, although the Committee itself was not prepared to lay all the blame on government for such failings. The CRE itself had to bear some responsibility for the state of race relations, despite the increased pressures placed upon the Commission by economic and social problems in society.

The CRE's 'gravest defect' according to the Committee was what was described as 'incoherence'. The Commission was seen to operate without any obvious sense of priorities or any clearly defined objectives:

There are few subjects on which they [the CRE] prove unwilling to pronounce and few projects upon which they are unwilling to embark. Where specific policy objectives have been established, they are rarely translated into concrete activity. Commission staff respond to this policy vacuum by setting their own objectives and taking independent initiatives, which not surprisingly peter out or go off at half-cock. A distressing amount of energy which should be channelled into a coherent and integrated programme leading to clearly-defined objectives is thus frittered away (HC 46-1 para. 8).

This highly critical view was presented despite Commission claims that they *had* become aware of the need for more effective planning and objective-setting. Government was blamed by CRE staff for refusing to allow required staffing increases. For the Commons Committee, however, the problems were structural in nature. The major question was whether the Commission should continue to have the dual objectives and functions of a law enforcement agency and a promotional, persuasive body initiating a wide range of race-related activities. The promotional side of the CRE's work had come to predominate, it was argued, and an organizational split had occurred between that side of the agency's work and the law enforcement side. For the Parliamentarians this issue was one which directly related to the CRE's ability to promote good race relations:

Whilst they [the CRE] have a significant part to play, the task of promoting good race relations lies mainly with government and local government. Only they have the power and resources to make the necessary impact. The pretence that a small statutory body can undertake that task assumes a responsibility it cannot discharge and the attempt can only lead to frustration amongst the staff and disillusionment amongst the black minority (HC 46-1, para. 11).

The Committee's response to this was something of a compromise between a return to a separate law-enforcement agency and the CRE's desire to maintain its existing structure together with a strong promotional commitment. The Committee endorsed the establishment of a single statutory body, and recommended that the Commission's dual role should be continued provided that promotional work was 'solely dictated by the need to eradicate racial discrimination' (HC 46-1 para. 14). In practice this meant that the

Committee remained deeply concerned about the balance between promotional activities and law enforcement work and about the lack of connection between the two. The CRE was seen to be involved with promotional work which generally did not arise from law enforcement and which was frequently unconnected with implementing anti-discrimination legislation. Housing and education were cited as areas in which this situation existed, with the CRE having completed no housing or education investigations, despite the commitment of staff to concerted promotional work in those fields.

In order to overcome the separation between enforcement and promotion the Committee suggested that a more corporate approach within the CRE would encourage a greater inter-relation between staff working in the two areas. A rearrangement of the CRE's internal divisional structure was proposed so that staff could relate more easily to the two sides of the CRE's work. Commission witnesses to the Committee claimed that there already existed a satisfactory liaison between those on each side, but this failed to impress the politicians, who wanted to see a more clearly defined role for the CRE set within the parameters of government legal provisions in the race field.

Criticism of the CRE's promotional work went deeper still, however. Of particular concern to the Committee was the way in which the CRE was alleged to 'adopt the role of spokesman for what they interpret as the views of ethnic minorities, and to prefer this role to their true one of a quasi-judicial statutory Commission' (HC 46-1 para. 18). Moreover, perusal of press releases by the Committee:

confirmed our impression that the Commission are at times unduly eager to engage in instant analysis of current political controversy to the detriment of their main statutory duties and at the cost of the reputation for scrupulous impartiality which many of their functions demand (HC 46-1 para. 18).

Significantly, the Committee revealed here one aspect of the effect of the CRE's centralization which often annoyed minority groups. The Committee pointed to minority group complaints about under-representation of their numbers in the CRE and to possible political differences between the CRE and voluntary groups. On the other hand, there were those in the black community who regarded the CRE as acting on behalf of minorities in a very direct sense and who were not unduly disturbed by the Commission's public pronouncements where they appeared to promote the interests of the black community. This reflected the diversity of group attitudes alluded to in Chapter 3 and serves to indicate the balance between black groups which have been quite happily accommodated within legitimate political channels and those which remain suspicious of bodies such as the CRE which may adopt policies contrary to black group commitments and ideologies. The Home Affairs Committee view that the CRE should temper its political statements and at the same time become more orientated toward enforcement, however, implied a potentially *more* centralized body, possibly producing even greater longer term group suspicion of its political connections and commitments. A more acquiescent CRE could be seen by many groups as a direct appendage of government and an enforcement body directly linked to the implementation of government strategy on race and, by implication, on immigration. Structural changes since the Committee's Report have not, however, significantly pushed the CRE closer to the centre, since the Commission still maintains what it regards as its duty to make its own policy pronouncements. The very fact, however, that the Home Affairs Committee Report stimulated Government thinking about the CRE's role and, in turn, brought about intensified internal discussion within the CRE itself, actually underlined the agency's reliance upon a favourable political climate and its ultimate responsibility to remain accountable to the government of the day and to Parliament.

CRE's response to criticisms

The Commons Report was not, however, highly regarded by CRE officials. They generally tended to regard the Report as superficial, uninformed or straightforwardly political in tone and content.[1] The discussion about internal change in the CRE had, anyway, preceded the Report and had been a matter of action within the CRE for some time. In this way many in the CRE regarded the Report as largely unhelpful in the development of new approaches to combating discrimination and evolving effective organizational structures to achieve this end.[2]

The CRE made its views clear to the government when the government was itself considering its own response to the Home Affairs Committee Report. The government White Paper (Cmnd 8547, 1982) reflected considerable sympathy with the CRE's view of what should be done to enhance its efficiency and effectiveness and, at the same time, accepted the main conclusion of the Home Affairs Committee that the CRE should remain as a single agency charged with the dual functions of enforcement and promotion of equality. The government did not agree with the Home Affairs Committee that promotional work should be narrowly defined in terms of being *solely* devoted to combating unlawful discrimination – an outcome which the CRE welcomed as an indication that its past record in these fields had been generally vindicated. The government accepted the need for the appointment of more legally qualified staff and also accepted the need for certain internal staff restructuring which the CRE was itself willing to take on. However, the Home Affairs Committee view that the Commission should examine the possibility of allocating some specialist staff to regional offices, if necessary in place of existing fieldwork officers, was seen by the CRE to be detrimental and the White Paper implicitly endorsed the CRE's view which, in effect maintained the CRE's firm involvement with local CRCs.

The Home Affairs Committee recommendation that the Home Office and the Commission should jointly review the CRE's practices in the conduct of investigations to reduce delays was accepted and such a review was initiated. The CRE was itself keen to improve the investigative side of its work, although its task was made difficult by resource limitations and by the very complexity of investigations. The government appears to have noted this point by quoting the CRE view in the White Paper (Cmnd 8547, 1982, p.8).

The Home Affairs Committee recommendation that the CRE's project aid programme should be terminated was rejected in the White Paper. The government's view was that the CRE's grant-making function was of central importance to ethnic-minority groups and that such funding could not be substituted through either Section 11 money (see below) or through the Urban Programme (Cmnd 8547, 1982, p.11). This was an implicit recognition of the CRE's rather special role in funding race-relations work and its unique position in relation to ethnic-minority groups.

Taken together, the White Paper's recommendations marked a change for the CRE, but not the kind of fundamental change envisaged by the Home Affairs Committee. There was, therefore, no direct connection between subsequent CRE reorganization and the Home Affairs Report. Reorganization can be understood only in terms of an *interplay* between the CRE's own thinking, the government's view and the climate produced by the Home Affairs Report, which stimulated discussion about the CRE's role.[3]

The CRE's own view had been summed up as follows:

In our efforts to increase our efficiency and use our powers and resources to maximum effect, we hope to turn to advantage some of the [Home Affairs] Committee's constructive recommendations which have been accepted by both Government and ourselves. We have set up special working parties on such problems as the speeding up of formal investigations, the greater involvement of outside bodies in assisting complainants, and strengthening the thrust of our promotional work (CRE, 1981a, p.42).

The CRE stressed its commitment to enforcement. The legal side was seen to be 'central to our work', although it was recognized that enforcement had to be swifter and more effective and that the CRE had to 'reflect the influence of the law more fully in our other activities' (CRE, 1981a, p.42). To this end the CRE decided to concentrate on five areas:

(1) elimination of discrimination in major fields of employment and improvement of the employment prospects of young blacks;

(2) changes in the schools' curriculum to reflect more positively the multi-cultural character of today's society, and ways of raising the educational attainments of ethnic minority pupils through the recommendations of the Rampton/Swann Committee;

(3) a greater contribution by the Commission to measures for the effective policing of a multi-racial society in the 1980s and the improvement of relationships between the police and young blacks;

(4)   the completion of area profiles and the implementation of the Commission's policy on the funding of the CRCs;
(5)   the promotion of policies and practices designed to assist the rapid development of black businesses (CRE, 1981a, pp.42–3).

Commitment was given to the urgent implementation of the recommendations of the Scarman Report which detailed proposals for dealing with the problems which had led to urban disorders in 1981, but how far these points actually implied that the CRE was becoming anything other than a managerially aware organization must remain open to debate. It is arguable that the internal reorganization and the setting of objectives enabled the Commission to define its role more positively, but in fact it still did little to change the agency into a driving force for social and economic change.

Benefits and incentives

Despite this prevailing weakness of the CRE, black groups *do* still co-operate. The benefit side of the cost/benefit equation still seems to predominate, with many groups seeking to gain access to funds and to certain decision-making processes. Indeed, the CRE's reorganization provided new incentives for some groups to work with the body, in view of the prospect of improved agency effectiveness and a stronger commitment to legal investigation and enforcement. In addition, many black leaders were impressed by the CRE's apparently more determined and 'dynamic' top management team.

In 1982 the Home Secretary appointed Alan Gayton, a Public Relations consultant and Chairman of the Juvenile Bench in Leicester, to the Commission. Gayton was joined by Edward Gilmour Jones, Director of Personnel at Smiths Industries, and Gerald Tyler, a solicitor and former member and Deputy Leader of West Yorkshire County Council. David Lane, the CRE Chairman, retired in August of the same year, to be succeeded by Peter Newsam, who had been at the Inner London Education Authority in the capacity of Education Officer. With this infusion of new blood the Commission appeared to be well placed to implement further internal change. Indeed, the review of the agency's internal structure led, in November 1982, to the establishment of a stronger Legal Section under the leadership of a newly appointed Legal Director.

Table 4 shows the new CRE structure and indicates the traditionally wide range of activities which provide services and financial assistance to black groups and individuals. Such activities, combined with the administrative functions of the CRE, required funding (as shown in Table 5) from a budget of around £8.75 million for the 1983–4 financial year. The approved Home Office grant for the Commission for the year was £8,720,000 which was supplemented by the CRE's own income of just over £33,000. Given the fact that expenditure was really quite modest (particularly as 31% went to CRE salaries), it is noteworthy that the CRE actually managed to sustain such a

Table 4. *CRE structure following reorganization*

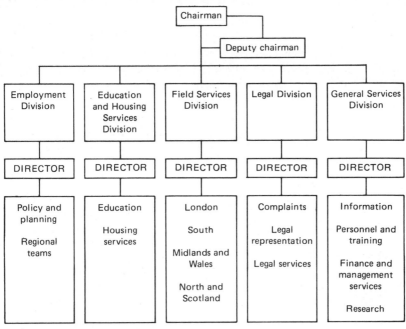

Source: CRE Annual Report, 1983.

Table 5. *Analysis of CRE expenditure 1983–4*

		£	%
1.	Staff salaries	2,726,833	31
2.	Grants to CRCs	2,478,541	28
3.	Grants for projects: self-help groups, project aid and bursaries	1,145,225	13
4.	Overheads: accommodation, travel, staff training, printing, stationery, furniture and equipment	1,434,499	16
5.	Information services, publications and conferences	404,897	5
6.	Research	136,873	2
7.	Legal and professional costs including external training	391,586	5
	Total expenditure	8,718,454	100

Source: CRE Annual Report, 1983.

variety of programmes for minorities. The main current provisions may be briefly summarized as follows, bearing in mind that these provide incentives for black groups to work with the CRE.

1.   *CRE legal work*

The Commission has power under Section 48 of the Race Relations Act to conduct formal investigations relating to race relations and the meeting of the CRE's general obligation to promote racial harmony. During 1983 seven final reports of investigations were published, one dealing with discrimination in the allocation of the London Borough of Hackney's council housing (see Chapter 5). Since 1977 the Commission has initiated 46 investigations: 24 in employment; 11 in housing; 2 in education; 8 in the provision of goods, facilities and services; and 1 relating to immigration (CRE, 1983, p.10).

Under Section 66 of the Race Relations Act the CRE is empowered to investigate situations in which individuals make complaints about discrimination. During 1983, 994 such complaints were received, many from those working in the private sector in small firms (CRE, 1983, p.12). Public houses and clubs have almost traditionally provided grounds for complaints about discrimination and the CRE's work in this area has often been supported by community groups which themselves seek to protect the interests of their own members or supporters.

2.   *Employment*

A major concern for the Commission has been the combating of discrimination in employment. The CRE's Code of Practice, approved by the Secretary of State for Employment, contains recommendations which are intended to promote 'racial equality at work' (CRE, 1983, p.15). The CRE held a number of seminars and conferences during 1983 which were designed to open the debate about the Code and to involve employers and trade unions in promoting its objectives. In line with this, black groups have been encouraging their members to join trade unions and actively participate in union branches. The CRE's Code thus provides them with a valuable focus in union-based activity.

The CRE has recognized that discrimination at a time of high unemployment is a crucial problem, affecting young blacks in particular, and points to the government's own research which indicates that around 50% of black 16- to 19-year-olds face the dole (CRE, 1983, p.17). The CRE has therefore concentrated much of its youth-related work on gaining equal opportunities for blacks in the Manpower Services Commission (MSC) Youth Training Scheme (YTS) and in advising the MSC on the need for the monitoring of equal opportunity provision on the YTS. In addition, the CRE has pressed for greater ethnic-minority involvement in MSC programme planning and for minority representation on MSC central and area boards.

The CRE is also encouraging the establishment of black businesses as one way round the problems of unemployment and the uncertainties of the YTS. Black organizations at local level have been keen to support the CRE's Black

Business Programme, which in 1983 had consolidated links with the private sector to assist individuals and groups to establish their own enterprises. The National Westminster Bank seconded a senior banker to advise the CRE in this area and local authorities also indicated their support.

3. Education

During 1983 the Commission published the findings of its first formal investigation into education (CRE, 1983, p.21). This followed allegations, in 1978, that black children were being discriminated against in terms of their allocations to particular schools in Reading. The Local Education Authority (LEA) accepted the CRE's recommendations and this proved to be an important precedent for other authorities. By 1983 around 25% of LEAs had developed policies on multi-racial education and the CRE is currently monitoring these (CRE, 1983, p.22).

4. Housing

Housing, like education, is a centrally important indicator of the condition of society. In the inner city the quality of life for blacks is defined largely in terms of the degrees of deprivation experienced in housing and education and with reference to the level of unemployment. The CRE's modest resources prevent it from initiating an extensive campaign to tackle housing in much more than a legal context. The CRE's approach has thus stressed the achievement of 'equal access' to and equality in housing (CRE, 1983, p.24). These objectives have been pursued through the CRE's investigative powers and through promotional work conducted in conjunction with black organizations, local authorities, housing associations and building societies. In line with this, the Commission has produced guidelines for local authorities dealing with the implications of the Race Relations Act and advising local authorities about issues concerning race and housing. The Commission also assisted with the establishment of the National Federation of Housing Association's Working Party on Race and Housing, which itself produced guidelines for local authorities on the activities of housing associations. The CRE has, in addition, provided funds for two conferences which led to the formation of the Federation of Black Housing Projects.

5. Immigration

The immigration issue continues to be a persistent problem for blacks and the CRE and local CRCs remain heavily committed to complex investigative work in this area.[4] Black voluntary organizations of numerous political colorations have come to rely upon the expertise of community-relations officers and the background of casework experience which they have at their disposal. Indeed, the CRE's record in this area illustrates the fact that it and the CRCs offer black organizations and individuals a wide area of technical/legal information which effectively increases group resources when confronted with immigration authorities and other government agencies. As indicated above, this also applies in employment, housing and education, where the CRE and CRCs provide groups with a useful source of information, advice and even funding.

6.   Police relations

It will be seen in Chapter 6 that many black organizations are keen to maintain links with police authorities. The CRE has also maintained contact with the police and voiced many of the demands and opinions of those in the black community who have pressed for improvements in police/community relations. The CRE has also participated in courses on race awareness at police training colleges and encouraged research into representation of blacks in the magistracy (CRE, 1983, p.29). The police have benefited from this co-operative attitude and have sought to enlist the support of the wider black community as a foundation upon which consent to 'physical' measures may be consolidated. In this, and the field of immigration policy, the CRE thus acts as an important agency which offsets the political consequences of the 'physical' side of public policy in the race field. Black groups are therefore able to point to what they regard as the positive advantages of co-operation with an agency which is seen to be campaigning for better treatment of immigrants and improved relations with police at local level, thereby undermining militant criticisms of overt physical controls and police actions.

7.   Links with local government

The close relationship which the CRE has with local government enabled black leaders to lobby more effectively for their demands and to obtain funding from government sources. The CRE was represented on a joint central government/Local Authority Association working group which led to a number of initiatives, including the establishment of a clearing house in local authority practice in race relations – the Local Authorities Race Relations Information Exchange (LARRIE) – and a local government Race Relations Training Development Group.

   In 1983 the DOE agreed that the independent Policy Studies Institute should carry out a feasibility study to assess the range, type and extent of local authority information needs in the race field. The clearing house idea, in line with this plea for improved information, appeared to hold out the prospect of better dissemination of experiences between authorities, despite the dangers of simply producing 'imitative' policy-making divorced from the specific needs of different communities (Young, 1984, pp.13–14).

8. *Funding the black community*

The CRE's financial assistance to black organizations clearly provides tangible benefits to groups which perhaps do not always stand to gain directly from the range of CRE provisions so far mentioned. The Commission's Project Grant Aid Scheme provides funds under six headings: Youth Training and Counselling; Employment Campaigns and Projects; Advice Services and Community Centres; Education; Ethnic Minority Arts; and Elderly Members of Ethnic Minorities. For 1983 the CRE provided £688,639 worth of aid under these headings directly to minority organizations, to help with salary and administrative costs, project financing, the holding of conferences and costs of publicity material. A total of 137 organizations benefited from this kind of assistance, including a number of Community Relations Councils which financed certain specialist projects from this source.

The Commission's Self-Help Fund mainly assists educational, counselling advice and training projects designed to meet the needs of black youth in the 13–25 years age range. £753,663 was allocated through the Fund in 1983 to organizations such as the Southall Youth Movement (see Chapter 6), local Harambee Associations and the Federation of Bangladesh Youth Organizations (London).

Finally, the Commission accepted 17 applicants under its Bursary Scheme. This scheme is intended to assist individuals conducting research into youth, community, ethnic businesses and other race-related topics. The Bursary recipients are generally affiliated to British community-relations agencies in both the public and private sectors and pursue their research in overseas (usually North American) 'placement' agencies. This range of funding sources is supplemented by the funding of the local CRCs and by the CRCs' own programme provisions. Co-operation with the CRCs is thus again defined in terms of benefits which colour the political attitudes of black groups seeking to enhance organizational resources.

The local CRCs

While this provides a picture of benefits available to groups at national level, it is important to remember that group attitudes are also influenced by provisions at the local level, which themselves have been the subject of much controversy. Indeed, as already indicated, the local CRCs should actually be regarded as the most important way in which black organizations can operate politically within official race institutions. The 1981 Home Affairs Committee Report, however, pointed out that ever since the establishment of the CRE there have been problems about its relationship with the CRCs:

The relationship both in general and in particular cases has been bedevilled by accusations of mutual discourtesy, lack of consultation and bad faith. Both the Commission and CRCs recognize the broad similarity of their tasks and their mutual dependence. CRCs need the Commission's money, the expertise of its specialist officers and the power deriving from its national statutory position. The Commission recognize that CRCs are their 'major partners in the work for equality of opportunity and good race relations', and that they can be the major channel for promotional work with local bodies and the means of keeping the Commission in touch with the state of race relations nationwide (HC 46-1, para. 96).

This centralist definition of CRE/CRC relations was not given to imply the *exclusive* dependence of one level upon the other. The Report mentioned the fact that some CRC staff were funded by local authorities and central government agencies and that CRCs had developed areas of work which would not normally be covered by the Commission. In addition to this, the CRE had developed direct links with local voluntary bodies particularly by way of funding 'self-help' community projects (HC 46-1 para. 97).

However, this does not alter the fact that *ultimately* the CRCs do have to respond to the general financial and administrative requirements of the CRE. The CRE does, for example, require some accountability over funds allocated to the local level and in administrative matters political tensions between the CRCs and the CRE can emerge when the latter attempts to influence practices or staff appointments. A recent example of such a conflict occurred in Wolverhampton, where the CRC's decision to appoint a new Senior Community Relations Officer (SCRO) late in 1979 led to the CRE threat to cut off their funds.

The dispute between the CRC and the CRE brought to a head issues which had been evident locally and nationally for some time. The conflict involved not only disagreement between the CRE and the CRC Executive Committee over the suitability of the SCRO, but also a clash between the Executive and the full-time staff at the CRC. The Executive wanted a more dynamic person for the post and this displeased the CRE, who regarded the appointee as altogether too outspoken and controversial. The CRC's staff supported the SCRO by joining a national strike of CRC staff over the CRE's attitude on the issue, but they remained displeased with their Executive's alleged lack of consultation and general lack of support from the black community. In April 1980 a meeting between the CRC, the CRE and the local authority failed to resolve the funding issue arising from the dispute. The local authority and the CRE did, however, decide to establish a so-called Trust Committee which would oversee the funding of race-relations work in Wolverhampton. This would involve funding of the CRC and also of other organizations involved with race relations in the town (Jacobs, 1980, p.421).

The Home Affairs Committee referred to the general situation existing between CRCs and the CRE in the following terms:

We are disturbed at the picture presented of industrial relations between CROs [Community Relations Officers], their nominal employers – the CRCs, and their paymasters – the Commission. Even allowing for a tendency to exaggerate, the ASTMS [Association of Scientific, Technical and Managerial Staff] description of these relations as a 'morass' where 'the climate of negotiation has become increasingly bitter' and 'manipulation and mendacity' have flourished paints a grim picture. The amount of energy which is thus wasted in conflict is appalling: CRCs trying to get rid of their CROs; CROs losing their jobs when the Commission withdraw support from a CRC; junior CROs undermining their superiors – these and other tales retailed in evidence to the Sub-Committee give cause for concern that the effectiveness of local race relations work is being seriously undermined by an atmosphere of bickering and backbiting (HC 46-1, para. 99).

The Committee stressed that it did not wish to exaggerate the situation and that major disputes were infrequent in most CRCs. However, in addition to Wolverhampton, Islington, Newham, Brent, Crawley and Oxford had all experienced problems and this pointed to a growing trend towards organizational conflict.

Benefits of CRCs

Despite these problems, black organizations persist in their co-operation with the CRCs, as they do at a national level with the CRE. One explanation is that black community representatives have simply become an integral part of local CRC 'bureaucracy' and are themselves actively involved in the bickering described by the Home Affairs Committee. While this may be the case in particular situations, it does not explain the co-operation of groups which prefer to stand aside from the inner politics of the CRCs. In Wolverhampton, for example, an attempt had been made to form a breakaway CRC, but this failed, and in many localities groups have made similar abortive attempts to establish independent umbrella formations. The answer to the question why groups decide to 'stay in' seems to relate – again as in the case of national co-operation with the CRE – to the political and financial incentives afforded to groups by the CRCs. These may be limited, but they are significant.

This may best be illustrated by looking at the CRCs' finances and activities. Under Section 44 of the Race Relations Act the CRE may provide financial assistance to the CRCs. The CRE currently provides grant aid (see Table 5) towards the full-time staff of 84 CRCs (out of a total of 99), while CRC funds are also supplemented by other bodies (such as the MSC). There is, therefore, money flowing from the centre to the locality which helps to sustain a range of activities listed under four main categories:

(1) Policy development – providing a review of provisions at community level and relating policies to the promotion of equal opportunity.
(2) Public education – CRCs campaign to influence decision-makers for changes in public policy to achieve racial equality.
(3) Community development – CRCs assist ethnic-minority groups in their development and their provision of assistance to minorities.
(4) Community service – CRCs promote projects which are intended to assist communities and also help with referral work relating to the personal problems of ethnic-minority groups and individuals.

The CRE's funding of CRCs is now based upon assessments of the nature of CRC programmes and local area characteristics. CRE Field Officers assist the CRCs in reviewing their internal arrangements for monitoring and evaluating their programmes and the National Association of Community Relations Councils also receives CRE funding for staff to deal with CRC work. This expertise to some extent offsets the constraints imposed by financial stringency and filters through to organizations participating in CRC activities by offering important support services to groups engaged in community-development programmes.

Co-operation with CRC programmes may be achieved through two kinds of working association between the CRCs and voluntary organizations. Groups may formally affiliate to CRCs (such as in Wolverhampton), thereby directly associating themselves with CRC activities (a possible cost of participation where the CRC identifies itself with controversial policies) and facilitating representation on CRC committees. Alternatively, groups may decide to keep a more informal relationship with the CRC, maintaining contacts with CROs or by attending open committee meetings as observers or co-opted members. Affiliation, where applicable, implies that groups are prepared to become more involved in the political, social and cultural activities of the CRC and expect to have the opportunity of making a direct impact upon CRC policy and upon the direction and objectives of community projects. Chapter 5 illustrates the way in which organizations display different degrees of involvement in CRC activities and political life and how this effects different levels of influence over policy questions.

This author's study of affiliation in Wolverhampton between 1967 and 1979 showed that, although only a limited number of black organizations were formally affiliated to the CRC (16 in 1978–9 out of a total of 35 black organizations in the town), this did not mean that the non-affiliates lacked contact with the CRC. According to one CRC official interviewed, every black organization known to him in Wolverhampton had at some time made representations to the CRC and a substantial proportion of groups regularly sent observers to committee meetings. In addition, a number of individuals affiliated to the CRC (138 in 1978–9) and many of these were members of non-affiliated organizations (Jacobs, 1980, pp.408–9).

This pattern of group involvement reinforces the proposition that the costs and benefits of co-operation may be weighed differently by organizations with differing conceptions of their political role, but that there is a strong general desire amongst group leaders to link their organizations in some degree to active CRCs. Group assessments of their relations with CRCs tend to change over time and this may herald a closer or more distant relationship depending upon circumstances. It will be seen, in Chapter 5, how groups are often successful in influencing the formal policy attitudes of a local CRC and this may encourage them to become more favourably disposed to using the CRC as a platform for their views and as a valuable agency for change in, for example, local authority housing, education or social policy. The 'cost' of entering into this kind of more intimate relationship, however, will generally be expressed in terms of a degree of necessary compromise with other groupings represented on the CRC committees, or a gradual moderation of demands where the relationship involves close liaison with local-authority officials, local councillors or with the police. Again, Chapter 5 illustrates this with reference to group attitudes to education policy in Wolverhampton, where militant group demands were eventually replaced with a commitment to more ordered co-operation with the local authority.

The wider context

Despite the CRE/CRC provisions mentioned above, black groups are now more aware of other areas of liaison with local government which hold out the prospect of enhancing the resources of the black community beyond the CRE/CRC orbit. CRCs encourage groups to participate in projects funded under the government's Urban Programme (see Chapter 7) or Section 11 of the Local Government Act 1966. Section 11 funding arose from the 1964–6 Labour government's urban policy and, like the Urban Programme, it provided government funding contributions which supplemented local expenditures. Unlike Urban Programme money, however, Section 11 allocations were specifically intended for race-related activities and provided money only for local-authority staff costs where local authorities made special provisions for minorities in areas with 'substantial numbers of immigrants' (Local Government Act 1966, Section 11). In such cases authorities could obtain 75% of the total eligible expenditure, which until recently had generally been allocated for educational purposes and to a lesser extent for housing, social services, recreation and libraries (Young, 1983, p.294).

Following the 1981 disorders extensive changes were made to Section 11 provisions. Section 11 expenditure rose from £40 million in 1978–9 to around £90 million in 1983–4 and in 1982 the government announced that important aspects of the scheme would be revised within the limits of existing legislation. After 1982 a wider range of local-authority staff appointments could benefit from Section 11 funding, including the appointment of race-relations advisors and the establishment of units concerned with the development of new race-related administrative practices. In addition, the Home Office undertook to review existing posts funded under the scheme, with a view to establishing whether or not posts were actually representative of special provisions to minority communities. In this way the Home Office sought to transform Section 11 from being a supplementary provision into one which could effect positive policy and administrative changes at local level.

Apart from Section 11 there is also a 'hidden' level of expenditure which goes to areas with high black populations and this spending comes under the jurisdiction of virtually all local authority committees – housing, education, social services, recreation, etc. No estimation has been made of this contribution to urban black communities and many would argue that such spending should remain non-race-specific (Young, 1983, p.296). The argument maintains that ethnic minorities should be treated equally with, say, the white inner-city working class when it comes to grant aid and service provision. The alternative approach, however, would produce a clearer identity of need in black working-class areas, since by analysing expenditures directly in terms of how they affect specific groups it would be possible to make clearer calculations of the actual magnitude of social disadvantage experienced.

The fact that moves have been made in this direction in the housing and education fields is indicative of the political desire to have a more accurate picture of urban deprivation. It will be seen in the following chapter that black groups have been supportive of the CRE and CRC attempts to obtain better ethnic statistics and have followed the CRE initiating studies into precisely how blacks fare in areas such as housing. Further research needs to be done into the economic share which blacks achieve in programmes, since this may lead to a greater understanding of the frustrations felt by unorganized black youth during periods of communal strife. It may also provide a more thorough explanation of the unease felt even by moderate black community leaders in co-operating with those local authorities which often appear to adopt a minimalist attitude towards ethnic-minority assistance, either over the whole range of local services or within particular services where additional minority provisions may prove economically costly or politically unpopular with the wider community. The case studies of housing and education in the following chapter consider the responses of black leaders in a situation where different local-authority attitudes prevailed in these two policy areas and where such economic constraint adversely affected group/authority relations for a period during the 1970s.

Under these circumstances it appears that while the CRE and CRCs themselves provide incentives to black groups, which encourage a significant degree of co-operation between groups and government, there are many opportunities for groups to place their own direct demands upon local-authority resources. The CRE/CRC structure is often unable to provide anything other than limited assistance, which may have relatively little impact in stemming the effects of local expenditure cuts and reductions in the Urban Programme. However, the next chapter reinforces the contention that the CRE and the CRCs do afford *some* tangible returns to groups, which may be regarded by those groups as crucial, and that the CRCs may still be one of the more effective ways of articulating black demands to obtain resources and of projecting the interests of the black inner-city community.

5 Housing and education: compromise and consent

This chapter illustrates the interaction of voluntary groups at local level with local government.[1] Housing and education are two policy areas where black groups compete for scarce resources within the context of urban public-expenditure constraints, pressures upon government-funded services and various degrees of material deprivation. It will be seen that, in line with the attempts of groups to maximize the benefits accruing to them in this situation, they generally feel it in their interest to give their consent to policies which arise from compromises between groups themselves and between groups and public decision-makers. In this respect local Community Relations Councils can play an important role in providing a forum for debate about public policy and for mediating between the often conflicting interests of groups and politicians keen to defend particular policy commitments.

Housing and education provide but two areas of research within a wide range of urban service provisions. They are of central importance, however, because they impinge upon so many aspects of black peoples' experiences in the urban environment. They affect the general well-being of inner-city dwellers and relate to the ability of black minorities to improve their status in society and to progress in terms of their access to employment opportunities. By concentrating upon these two policy areas in Wolverhampton (in the British West Midlands), this chapter identifies the way in which black groups and black community leaders try to ensure that they have a stake in influencing decisions affecting minority interests made by public authorities and how public officials and politicians react to group demands. The chapter is thus *not* about the social and economic impacts of particular policies, or about the moral or other justifications for those policies. The objective is to provide an account of the way in which groups interact with local government and how they generally attempt to maintain the conditions conducive to relatively ordered group/government consultation.

The examination of these themes within a time-scale going back to the mid 1970s helps to establish the general character of group/government relations over time and provides a perspective which explains periodic changes in group attitudes and political dispositions. These variations should be analysed within the framework provided in Chapter 3, 'Black political action', and will be seen in terms of the institutional costs and benefits associated with the community-relations bodies detailed in the previous chapter.

Another advantage of using a longer time-scale relates to the ability to study the development of group/local authority relations in terms of the emergence of more formal local channels of access. The Wolverhampton case-study traces some of the early attempts of policy-makers and groups to establish effective lines of communication with each other, which by the mid 1980s have become part of the regularized process of consultation and negotiation. The present character of minority-related consultation in Wolverhampton, and in other British towns and cities, has therefore been formed by a pragmatic process of bargaining and compromise adapted to prevailing local circumstances. In the Wolverhampton case, this has produced a diverse set of group/local-authority contacts and a variety of political responses from those affected by the political constraints and opportunities inherent in these arrangements. In many instances these responses have not yet 'hardened' into what may be termed 'predictable' responses, precisely because the local policy-making and consultative provisions involving black groups are still relatively new and untried.

Black groups have generally had to struggle hard to obtain a voice in local affairs and, although many blacks have become successfully integrated into local policy processes, there still remain wide areas where black representation is minimal or at best token. Many local authorities still tend to regard blacks as a category which may be allowed access to certain parts of the policy process but which should be regarded as essentially peripheral to the important decision-making undertaken by councillors and local-authority officials. There was an element of this with the Wolverhampton case, although by the mid 1970s many local councillors and officials were keen to extend black involvement in decision-making and were prepared to allow blacks to take on a greater degree of responsibility for running local programmes and to take part in the management of public and private initiatives.

The Wolverhampton study presented here, of course, illustrates the responses of only one local authority. While this book seeks to provide a wider context within which local political situations may be understood, it is recognized that this particular chapter should be seen as providing but one contribution to research on local responses to minority needs. Much valuable research into a range of local authority provisions for ethnic minorities has been carried out by the Policy Studies Institute (PSI). This work has highlighted not only the differences between authorities, but has also indicated the similarities between local situations, particularly with respect to the willingness of black groups to enter into closer liaison with local government. Ken Young and Naomi Connelly, in a 1981 PSI study, argued for the Department of the Environment to play a leading role in development strategies which would produce greater co-ordination of central and local efforts to implement policies designed to combat racial disadvantage more effectively. This would lead to a lessening of the discrepancies between authorities and better co-ordination of race-related policies (Young and Connelly, 1981).

PSI research undertaken since 1981 has sought to map the pattern of local provisions more fully (Young, 1983). The categorization of local authorities into so-called 'thrusters, learners, waverers and resistors' has provided a rough framework within which to understand and possibly even to predict policy responses. Ken Young's 'thruster' authorities (largely London Boroughs) are those which have adopted highly innovative policies to meet the needs of multi-ethnic communities, creating new local-authority posts, committees and machinery to implement policy and assist with policy development. A growing group of authorities, however, appear to be 'learners', which have recognized the need to adapt current practices to cater for ethnic minority needs, but which still have to produce well-defined policy strategies in this area; individual committees generally are left to work out their own approaches (like Wolverhampton in this study, but see note 14 also).

The 'waverers' are different from the 'learners', not so much in terms of their actual provisions, but more in terms of the absence of any agreement on the need to review and adjust practices. In such authorities the presence of racial disadvantage in multi-ethnic areas may be recognized, but no major adaptations are evident, possibly because councillors and officials do not wish to alienate local white opinion (this contrasts with Wolverhampton, where important council initiatives led to significant special administrative arrangements to handle race-related policies). 'Resistor' authorities go beyond the waverers in that they simply refuse to accept that the presence of minorities in their areas has any important implications for local-authority provision. The consequence of this attitude is a restricted interpretation of the 1976 Race Relations Act amounting to a virtual non-response in policy terms (Young, 1983, p.297).

Table 6 shows something of the diversity of local-authority approaches, although it by no means provides a comprehensive survey. It simply illustrates the degree to which the London Boroughs provide special race committees, race advisers and funding under Section 11 of the 1966 Local Government Act. The Table is intended to emphasize that there is no common standard of provision for ethnic minorities at local level and no generally accepted agreement on the nature of committee arrangements handling race-related issues.

Wolverhampton's approach depended largely upon the nature of black group attitudes and upon the implications of centrally produced policy statements and guidelines from the CRE (and the former Community Relations Commission). As the PSI research suggests, this learning might have been far speedier if those central guidelines had been more positively applied, but whether this would have carried black opinion quite so well is a

Table 6. *London Borough race provision, October 1983.*

London Borough Councils	Majority party	Race committee	Adviser posts	Section 11 money use (80/1) (£s)	Population (X)
Barking	Labour			71,461	4.1
Barnet	Conservative			320,201	12.6
Bexley	Conservative				4.2
Brent	Labour	Sub	Principal & Unit	2,002,269	33.0
Bromley	Conservative				3.6
Camden	Labour	Full	Principal & Unit	71,074	10.1
Croydon	Conservative			550,922	11.9
Ealing	Conservative			2,004,512	25.0
Enfield	Conservative			199,571	13.9
Greenwich	Labour	Sub	Principal & Housing	130,091	7.9
Hackney	Labour	Sub	Principal & Unit	131,107	27.5
Hammersmith	Conservative	Full	Principal	20,087	14.8
Haringey	Labour	Consultative	Principal	1,744,345	29.4
Harrow	Conservative	Sub		271,187	15.2
Havering	Conservative				2.4
Hillingdon	Conservative			117,032	6.5
Hounslow	Labour			386,169	16.9
Islington	Labour	Sub	Principal & Unit	45,791	16.5
Kensington	Conservative	Sub	Principal	81,088	8.9
Kingston	Conservative				5.3
Lambeth	Labour	Full	Principal & Unit	116,681	23.0
Lewisham	Labour	Full	Housing, Social Services	29,612	15.0
Merton	Conservative			138,828	10.6
Newham	Labour	Sub	Principal & Housing	750,116	26.5
Redbridge	Conservative			270,057	11.0
Richmond	Conservative				4.5
Southwark	Labour	Full	Principal	96,362	16.2
Tower Hamlets	Labour	Sub		99,600	19.8
Waltham Forest	Conservative		Principal	929,597	17.3
Wandsworth	Conservative		Housing, Personnel	23,785	18.4
Westminster	Conservative			14,422	11.5

Note: X = % of the population with head born in New Commonwealth (including Pakistan), 1981 Census. No information provided for Sutton.
Source: GLC, 1984.

question which the PSI neglects. More centralization, particularly in the early and mid 1970s, might well have simply alienated some black groups and 'forced' local authorities to adopt measures which at that time were out of step with minority expectations as to the role government should play in their affairs. The housing issue in Wolverhampton illustrates this point, as black groups were reluctant to preside over any radical or innovative local-authority initiatives or even to echo central concern over the housing issue.

Race and housing: the background

In 1977 a Home Office/Community Relations Commission Report entitled 'Urban Deprivation, Racial Inequality and Social Policy' outlined some of the most pressing problems facing ethnic minorities in Britain. The report also indicated policy areas of particular concern to the leaders of black communities and to local and national government. It relied upon information contained in academic literature, census data and various research projects and on results from government-sponsored fieldwork specially undertaken in eight 'project' areas'.[2] The research embodied in the report suggested that the ethnic-minority groups were concerned to make representations to local authorities over a wide range of issues, but that in particular housing, employment, education and the social services were areas where groups were keen to strike up relationships with local government. Moreover, local authorities were themselves willing to concentrate resources into these problem areas.

The policy commitments followed by all local authorities with regard to education and housing were seen in the mid 1970s as dependent upon the recognition of black community needs as being 'special' when compared with the rest of the community. Local authorities to this day are disposed to regard blacks as 'special cases' with special needs and interests with respect to their communities.

Race-relations legislation in Britain provides virtually no opportunity for the direct implementation of American-style 'affirmative action', although many local authorities have translated special needs into programmes of 'positive discrimination' in favour of blacks (Home Office/CRC, 1977, p.31). In housing and education, opportunities abound for such an approach and the general policy environment in these two areas has traditionally been one in which local authorities have tended to be more favourably disposed to conducting policy-making with the assistance of black groups. Groups can help in identifying the extent and nature of the 'needs' of the black community, thus facilitating the most effective strategies for policy implementation.

The early 1970s was a period conducive to the improvement of group/government relations over housing policy, not only because central government was concerned to improve the effectiveness of its policy implementation, but also because the economic climate was still one of moderate expansion on the housing front. The 1980s were to see severe reductions in public housing expenditure which inevitably limited discussion of expanding housing opportunity. In September 1975, by contrast, the Labour government issued a White Paper, *Race Relations and Housing,* which commented on a 1971 House of Commons Select Committee Report dealing with housing and minorities:

The Government's view is that it is essential for the development of healthy social conditions, particularly in the old urban areas, that there should not be ethnic, racial, religious or class discrimination in the formulation or the application of housing policies and practices. People in housing need should have, and feel that they have, a better opportunity than they have had so far of access to decent housing, whether public or private; and of sharing in the improvement of housing conditions. It is the Government's policy to secure this (Cmnd 6232, para. 5).

Following the publication of the White Paper, the government indicated that, as part of an overall information system, it wished local authorities to collect information about the numbers and needs of black communities, to enable them to make informed judgements about the effect of central policies and programmes in relation to the local situation. At the same time as this White Paper was published, a Political and Economic Planning (PEP) Report suggested that there was no evidence of deliberate discrimination against racial groups, although 'the system' tended to work, unintentionally, to the disadvantage of minority communities (PEP, 1975, p.10). The PEP and government Reports singled out the questions of need, dispersal, record-keeping and language as the main areas in housing where immigrant communities experienced difficulties and effectively defined these questions as the minority housing problem.

Influencing policy: group access in Wolverhampton

Groups naturally responded favourably to central attempts to meet the minority housing problem and, like many local authorities, reacted with an expansionist perspective. Despite the Labour government's intentions, however, local authorities were by 1975 facing some less optimistic realities, as they were now being urged by central government to maintain tighter control over their expenditure. The expansionist expectations of black groups would be frustrated over the coming period, not only in the housing area but also in education, social service provision and employment.

The question of how to formulate a policy under these changing conditions which would identify correctly the extent of the ethnic-minority housing problem in Wolverhampton was therefore of critical importance to the Labour-controlled local authority. The economic constraints facing the authority would inevitably produce longer-term problems in the 1980s and 1990s, and so effective short-term policies were required which would offset, to some extent, any future difficulties. Minority groups themselves could supply important information about short- and long-term needs, about attitudes towards change and about potential improvisations where resources were scarce. The quality of such information could be enhanced by the Wolverhampton Council for Community Relations (WCCR), which assumed an important role in the process adopted by policy-makers in assessing minority needs and the extent of material deprivation.

According to the above-mentioned Home Office/CRC Report, most local authorities in 1977 had no special formalized channels of communication with black ethnic-minority organizations with regard to housing, even though authorities had attempted to identify areas of need within the black community. Despite the fact that this report failed to take account of the local Community Relations Councils, such as WCCR, as providing links with local authorities over housing (Home Office/CRC, 1977, p.42), this still illustrated a quite remarkable lack of concern by local government over an important issue affecting blacks in particular and the future of Britain's inner cities in general.

In Wolverhampton at that time there were a number of contact points between black groups and the local authority through which consultation on housing could be achieved, although these could not all be described as constituting formal consultative contacts (see Chapter 3). This liaison could be summarized as follows:

(1) Groups had contacts with councillors and housing officials through the WCCR committee structure and its day-to-day contacts with the local authority. Some black leaders also had partisan contacts with councillors through the local Labour Party, which meant that direct approaches to councillors could be made without prior reference to WCCR.

(2) The local authority initiated a series of housing seminars which provided an *ad hoc* channel of communication to councillors and officials.

(3) Groups could have access to the authority's Homeless and Exceptional Needs Committee, which acted as an informal open forum advising councillors on matters relating to housing. In 1977, however, no black groups had actually taken advantage of the opportunity to participate in the committee deliberations (except for the Marcus Garney Advice Centre). This reflected the general passivity of the black groups in Wolverhampton on the housing question and their general lack of confidence in the Homeless and Exceptional Needs Committee.

Insofar as groups had access to information, there were several ways in which this could be obtained and communicated to councillors and officials. A CRC report (1976) pointed to four possible group activities directly related to the ability of groups to ascertain and disseminate information. These points were relevant in Wolverhampton:

(1) Use of the relevant ethnic press and local radio stations which carry programmes in a variety of languages.

(2)   Door-to-door canvassing in areas of high ethnic-minority concentration (to gain support for campaigns, petitions, WCCR initiatives, etc.).

(3)   Groups distributing translated material to the local Community Relations Councils, case-workers, language tutors at neighbourhood English classes and local religious and commercial organizations in the black community. These agencies can, in turn, distribute material to individual households.

(4)   Dissemination of information through those who are considered to be community leaders and the reverse flow of information from community leaders to groups and eventually to decision-makers (CRC, 1976, p.14).

These points relate to other policy areas as well as housing and indicate that the relationship between groups and local authorities can be a two-way process involving group inputs (information and demands upon the local authority) and local-authority policy outputs, which may be communicated to the black community by black organizations. This implies a form of co-ordination between authorities and groups, involving the 'association' of groups with local-authority policies. Information supplied by groups can be functional to the activity of the authority and also highly advantageous where groups are prepared to transmit decisions back to the community.

In Wolverhampton there appeared to be a distinct lack of enthusiasm by black groups to perform this role in the housing area. It is not surprising, therefore, that discussion surrounding the issue of housing for ethnic minorities was initially instigated by the local authority, in response to the various central governmental reports and policy initiatives referred to above. Black groups were not, therefore, applying any significant pressure on the authority before the Housing Management Committee launched its housing 'campaign' in 1976.

There were two reasons for the passivity of groups in Wolverhampton on this issue up to early 1976.

(1)   The minority communities were concentrated into particular areas of the town. This gave black organizations specific 'constituencies' where their support was easily identifiable and where community identity contributed towards a certain 'consciousness' which could be capitalized upon by leaders seeking political support. The measures to disrupt these communities, as implied by local-authority proposals for housing dispersal, were considered by group leaders to be potentially harmful, threatening to split the cohesion of their 'constituencies' and to undermine their political support.[3]

(2)   The majority of black householders were owner-occupiers and were not directly affected by council policy concerning public-authority housing. While black owner-occupiers did tend to live in the most run-down areas of the town, they nevertheless tended not to apply to local authorities for re-allocation to other areas. Those who did apply appeared to be more successful in obtaining council accommodation than in other cities with a high percentage of immigrants.

With regard to owner-occupation, the Runnymede Trust had found that in Wolverhampton 65–66% of black households were owner-occupiers compared with only 39.9% of non-black families, but many more black families were overcrowded, although their standard of housing was better than in some other towns studied (Runnymede Trust, 1971, p.6). The problem concerning Wolverhampton was essentially concerned with the distribution of black families in the poorer-quality housing in central areas. According to the Runnymede Trust, twelve wards in Wolverhampton had a less-than-proportionate share of black households compared with the total household distribution. This disproportionate distribution implied a need to 'disperse' black families to other areas of the town, but the twin issues of concentration and housing dispersal were not of urgent concern to the black community. On the one hand concentration added strength to the ethnic-minority communities as 'whole units', while on the other dispersal implied the shift of at least some owner-occupiers into council properties segregated from the major immigrant concentrations. For the local authority, however, the social effects of potential ghettos and the dissatisfaction of the WCCR and black groups with at least the lowest-quality council accommodation meant that a change of policy on ethnic-minority housing was seen to be desirable.

The attitude of black groups on dispersal was an implicit endorsement of the *status quo*. The policy in Wolverhampton was for many years to give preference to re-lets (i.e. dwellings that became available for re-letting), first to those to be rehoused as a result of slum clearance or redevelopment, secondly to transfers from other council dwellings, and thirdly to the General Needs Waiting List. For new dwellings, preference was given to those displaced by slum clearance or redevelopment and the remainder was usually allocated half to transfers and half to the General Needs Waiting List. In practice, transfers had some priority over the Waiting List, which meant that those transferring tended to move to higher-quality housing and the Waiting List to poorer-quality housing (Wolverhampton Borough Council, 1977a).

Black families were to be found in greater proportion on the Waiting List than amongst transfers, so they tended to move into the poorer-quality housing. Those in greatest need, including many black families, were less able to wait for the estate of their choice. From April 1976, the Housing Management Committee in Wolverhampton began to give more opportunities to those on the Waiting List compared to tenants transferring and this helped to correct the imbalance during 1977. The revised Points Scheme for the General Needs Waiting List, introduced in 1976, emphasized need rather than waiting time (and not residence in Wolverhampton), so that the allocation could help those who had 'an above average housing need' (Wolverhampton Borough Council, 1977a, pp.1–6).

By 1977 the Housing Management Committee was reconsidering its general policy on housing owner-occupiers in order to make provision, with suitable safeguards, for those who purchased at the 'bottom' of the housing market and found that they could not achieve 'decent' housing. The need in this area could in some measure be met if the Points Scheme provided for owner-occupiers of houses below a given rateable value to be housed on the same basis as tenants who applied on the General Needs List (i.e. in cases of over-crowding or medical need). The Council's programme of Housing Action Areas would also assist owner-occupiers to improve their housing.

The Committee was again particularly concerned about the concentration of black families in certain parts of town and also on the less popular and run-down council estates. The Committee generally found this to be undesirable but, by 1977, had recognized the controversial implications of such a policy for the white native community and the reluctance of black groups to adopt dispersal in view of the disruption of their own communities.

The idea of a fixed-percentage dispersal of immigrants to housing estates had been mooted originally, but it soon became clear that this would prove to be unworkable in practice and would possibly be unlawful if applied in the strict sense of proportional entry onto particular estates. The Housing Management Committee Chairman, Councillor Ken Purchase, strongly favoured a new policy approach and suggested a strategy which would bring about voluntary dispersal of families, arrived at through consultation with ethnic-minority organizations; but opposition to the launching of a campaign on dispersal came from within the Labour group itself. Purchase, however, managed to obtain the support of the group and dispersal became a central issue in the housing debate.

Another issue raised by the Housing Management Committee was that of record-keeping. The view expressed was that there was no reason why records relating to the origins of housing applicants or tenants should not be maintained by Housing Directors. The need for records arose from the misgivings that surround any process of selection by public bodies. The Committee decided that separate basic housing statistics should be kept for white and for black families because they were needed for the monitoring of the performance of housing policies in Wolverhampton.

The housing seminars: consensus emerges

These issues were to be considered in depth at two Borough-Council-initiated housing seminars, which enabled ethnic-minority groups to contribute to the debate on housing policy. Prior to the seminars, the WCCR met with local councillors and council officials who agreed to prepare a paper outlining 'the view of the black community' relating to housing policy over a whole range of issues (dispersal, records, Housing Department personnel etc.).[4] The WCCR published their own views under the title 'Observations on a Fair Housing Policy for Wolverhampton', which supported the local-authority initiative and marked the culmination of a series of internal WCCR debates on housing, mainly conducted by the WCCR Housing Panel. The paper supported local- and central-government thinking on the questions of 'needs', record-keeping and language difficulties but only gave guarded support to a dispersal policy:

If the council were to attempt to disperse council tenants from the black ethnic minority communities on a percentage basis throughout the streets of the town, this would amount to compulsory dispersal and will be ill conceived.

But:

If the Council were to attempt this same dispersal based on the personal choice of the applicant/tenant, this is acceptable (WCCR, 1976, p.1).

The WCCR conceded that this position stressing personal choice reflected a compromise between the original line taken by Ken Purchase and the views of individual affiliates on the WCCR; many, such as the temples, remained hostile to dispersal and even those such as the IWA (GB), which were prepared to support the general principle, did so only tacitly. The IWA (GB) adopted what amounted to a 'wait and see' attitude on dispersal policy and the Harambee Association, which like the IWA (GB) had not taken any previous initiatives on the major issues raised in the WCCR paper, also reserved detailed comment. These attitudes effectively placed the major responsibility for the WCCR housing policy on the then Senior Community Relations Officer, Chris Le Maitre, who drafted the WCCR paper and who acted as WCCR's most prominent housing spokesman.

The muted black response was an early indication that local-authority housing policy proposals would not be seriously challenged by any black organizations in the town, provided that any dispersal was carried out on a voluntary basis. Voluntary dispersal – almost by definition – provided little immediate threat to black 'constituencies', since it was highly unlikely that significant numbers of blacks in central areas would actually want to move to estates where they would be in a small minority and where there were no facilities to cater for their special ethnic requirements (places to worship, to shop and to be entertained, for example). For black groups, therefore, the local authority housing 'campaign' was best treated as a political 'non-event'.

At the first housing seminar held in November 1976 it was the WCCR officials who were the main contributors on the ethnic-minority side. They were left with the task of articulating a range of individual group attitudes, while at the same time attempting to make a positive and constructive contribution to the debate. It soon became clear that the lack of controversy at the meeting facilitated the convergence of WCCR/local authority views. The WCCR did not place 'demands' upon the authority, but merely played the role of commentator and supplier of information relating to the needs of blacks in Wolverhampton. The Annual Report of the WCCR for 1976–7 further indicated the reluctance of even WCCR officials to 'demand' specific action on housing: 'We have no specific strategy on housing but work very closely with the Housing Department' (WCCR, 1977a, pp.27–8). Indeed, the very title of the WCCR submission at the 1976 housing seminar stressed that they were making 'observations' on a fair housing policy rather than presenting a programme of action for implementation in Wolverhampton. The WCCR was content to rely upon government reports and Housing Management Committee initiatives and to consolidate its good relations and support *vis à vis* the local authority.

Even though little was being achieved with respect to innovative policy formulation or implementation by the WCCR, the stance of the body was significant because it facilitated the access of black groups and the WCCR to local decision-makers influential in housing and other fields relevant to blacks. Groups benefited from a closer association with the local authority and, to a limited degree, gained 'standing' from having been consulted on the manner in which proposed policies could be implemented. The passive resistance to dispersal had in fact impacted upon the local authority, which had discovered through consultation that such an approach would be unacceptable to black groups. In that respect groups *had* influenced policy in a negative way and without the placing of specific demands. The feelings of black groups on the dispersal question had the effect of alerting the Housing Management Committee to the likely community response to such a policy and this avoided any potential conflict. The Housing Management Committee were themselves undecided about future policy and this itself made the virtually meaningless 'voluntary dispersal' approach more amenable.

A second, and more important, housing seminar was held in April 1977. The seminar was attended by ethnic-minority and other groups directly and indirectly concerned with housing. Many non-black groups were present but, again, it was the WCCR which tended to dominate the seminar, although other individual black groups were quite vocal. The seminar, like the one in 1976, had no formal policy-making authority, but it did produce a number of recommendations which were to be placed before the Housing Management Committee. The WCCR and black groups were also able to provide the Committee with information, even though much of this tended to be impressionistic and unsupported by factual material.

Once again the voluntary dispersal policy was welcomed by the WCCR, whose submission praised the local authority for initiating the debate on housing and Chris Le Maitre's contribution ended with an expression of virtually uncritical admiration for the local Labour record on housing. This support was endorsed by other participants, who tended to avoid overtly political arguments in order to concentrate upon often rather abstract notions about the rights of blacks in housing. Apart from an intervention by the Commonwealth Citizens' Association, no black organizations took part in the dispersal debate, thus again leaving the WCCR to present the view agreed by its Housing Panel. Silence was maintained even by the IWA (GB), despite the complete opposition to dispersal expressed by the white tenants' associations present at the seminar (WCCR, 1977b, pp.1–2).

Discussion turned to the question of the keeping of records. The WCCR 'strongly' advocated the keeping of records on ethnic-minority applicants, but argued that this should not be applied to blacks alone (WCCR, 1977b, p.2). This view was in line with the Race Relations Board policy outlined in a paper distributed to all local Community Relations Councils just one month before the seminar.[5] The WCCR assumed the most prominent role in this debate – a pattern which was repeated in the debates on staffing (appointment of black persons to the staff of the Housing Department), development of older properties, single-person accommodation, co-option of community representatives to the Housing Committee, the role of tenants' associations, owner-occupiers and the question of mortgages for immigrants.

Outcomes on housing: the benefits of group involvement

Given the attitudes of the various groups, the following points may be drawn up, which help to define the nature of group/local-authority relations over housing at that time:

(1) Where a broad consensus could be reached, the WCCR was able to act as a spokesman on behalf of affiliate groups – groups tended to let the WCCR articulate views about issues on which they themselves adopted a cautious stance (such as dispersal).

(2) Only one *non*-WCCR *affiliate* organization (the Krishna Temple) attended the second seminar. This reinforces the impression that non-affiliate groups tended to be suspicious of WCCR/local-authority liaison, or were simply uninterested in the housing issue.

(3) On issues other than dispersal, but connected with housing, the WCCR adopted 'acceptable' policy commitments which were supported by affiliate organizations and which helped the WCCR to broaden its links with councillors and officials. These links provided the basis for future contacts between the parties involved, but their *ad hoc* nature made them susceptible to strain under less favourable conditions. In education, for example, *ad hoc* arrangements were for many years inadequate as effective channels of communication over local educational policy and in Wolverhampton after 1978 they allowed housing to be virtually removed from the policy agenda as far as blacks were concerned.

(4) The local authority evidently benefited from the housing seminars. A report was presented by the Council's Housing Manager to the Housing Management Committee at the end of May 1977. The report referred to the 'general agreement' between the local authority and groups and acknowledged that this was representative of opinion in the black community. In this way WCCR's 'representativeness' was seen to be proven.

The Housing Manager's report mentioned above gave details of recommended action which the Housing Management Committee saw as a logical follow-up to the seminars. On dispersal the report stated:

that dispersal must be voluntary and that at this stage the most important action will seem to be to ensure that coloured people have full information concerning what housing opportunities are open to them (Wolverhampton Borough Council, 1977b, p.1).

The Committee was unable to take any firm decision on the question of records, although in principle councillors were in favour of the keeping of separate records on ethnic-minority groups and others. On staffing, the report similarly reflected the views expressed at the seminars. The Committee would continue to advertise suitable posts in the Housing Department 'in ways that help coloured people to become aware of the opportunities available' (Wolverhampton Borough Council, 1977b, pp.1–2). Finally, a firm commitment was given to improving the quality of the existing housing stock – a measure that was seen to be of direct benefit to owner-occupiers and local voluntary housing associations assisting black people.

The significance of the report lay in the support which the Committee was now apparently giving to the requirements of the black community in housing, and in the limited but nevertheless quite tangible benefits which black groups could point to as having been gained through support of the housing seminars. The impact of the seminars, as far as groups were concerned, had been felt in terms of their contribution to discussion on a range of problems and the shifting of resources in their direction through Housing Action Areas, by way of improved staffing arrangements and an increase in the number of homes in tenancy possession by black people.

Housing off the agenda

The relative lack of controversy over the limited initiatives in the housing area effectively reduced the importance of the whole issue in relation to other WCCR policy interests after 1978. The seminars represented a kind of 'settlement' between the local authority and black organizations. This contrasted strongly with the education issue, which was highly charged during the 1975–8 period and which to some degree diverted political attention away from housing during and after that period. Group acceptance of the WCCR's 'settlement' also reflected their view on housing and the desire by some groups to let the whole issue die. Many within the black community were of the belief that it was minority communities themselves who could and should provide acceptable housing within those communities and that external involvement was irrelevant to this task, particularly where local 'self-help' was being encouraged by housing associations and groups such as Harambee (Jacobs, 1978).

WCCR Annual Reports for the years up to 1982 indicated the lack of urgency over housing – the issue being relegated to one of secondary importance. The WCCR's own Housing Panel became inactive, to be reconvened only in late 1982 as a number of housing-related matters demanded attention. The WCCR did of course maintain an active interest in individual housing problems through its casework and advice to the public, but the point here is that housing was not a central political issue during the late 1970s and early 1980s.

The lack of activity of the WCCR's Housing Panel had serious practical consequences. The *ad hoc* liaison between the Panel and the local authority gave way to informal WCCR contacts between councillors and officials either by telephone or through non-housing WCCR committees and panels. Black groups had to make their own approaches to the WCCR or directly to the local authority. Consequently, the new 1982 Housing Panel 'set out first to introduce itself to the main housing agencies in the town' (WCCR, 1982–3, p.32). This meant re-establishing its good name with the local authority and making new contacts with the Housing Corporation and local housing association. The focus of WCCR interest was to centre upon the encouragement of these agencies to provide opportunities for special-need groups, such as the homeless and the elderly. The Panel was inspired in this by the National Federation of Housing Association's policy of encouraging a 'fair housing policy' for ethnic minorities. This objective was impressed upon the local authority by way of its recently established Race Relations Committee. The Panel's approach was thus much more in tune with the kind of community-based approach favoured by black groups, while at the same time conducive to the enhancement of the Race Relations Committee's involvement in housing matters. Also implicit in the Panel's general approach was the feeling that the WCCR's inactivity on housing had produced a general complacency in the town over the housing issue. The Panel's observations on this were stated as follows:

(1) There is no general housing forum in the town incorporating the statutory and voluntary sectors committed to a fair housing policy. It is hoped that the Panel can to some extent meet a need here.

(2) It is clear from initial discussions that the whole question of race and housing is ridden with assumptions held particularly by those who provide housing. For example it is often quoted that 'All Asians are home owners' and 'all ethnic minorities prefer to live in inner cities'. Unless such assumptions are challenged more often, policy is likely to become arid and stale.

(3) It appears that:
    (a) Where data on minorities has been collected by the Local Authority this has been under-used, and
    (b) In many housing associations no data is kept at all.
    Considering that the Local Authority has been collecting data on ethnic minority housing since 1978, it is worrying that there appears to have been little analysis of such data . . . (WCCR, 1982–3, p.32).

The Panel thus launched what it called 'a modest campaign' to promote fair housing and to warn against racism in the housing field. This modesty reflected the same conditions which had prevailed during the 1970s, namely a desire to maintain an ordered consultation with other agencies and a desire not to demand radical changes when such demands were not forthcoming from the local black community itself. Despite the inadequacy of housing in inner city areas and the difficulties faced by blacks in those areas, black community leaders were not prepared to disrupt their constituencies or, indeed, their relations with the local authority over, for example, employment, social services and police/community relations. It is arguable, therefore, that in Wolverhampton black leadership reticence over housing often seemed to perpetuate some of the problems facing their communities relating to overcrowding, ghettoization and poor living conditions. This was in return for political benefits related to leadership access to local decision-makers and the preservation of community cohesion.

Education and race: raising the stakes

Does a similar situation arise from the political debate about education? Here the situation facing moderate black leaders is different, since in Wolverhampton, as in other British cities and towns, the problem of race and education is an issue which has become heavily politicized. It is also an issue over which some moderate black leaders have made very militant demands, which mirror to some extent the opposition of black radicals.

In Wolverhampton, like other local authorities, the general approach was to consider 'material deprivation' as a significant aspect of the educational disadvantage faced by black ethnic-minority pupils. This deprivation was linked to the issue of solving problems concerned with racial discrimination in education and in society in general (Home Office/CRC, 1977, p.58). Local authorities differed in their judgements of how far educational disadvantage results from the distinctive position of ethnic minorities, but it was widely acknowledged that there were issues which arose in providing an education for ethnic-minority children which differed from those relating to white inner-city children (Home Office/CRC, 1977, p.66).

In line with this thinking, the 1976 Race Relations Act embodied two important provisions which affected the approach adopted by local education authorities (LEAs). The Act extended the definition of racial discrimination to include inadvertent discrimination which could 'put into question educational practices which neglect to implement positive policies to remove handicap' (Home Office/CRC, 1977, p.66). This provision could actually be used against local authorities not engaged in the formulation and implementation of policies designed to improve the position of minority educational advance.

Secondly, the Act rendered lawful any provision made specifically for ethnic minorities to meet their 'special needs in education and training' (Home Office/CRC, 1977, p.68). The provisions of the 1976 Act thus allowed education authorities to adopt policies which gave greater emphasis to meeting the needs of minority pupils and claimed to be a more effective method of achieving racial equality.

The degree of support given by central government and their success in encouraging local authorities to implement such policies was rather limited up to the 1976 Act. Education authorities looked to the Department of Education and Science to support them in developing and implementing strategies to overcome racial problems within the educational sector and obtained the backing of the Community Relations Commission for such initiatives. In Wolverhampton the record of the local authority in this area was, by national standards, noteworthy and was, in part, attributable to the identification of issues raised initially by black organizations themselves. Wolverhampton's record was one of regular consultation between the LEA and black groups, particularly through the WCCR.

The history of such consultation involved the adoption by the WCCR and the LEA of a general consensus on educational policy issues, which lasted up to 1975, when the WCCR and affiliate organizations, led by the IWA (GB), broke with the consensus and adopted demands which fell well outside the scope of LEA commitments. The contrast with the study of the housing issue provides a useful point of reference in highlighting the actions of groups and decision-makers under different conditions. The distinction between housing and education was related to differences in black organizations' interests and demands *vis à vis* housing and education, and dissimilarities between the two policy situations themselves.

Firstly, the question of group interests. The WCCR and affiliate bodies were naturally concerned with educational issues because of the large proportion of immigrants in the town's schools: a clear interest thus existed within the black community. In the case of housing, it was suggested that consensus was achieved because black organizations were keen not to disrupt their communities or challenge rights of property ownership. In education the challenging of the *status quo* and the raising of demands for better educational provision were linked to the potential benefits to the black community of a substantial increase in the resources devoted to black education. The needs of black children were readily identifiable in terms of a relative disadvantage when compared with white children and with the relatively poor performance of blacks in educational terms. These problems were of immediate concern to black (particularly Asian) families, traditionally keen to see their children advance in a white society. Black organizations, especially the IWAs, were certain to find popular support within the community for demands for an extension of educational provision (particularly when related to unemployment and the question of black crime).

The second difference between the two policy areas arose from the fact that in housing between 1976 and 1977 the local authority was engaged in *changing* or re-formulating its commitment on the provision of homes for the ethnic minorities. In education, groups were faced during this period with an LEA which was *defending* its policy and resource commitments in the face of group demands:

(1)   There was an economic constraint on the degree of policy change which

was possible. In housing, new policies on dispersal and record keeping etc. could be implemented largely through changes in administrative procedures, whereas expansion of educational provision implied the revision of resource commitments on a relatively large scale by the LEA.

(2) The LEA claimed that educational provision for ethnic-minority children was already adequate given limited resources and was (by 1977) providing certain members of the black community with the opportunity of actually participating in the implementation of policies designed to promote multi-cultural education.

(3) Central government, again for economic reasons, was less anxious to promote positively an extension of specifically ethnic-minority-orientated education and tended to rely on vague exhortations which allowed LEAs to pursue widely flexible approaches to the problem.

(4) The LEA argued that it was concerned to protect the interests of all Wolverhampton children. The demands being raised by black groups would inevitably have conflicted with the desires of parents in the white community. This could also be applied to the housing issue where dispersal was concerned, but in housing the dispersal process was to be slower and almost imperceptible compared with the impact of multi-cultural education in the schools.[6]

(5) In a relatively defensive policy situation, permanent officials of the Council tended to play a more prominent part than on the housing issue. These officials were less likely to favour black groups than councillors (Jacobs, 1978).

Temporarily breaking the consensus

The launching of the black group campaign for an extension of multi-cultural education came as a response to numerous policy statements issued on the subject by the then Community Relations Commission (CRC). These statements were in line with the Labour government's rather non-committal 'request' for action to extend provision for ethnic minorities in the educational sector.[7] The recommendations made by the Commission were not binding on local authorities and so Wolverhampton, for instance, was not obliged to adopt the proposals. The reluctance of the local education authority to do so resulted not so much from a neglect of multi-cultural educational needs, but from economic constraints which limited the scope of the LEA's policy commitment to an area much narrower than that envisaged by the CRC. Group demands on the other hand were based upon a disregard of the economic factors inherent in the situation and, eventually, upon an apparent disregard for the political consequences of challenging certain interests of the white community.

In October 1975 the IWA (GB) organized a conference in Wolverhampton on education and race. The conference was attended by numerous groups representing both moderate and militant political opinion and although a militant tone was adopted during debate, moderate resolutions, intended for presentation to the Wolverhampton Education Department and to WCCR, were passed. Typical of some of the contributions to the debate was the following:

[The] majority of the Headmasters (some without heads), Inspectors, H.M.I.s, Education Officers and Directors of Education, being the 'proud' products of Grammar Schools, Public Schools and Oxbridge Universities, behave like the Colonial bosses. Their attitude has to be tamed, they have to be re-educated and re-orientated in tune with the needs of the dynamic society. They might have something to learn from the diversity of cultures and the cross-fertilization of ideas. The Wolverhampton bosses need this 'treatment' more than anybody else.[8]

In contrast to this militancy from 'the floor', the 'platform' presented what was to be the public face of the conference embodied in the resolutions. The moderation of demands assured a broad degree of support from the temples, religious societies and moderates in the Labour Party. The resolutions, broadly in line with the CRC recommendations, could be summarized as follows:

(1) The conference demanded from the Department of Education and Science that all literature containing words such as 'black' with racial overtones must be withdrawn from schools, libraries and other public places and that 'deliberate' attempts to incite racial conflict through literature or the mass media should be punished by law.

(2) The conference opposed any cuts in resources devoted to education and called for an extension of nursery education 'for all working-class children'.

(3) A call was made for the establishment by the LEA of an advisory team empowered to 'define a philosophy' for multi-cultural education. This would advise the Education Committee on matters concerning school organization, lesson content and counselling and would represent teachers, the education authority and black organizations.

(4) The LEA was urged to improve the promotion prospects of ethnic-minority teachers in Wolverhampton.

(5) Most importantly, the conference called for a re-orientation of school curricula to include the study of the literature, religious backgrounds, geography and history of the black ethnic minorities. All multi-racial schools, it was stated, must encourage and make provision for the teaching of Asian Studies for all children and for the teaching of Asian languages as a second language. There should be no separate schools for whites or for blacks.

(6) Teachers should attend courses prior to implementation of the above proposals.

Thus the scope of the conference's demands was wide in comparison with the

LEA's commitment to a *status quo* position in the ethnic-minority education sphere (particularly on points 3 and 5).

It has been stated that the LEA claimed that it was already making a substantial provision for multi-cultural education. In 1970 the Education Committee issued, a statement entitled 'Immigrants in Education', which alluded to the usefulness of liaison between the Committee and the WCCR and which committed the LEA to extending the provision of facilities designed to enhance racial harmony through the educational system. 1974 had seen the establishment of working groups following a LEA-sponsored initiative which brought together WCCR and LEA representatives with a view to formulating future educational strategies. These *ad hoc* working groups, taken together, led to the establishment of the Multi-Racial Education Service (MRE), which became operational shortly before the IWA (GB) Education and Race Conference.

The MRE was placed under the directorship of a special advisor who was responsible for the co-ordination of all aspects of multi-racial education in Wolverhampton and who was empowered to co-opt teachers and members of school governing bodies to the Committee (with the overall sanction of the Director of Education). However, by adopting a structure which effectively excluded black voluntary *groups* and by acting only in an advisory capacity, the MRE inevitably invited criticism from the IWA (GB) conference. The conference claimed that the MRE was rendered ineffective and was 'totally manned by the so-called experts'.[9] Indeed, the policy-making function of the LEA still remained with the councillors and officials and, with the termination of the *ad hoc* LEA/WCCR working groups upon the introduction of the MRE, the WCCR and black organizations were left with no formalized channel of communication with the authority apart from the WCCR Education Panel.

By the middle of 1976 it had become clear that the LEA/WCCR liaison which had existed when the working groups were established had given way to a situation where the LEA was now resting content with the MRE. The working groups had, however, shown the WCCR that it could make an impact on educational policy and that, as the Education and Race Conference had suggested, there were definite benefits to be gained from the establishment of a more formal consultative structure. At a WCCR 'Self-Assessment' Conference held in July 1976, resolutions submitted called on the LEA to give recognition within the school curriculum to religions other than Christianity and to ethnic studies. The conference also articulated more clearly its demand for an advisory group on multi-cultural education which would have group/ WCCR representation.

The 'self-assessment' resolutions were further discussed by WCCR's Education Panel in September 1976. The policy established at the Self-Assessment Conference was endorsed by the Panel, which urged that the matters discussed be taken up with the LEA, concentrating upon demand for:

(1)   Provision for Afro-Caribbean and Asian Studies and for Asian languages in schools (to be provided at GCE levels).
(2)   Provision of ethnic-minority religious education. A document on multi-racial education was produced and discussed by the Education Panel and recommendations were made to the LEA reiterating the demand for an advisory group – a demand which was to be made repeatedly throughout the whole of the following year, with no positive response from the LEA.

The main supporters of these initiatives were the IWA (GB), Harambee and the West Midlands Caribbean Association. Their success in legitimating the demands of the Education and Race Conference by formal adoption of them as WCCR policy was a significant factor in encouraging the groups and the WCCR to maintain a campaign on the educational issue. Although it was becoming increasingly obvious that the position taken by the groups and the WCCR was being strongly opposed by the LEA, the IWA (GB) in particular was gaining confidence in the pursuit of these demands as WCCR support was seen to be forthcoming. Enthusiasm was, however, combined with increasing frustration with the LEA's stance, which was leading the IWA (GB) to adopt more aggressive demands on the issue. By April 1977 the tone adopted by the IWA (GB) had changed from the reasoned resolutions of the Race and Education Conference to one articulated by the IWA (GB) local (later to be national) President, N. S. Noor, in a letter to the local press:

ethnic minority languages have been altogether ignored by the Wolverhampton LEA.
   The Indian Workers Association has been demanding the inclusion of ethnic minority languages and essential parts of their cultures in the curricula of schools. Unlike Coventry and other multi-racial towns, the Wolverhampton LEA is notorious for its scornful apathy towards the needs of the multi-racial society we live in.
   Perhaps the Director of Education is blissfully ignorant of the damage that has already been done to community relations, to multi-racial education and to the family life of the ethnic minorities.
   Posterity will never forgive the LEA for its multiple murder of language, cultures, religions and the self-image of the ethnic minority children.[10]

The response to this outburst soon followed from the Director of Education:

I refute what Mr. Noor has to say at the same time as I regret the polarisation of viewpoints which this letter exemplifies and which does nothing but harm to community relations.[11]

   Noor's attack was also rather too much for some of the more moderate black groups, which up to this point had sided with WCCR policy and the IWA (GB). The Sikh temples, the Dudley Road Guru Ravi Das and the Pakistan Welfare Association, together with WCCR permanent officials, were keen not to engage in such arguments with the LEA. While WCCR officials remained uneasy about Noor's position, the temples went further and dissociated themselves from the IWA (GB)'s new tone by expressing a now open opposition to Noor and his principal backer, Lance Dunkley of the West

Midlands Caribbean Association (WMCA), at WCCR Education Panel meetings. Education Authority officials frequently pointed to this conflict within the WCCR as a factor detracting from the important issues and reducing the WCCR's effectiveness as a bargaining and consultative body.[12]

The temples were keen to extend multi-racial education but a difference of opinion with the IWA (GB) emerged, since they believed that educational matters were, as the Director of Education had suggested, 'best dealt with by themselves'.[13] British educational methods, some argued, would only serve to dilute religious and cultural ties. Moreover, groups such as the Pakistan Welfare Association (PWA) (which was more restrained on the education issue) had links with the LEA which, if disrupted too seriously, could lead to a worsening of their chances for local authority support for other projects. The PWA was well placed with its Muslim Education Service operating in close conjunction with the LEA and even the more vocal Harambee was dependent upon LEA and WCCR support for its hostel projects. The IWA (GB) and Dunkley's WMCA had no such links with the authority and in that situation could afford to project a more strident image.

In August 1977 the LEA's School Management Committee held a special meeting in an attempt to restore a degree of consensus over educational policy. Committee members were concerned about the tone of Noor's statements and about the implications of the IWA (GB)'s influential attitude on relations between the Asian community and the local authority in the education sector. The LEA was effectively seeking to minimize the actual and potential disruption of group/authority relations and seeking to avert a conflict with the WCCR at a time when the WCCR was appearing to tolerate the IWA (GB)'s rhetorical demands.

The August meeting brought together representatives from the School Management Committee, officials from the Borough Education Department, the WCCR, the Wolverhampton Anti-Racism Committee, the IWA (GB) and allied black organizations. The meeting, despite the LEA's intentions, ended in what one Borough official described as 'uproar', marking a breakdown in relations between the LEA, the WCCR and the vocal black groups over the multi-cultural education issue. The contrast with housing was thus a dramatic one, particularly as it developed into an increasingly personalized argument between Noor and Wolverhampton's Chief Education Officer, D. Grayson. It was a conflict which was to leave its imprint on relations between groups and the LEA well into the 1980s, but which still did not prevent groups from reassessing their attitudes in the longer term. Indeed, by the mid 1980s even the more militant black groups were gradually adopting a more co-operative attitude on education, which reflected the impasse felt resulting from the lack of agreement over education and which related to a 'realistic' view of prevailing economic constraints (from the LEA's point of view) and which was therefore more likely to produce short-term returns for the black community. Group demands consequently tended more towards raising issues which had an immediate, practical impact upon the condition of black people and which could be approached within the context of existing race-relations legislation.

Issue for the 1980s and 1990s: the uneasy integration of groups

This change in attitude should also be related to a change in the general approach by groups and the CRE, which began concentrating more upon the broad implications of the racism issue. In Wolverhampton, as in other cities and towns with large black populations, the demands of black groups in the 1980s have concentrated increasingly on the need for local authorities to go beyond the relatively straightforward granting of improved conditions to the *eliminating* of alleged racism inherent in local-authority practices. Racist practices, it is argued, form the essence of the problems facing blacks in housing and education, since without attacking institutional racism there is little prospect of blacks participating in decision-making processes on an equal basis with their white counterparts.

Reflecting this concern, in May 1983 the CRE served a non-discrimination notice under the 1976 Race Relations Act on the London Borough of Hackney. This followed a CRE investigation into the quality of council housing allocated to different racial groups. Hackney Council co-operated with the investigation and responded positively to its finding by working towards full implementation of the requirements of the non-discrimination notice throughout its housing service provision (CRE, 1984).

The important thing was that the basis of the non-discrimination notice was that the Council had unlawfully discriminated against various people of West Indian, Asian and African origin by providing them with inferior housing to that given to whites in similar circumstances. The differences in allocations were not explained by any factors other than race.

The 1984 CRE report confirmed the impression evident in research published in the 1970s which indicated that ethnic minorities were concentrated in the poorest-quality council housing (GLC, 1976; London Borough of Islington, 1977; PEP, 1975; Runnymede Trust, 1975). More recent research showed that black applicants still had difficulty in obtaining access to council housing both in London and the provinces (CRE, 1984, p.17; Flett, 1979; London Borough of Lewisham, 1980; London Borough of Wandsworth, 1979; Simpson, 1981; Skellington, 1980). The Hackney findings were thus indicative of a widespread problem which was increasingly to concern black groups and local politicians dealing with the social problems and potential communal tensions arising from what were perceived to be racist administrative practices.

In education, also, increasing attention has been paid to the more fundamental racist aspects of the British educational system (CRE, 1981b), which persist despite the largely administrative and technical reforms of the

1970s. Under the 1976 Race Relations Act local authorities had an obligation to 'make appropriate arrangements' to promote equal opportunity in fields such as education and housing. The CRE's concern in the 1980s concentrated upon this provision and encouraged local authorities to eliminate more effectively inequality of opportunity, curriculum bias against minorities and discrimination in education (e.g. in teacher recruitment, training and promotion) by challenging negative attitudes and prejudices.

An essential pre-requisite for the implementation of a multi-cultural education policy was seen to be an increased awareness that racist practices were present and that educational and other local-authority services should, as a result, be evaluated in terms of criteria which defined good practice (CRE, 1981b, p.20). Indeed, such criteria are in part provided by Section 71 of the Race Relations Act, where it refers to the need to eliminate discrimination and to promote equality of opportunity and good race relations. With these guidelines in mind, some local authorities have established inter-departmental working parties on race relations as part of a 'corporate' view of the need to implement the spirit of the 1976 Act. In many cases, as recently in Wolverhampton, local authorities have involved black groups in these efforts and provided groups with access to councillors and officials involved in the evaluation of school curriculum development, language provisions and general policy development. The attractions of such liaison were hard for groups to ignore, since black organizations felt that they had much to offer local authorities in terms of specialist policy advice and assistance with their programme implementation.

The willingness of local authorities to actively pursue policies which promote 'good race relations' is therefore evident. This willingness may stem from an authority's desire to keep out of the CRE's bad books (such as Hackney) or, as in Wolverhampton, it may also relate to the persistent demands of black groups. For instance, the reconciliation between the LEA in Wolverhampton and black groups was effected in the 1980s as both groups and the local authority came to identify a greater *common interest* in working together to improve minority educational provisions. By the late 1970s the WCCR's educational campaigning began to complement the Commission for Racial Equality's desire, and the desire of many politicians at Westminster, to adopt policies which would require a much more concerted approach by local authorities towards tackling some of the problems faced by ethnic minorities. Wolverhampton's defensive attitude on education appeared to be at odds with these proposals and in many respects was seen to be lagging behind the more 'forward' thinking of some local black organizations.

Much of the debate about education into the 1980s has centred around discussion of the findings of the Rampton Committee of Inquiry into the educational problems of ethnic-minority children (Rampton Report, 1981). Rampton carried out a most comprehensive survey of the educational performance of West Indian, Asian and white children on behalf of the

Department of Education and Science. West Indians were found to fare particularly badly when compared with white children and Asian children, with only 1% of West Indians going on to study at university. Asians did perform rather less well than whites, despite their advantage over West Indians, although a number of gifted Asian children did even better than white children (Parekh, 1983).

A number of factors seem to have contributed to the disadvantage of minorities in education and the Rampton Report raised discussion of these factors at national and local level between politicians and black organizations. The impact of racism in society and the neglect by certain local authorities of the needs of black children were frequently quoted by black groups as contributory factors which, combined with other socio-economic variables, produced poor educational performances, poor career prospects and racially motivated criticisms of 'under-achieving' minorities.

In Wolverhampton, the Rampton Report inspired the WCCR and affiliate black organizations. The local authority was regarded by them as being backward in making special provisions for blacks when seen in terms of the Rampton Report's regard for multi-ethnic education (WCCR, 1980–1, p.1), but the report provided these groups with a firmer, 'legitimate' foundation from which to argue for educational change.

In the spring of 1982 Wolverhampton's then Director of Education accepted an invitation to speak to the WCCR's Education Panel and received the WCCR's comments about Section 11 allocations. The WCCR's attitude reflected the new mood of many black groups that consultation was to be preferred to confrontation. As the WCCR stated in its 1982–3 Annual Report, 'such consultative exercises are to be greatly encouraged if we are to make an impact on the policies of the LEA as they affect black people'. Further, and very significantly, the WCCR stated:

the [WCCR Education] Panel in the spring of 1982 submitted proposals to the Director of Education regarding multi-cultural education. In view of the recent (favourable) LEA policy statement on this subject it is apparent that the WCCR Education Panel's proposals have been of some influence (WCCR, 1982–3, p.11).

Clearly the Rampton Report had effected a change on both sides, with the LEA moving towards a firmer commitment to minority education and black groups seeking some practical solutions to prevailing problems. In line with this attitude, the WCCR and black groups were becoming more closely involved with the Manpower Services Commission (MSC), which implied the taking on of new responsibilities within MSC programmes for youth training and vocational education. Within these programmes, groups were assuming organizational and administrative roles which forced them either to adapt or to flatly opt out of the MSC orbit. The temptation to adapt was generally the stronger impulse, particularly as a growing number of black youths were joining the ranks of the unemployed. The WCCR's Education Team was established to work with the MSC in operationalizing a WCCR/MSC Youth Scheme, which formed part of the MSC's implementation of its own Youth Training Scheme (YTS). The Youth Scheme involved the WCCR in assisting the MSC to establish short vocational courses, day-release courses, courses in life and social skills and in providing guidance and counselling. For this the WCCR obtained a substantial amount of funding from the MSC (£440,000 in 1982–3, plus £755 under the MSC's Community Programme), effectively making the MSC the largest single contributor to the WCCR's budget for that financial year.

Black participation in such schemes in the mid 1980s had thus become an established part of Wolverhampton's race-related public policy commitment. With three black members on the Borough Council, participation in the borough's Urban Programme and with black groups active in Wolverhampton's large Voluntary Sector Council (representing another important link between the local authority and community groups), it could be argued that ethnic minorities were more fully represented than at any other time in the history of group/authority relations in the town. This point is further underlined by WCCR's representation on the town's Inner Area Sub-committee, the appointment of a Race Relations Officer and the establishment of a Race Relations Sub-committee upon which minority groups could be represented alongside ethnic-minority councillors. The Inner Area Sub-committee enabled minority groups active in WVSC to voice their opinions to the Inner Area Programme authority and to more effectively bid for finance from the local UP's so-called 'Community Chest', established to assist community projects.[14] As one council official in Wolverhampton told this author, 'by 1982 the climate has therefore improved greatly for black groups keen to work with the local authority and much of the consultation is conducted quite informally but nevertheless very effectively. Indeed the informality in Wolverhampton has often blurred the dividing line between group and local-authority interests.' A degree of real integration had therefore been achieved, but it was not indicative of a comprehensive assimilation of groups into 'the system'. In Wolverhampton, as elsewhere, blacks had still failed to gain representation on the council in proportion to the size of the black constituency. The WCCR was consulted, but still had not achieved wide representation of blacks on the more important local-authority committees. Many black organizations represented on the WCCR and many not affiliated to the body maintained their distance from WCCR policy and remained highly critical of local authority policies. Community development still implied central funding through government-supported agencies such as the WCCR itself and the MSC – this was hardly likely to overcome black suspicions of a government policy which still allowed relatively little local control over community projects and which was still associated in many minds with the 'physical' controls brought into effect by the police during the 1981 'riots'.

The Wolverhampton case illustrates very well the general character o integration in Britain when black groups tend to adopt a generally 'moderate' and co-operative attitude towards government at local level. It will be seen in Chapter 8 that this integration is less extensive than in the USA, but it is no less important politically, particularly with regard to governments' (both central and local) ability to promote 'harmony' within the urban policy-making context. The 'benefit' of participation (see Chapter 3) appears to be an important one for black leaders who are themselves anxious to maintain relatively well-ordered relationships with politicians and local officials. This commitment comes out strongly in the following chapter, where it will be seen that even some quite militant leaders and organizations can be drawn towards co-operation with existing institutions and local conflict-resolving mechanisms because it is those institutions and mechanisms which ensure the continuation of stability. It is stability which provides a 'culture' within which integration grows.

6   Riot and dissent

Having viewed the interaction of black organizations and government under relatively ordered conditions, it is necessary to consider political situations which present politicians and community leaders with acute problems associated with communal disturbance. It will be seen that black leaders are keen to maintain their links with government under disturbed conditions and that their political responses are conditioned by their desire to maintain ordered access and bargaining with politicians and officials. There are, however, pressures upon community leaders to defend positively the demands and local interests of their communities and this frequently pushes even moderate leaders to criticize government and to redefine their relationship with public agencies.

This chapter examines available accounts of urban disturbances in Britain which at present provide a record of urban violence. The accounts are to be treated with caution where they represent the findings of unofficial studies (Bethnal Green and Stepney Trades Council, 1978; NCCL, 1980). However, the detailed research embodied in such studies appears to be factual and accurate and quite consistent with reports in the serious press. Official studies (Scarman Report, 1981) will be treated as authoritative, although they, like unofficial reports, are based upon eye-witness observations, which proved to be the main sources of information apart from the press and the police. Academic research about the events themselves is limited, although investigations have been produced, again often using eye-witness sources, to provide interesting conclusions and case studies of events (Joshua, Wallace and Booth, 1983).

Urban disorder in Britain

The inner-city violence of summer 1981 was not an isolated phenomenon. There were numerous outbreaks of street violence prior to that summer which served as a warning of the events that were to follow. The build-up to 1981 suggested that the disturbances were the consequence of social tensions which were deeply rooted in the social and economic environment of the inner city in Britain (Benyon, 1984; Solomos, 1984). It is not, however, the task of this chapter to examine the causes of communal conflict but to describe the disturbances, in order to throw light upon the nature of black leadership attitudes and responses.

It is important to preface the discussion by identifying two broad categories of communal disturbance. The first type stems from the activities of those participating in organized political activity. It will be shown below that many of the disturbances prior to 1981 were the result of clashes between black organizations and either the police or extreme right-wing groups such as the National Front and the British Movement. Together with the influential Anti-Nazi League, many black groups joined locally based campaigns which were distinctly political in character (Cashmore and Troyna, 1982).

The second major type of disturbance resulted from the actions of the 'unorganized'. The summer 1981 disorders generally lacked the overt participation or stimulus of organized political groupings. The fire-bombing and looting which accompanied the attacks on police were rarely attributed to political activists. The actions taken by both black and white youths and others were spontaneous and undirected and frequently assumed the nature of simple hooliganism (Jacobs, 1982; Pearson, 1983). The extent of this kind of violence in physical terms went beyond anything so far experienced as the result of organized political protest and in this respect the 'riots' were more disruptive than political rallies and demonstrations. The directionless nature of the 'riots' led to their dissipation, but the after-effects of such serious actions, as with important political confrontations between blacks and the authorities, profoundly affected the relationships between community leaders, their rank-and-file members and local and national governments. Black leaders may have disclaimed responsibility for the actions of the unorganized but, as with political protests, they were forced to strike up defensive attitudes on behalf of their communities which often aggravated conflicts with politicians and government officials. Under these circumstances community leaders were vulnerable to criticisms from government, since they were expected to be representative of their 'constituents' and thereby in some ways responsible for their actions. The question of 'moderation' with respect to the attitudes of community leaders was an issue which came into sharp focus when groups were placed in a position where they had to take a public stand on matters which concerned many blacks who were clearly remote from their community leaders and uninterested in legitimate forms of political expression. Black militants tended to identify with the interests of the unorganized and moderate leaders raised the level of critical rhetoric to offset the political costs of association with agencies and programmes which had apparently failed to produce social harmony or significant economic gains for many blacks (Ollerearnshaw, 1983).

Southall 1979

Southall in west London provided an early example of a highly politicized conflict involving the black community, the police and extreme right-wing organizations. Southall has a predominantly Indian population with a smaller number of people of Caribbean origin. The Indian community has tradition-ally been highly organized politically through the moderate Indian Workers' Association (Southall) which is one of the largest locally based groupings representing the Asian community in Britain.

In April 1979 the right wing National Front (NF) held an election rally in Southall Town Hall. Community organizations decided to oppose the rally by organizing a so-called march for 'unity and peace' on the Sunday preceding the NF meeting. The next day, 23 April, the Metropolitan Police drafted more than 2,000 men into the area, sealing off Southall town centre and blocking the path of a second anti-NF demonstration. In the course of the events which followed serious clashes broke out, resulting in the death of Mr Blair Peach, one of the anti-NF demonstrators.

The death of Peach provided a spark which angered black organizations and the Anti-Nazi League (to which Peach had belonged). Accusations were made against the police claiming that acts of violence by them had been perpetrated upon the black community. The National Council for Civil Liberties (NCCL), in response to these charges, published a report of an unofficial Committee of Inquiry into the events in Southall which provides valuable factual information about the attitudes of black organizations before, during and after the demonstrations.[1] The picture which emerges in the report is one of black representative organizations seeking to place pressure on the local authority (Ealing Council) to take action to calm the situation and prevent disruption. Black leaders sought to persuade the Council to revoke their decision to allow the NF to hold their meeting in the first place. At an early date prior to the NF rally, and in line with this objective, the IWA (Southall) took the initiative by inviting representatives of local organizations to a meeting on 11 April:

in order to discuss the implications of the National Front rally and to chalk out a clear, united strategy against fascism coming to Southall and to mobilise maximum turn-out for organizing peaceful resistance against it (NCCL, 1980, p.23).

Efforts would be made to persuade the Conservative leader of Ealing Council, Mrs Beatrice Howard, to reconsider the authority's decision to sanction the NF meeting and Ealing Community Relations Council echoed the IWA call by giving its backing to the peaceful resistance campaign. The 11 April campaign meeting thus attracted the support of some 100 representatives from the IWA, the Community Relations Council, the local branch of the Anti-Nazi League (ANL) and a variety of political, religious and community groups. The ANL representatives spoke strongly in favour of organizing a demonstration against the NF, while the IWA took the cautious view that the NF rally should be ignored and that a wall of silence would be a more effective way of reducing the impact of the NF's activities. The Community Relations Council supported the IWA view, but the majority at the meeting wanted some form of direct action which, it was claimed, would draw attention to the threat which the NF were posing to the black community.

The meeting established a Co-ordinating Committee charged with the task of organizing the protest and issuing publicity calling on the Council to cancel the NF rally. The Southall Youth Movement (SYM) voiced their opposition to the Co-ordinating Committee with the argument that it was too late at that stage to influence the Ealing Council and that the march being organized by the Committee could easily be exploited for election purposes by local Labour politicians. The 'militancy' of the SYM thus amounted to mild criticism of the Co-ordinating Committee's tactics rather than to any differences of basic political strategy. Indeed, the SYM themselves decided to participate in the demonstration despite its alleged publicity boost for the Labour Party.

The campaign gained additional momentum when John Beeston, President of the Southall Chamber of Commerce, wrote to his members recommending that they follow the IWA in closing all shops on the day of the main demonstration. The boarding-up of shopfronts and the removal of Asian signs was seen to be a practical way of protecting property rather than an expression of solidarity with the organizers of the anti-NF protest. The Co-ordinating Committee itself also treated the shops' closure issue as a practical rather than a political one. Keen to minimize any financial losses to proprietors, the Committee appointed representatives to liaise with the police over shop-closure arrangements for the 22–23 April period – a move which followed police assurances that they would do everything in their power to prevent damage to property near the Town Hall. In general, therefore, the Co-ordinating Committee cast itself in the role of responsible defender of the black community, keen, wherever possible, to minimize communal tensions through non-violent protest against a local authority which was regarded as sanctioning a provocative NF political mobilization which would cause inconvenience to black traders, white traders and residents alike.

On 17 April representatives of the Co-ordinating Committee met with the Southall police and an officer from Scotland Yard. According to the unofficial Committee of Inquiry: 'the meeting was amiable and no objection was made by the police to the plans for a peaceful sit-down protest' (NCCL, 1980, p.26). In accordance with common practice, the police refused to give the Co-ordinating Committee any indication of the tactics that they would employ on the day of the protests. This disappointed the Committee, which had wanted to plan its own tactics to fit in broadly with police plans in an attempt to control tightly the anti-NF demonstration. This was an important point, not simply because of the Committee's increasing fear that violence would break out, but more importantly because it strengthened the demand for state intervention to ban the NF march.

Ealing Community Relations Council sent a telegram to the Prime Minister, the Home Secretary and the Chairman of the CRE expressing this fear and urging them to intervene to cancel the NF meeting. The negative response of the Home Secretary left the Co-ordinating Committee with the prospect of what was by then promising to be a massive protest which would be of national significance. This outcome would go well beyond the comparatively manageable protest originally envisaged by the organizers on 11 April. An eleventh-hour intervention by the Home Secretary could have relieved the Co-ordinating Committee of the onerous task of actually setting out on a demonstration directed physically against the NF, which was beginning to pose a threat to the more traditional ordered process of consultation and compromise which the moderates on the Committee were used to. The unease of the organizers is underlined by considering the meeting held between the Co-ordinating Committee's 'inner group' of negotiators and the Labour Home Secretary, Merlin Rees, on 19 April.

The 'inner group' consisted of: Vishnu Sharma (IWA, Southall); Martyn Grubb (Principal Community Relations Officer of Ealing CRC); S. Pulley (Southall Trades Council); Balwinder Singh Rana (Southall Anti-Nazi League); and the Revd Jim Parkinson. Rees agreed to meet with three members of this predominantly moderate inner group, together with Yinnon Ezra (Ealing CRC and Secretary of the Southall Rights group). The Home Secretary was informed that the demonstration was intended to be peaceful. Martyn Grubb later explained that:

> we wanted the police to know our plans at the highest level. We thought that Merlin Rees would not want community leaders arrested and that he might ask the Chief Constable to avoid it . . . (NCCL, 1980, p.27).

The refusal of Rees to ban the NF rally meant that the 'march for unity and peace' took place on 22 April in a tense atmosphere, with around 5,000 joining the ranks of the main demonstration headed by prominent Labour politicians and the somewhat anxious Co-ordinating Committee members. As the procession passed Southall police station a number of incidents occurred and several arrests were made for obstruction, but apart from that the march was uneventful and, indeed, 'rather a shambles due to poor stewarding and organization' (NCCL, 1980, p.29).

It was the second demonstration on 23 April, the day of the NF meeting, that proved to be the most violent and controversial. By the early afternoon most shops and businesses in central Southall had closed. At about 12.30 p.m. the SYM deployed some 50 of its supporters in the town centre in preparation for direct action to prevent people entering the NF meeting. The SYM proved only to be a minor irritant to the NF and the police – a contrast to the impact of the main body of the anti-NF demonstration. In evidence to the unofficial Inquiry one witness stated:

There was terrific anger among the crowd by this time [early evening of April 23] and one or two people . . . started to smash shop windows . . . Throughout the events, the police cordon had stood still, good-humouredly maintaining a show of force. In my view it was doing the correct thing. Nobody was going to penetrate the police line and nobody tried to. The cordon did not once charge the crowd and no missiles were thrown at it that I saw. Missiles that were thrown were reserved exclusively for the vans. People were provoked by the vicious driving. They threw missiles (mainly milk bottles, picked up on the spur of the moment) . . . I have never seen police behave this way in my life and I hope never to see such a thing again (NCCL, 1980, p.39).

It seems, therefore, that there was considerable antagonism against the large police presence and tactics in controlling the demonstration and that this was a contributory factor in sparking off the street violence. The Co-ordinating Committee, however, lost direction themselves, despite their attempts to calm people in the streets and maintain their close liaison with the police. Nor did the Co-ordinating Committee hold much sway with militant elements who had been attracted to the protest, or with militant ANL rank-and-file demonstrators keen to use force to stop the NF.

As the evening wore on, the situation deteriorated. The following quote, again from the unofficial Committee of Inquiry, is provided to illustrate the view of an anti-NF demonstrator. The role of the police Special Patrol Group (SPG) was criticized by many participants who complained of baton-wielding SPG men and police harassment:

Jack Dromey, Transport and General Workers' Union Officer, was on the Broadway about 8.15 p.m. 'I must say that I have never seen such unrestrained violence against demonstrators nor such hatred on both sides. The SPG vans were making stupid forays into the crowd, turning round and coming back. Moving the cordon forward might have cooled the situation but this was just insane . . . The SPG started running down the pavement. There was abuse from the kids and the police suddenly pushed a dozen of them into a shop window very hard with their riot shields. The kids naturally retaliated' (NCCL, 1980, p.41).

This quote provides a flavour of the intensity of the feelings held by many involved in street actions at the time. The eye-witness accounts also draw attention to the way in which increasing numbers of politically unaffiliated participants became involved with conflicts with the police as time passed. Certain localized incidents suggested that violence was initiated by what the eye-witness referred to as 'the kids', who had no formal relationship with either the Co-ordinating Committee or other political organizations represented on the main demonstration. On this occasion, however, these unorganized elements were influenced by events which had occurred as a consequence of the politically motivated and centrally organized anti-NF protest. We may propose, therefore, that the Southall disturbances were headed by a leadership seeking to impose a moderating influence, which had some impact on the conduct of demonstration participants, and that this important moderating group probably helped to contain subsequent events. This stands in contrast to the later disorders (Bristol, 1980; Brixton and Toxteth, 1981) which generated a momentum in the absence of such a calming influence. With respect to Southall, the following defines the importance of the intervention of certain moderating political activists:

Martin Craxton had been distributing literature in the Park for the Labour Party Young Socialists of which he is a member. 'Everything remained peaceful until some people began to throw stones at the [police] cordon. It was then that the riot shields came out and those of us in the Young Socialists were going around telling people not to throw stones . . .' (NCCL, 1980, p.50).

Another example of moderation by certain political activists present is evidenced by the Peoples Unite group:

The philosophy behind Peoples Unite had clear links with Rastafarianism. Though not explicitly such, it was non-militant – advocating love, harmony and peaceful co-existence (NCCL, 1980, p.55).

This organization maintained contacts with the ANL and the Socialist Workers' Party (SWP). Prior to the death of ANL supporter Blair Peach at 7.45 p.m. on 23 April, there was little evidence that any of these groups was prepared either to distance itself politically from the main Co-ordinating Commitee or from the conduct of the demonstration. On the contrary, they endorsed the moderate Co-ordinating Committee's plea for peaceful protest and for responsible policing of any future demonstrations. Immediately following the Peach incident, it appears that moderates and ANL and SWP militants were still keen to maintain this position, since both saw an immediate interest in defending their respective political integrities amongst the broad mass of protesters. This is shown by reference to the unofficial Committee of Inquiry report:

On 24 April at 2 p.m. the Co-ordinating Committee and the IWA called a press conference in the Ballroom of the Dominion Cinema. There was a large attendance of those who had been involved in the events of the previous day. Many had little or no sleep during the night as they awaited release from police custody or assisted in co-ordinating information and providing transport from distant police stations back to Southall. The Co-ordinating Committee had always been loosely constituted of representatives of local groups. Members of the Southall Youth Movement, IWA and Ealing CRC attended as did Paul Holborrow of the Anti-Nazi League and Tariq Ali of the Socialist Unity group. Individuals who had suffered arrest or injury gave their stories emotionally.

There were obvious worries about apparently impulsive reactions. There was also a desire to preserve political unity. Vishnu Sharma stated that concern:

was expressed about the conduct of the police and what appeared to be a bias in the newspapers' coverage of events. Without consultation Tariq Ali called for a demonstration on the following Saturday, 28 April. Vishnu Sharma told the enquiry: 'When Tariq Ali spoke he said: "We will fight in the streets of Southall. We will be carrying on the struggle." He called for a demonstration. No one knew of this. I took Tariq Ali and Paul Holborrow into a corner. I pointed out that the fury of the young people could flare up. We three agreed that we should have a demonstration but rather than just a demonstration we should organise in memory of Blair Peach, as a demonstration of sorrow.' The Co-ordinating Committee issued a press statement giving a brief account of events, announcing a Defence Fund, calling for an independent public enquiry into the actions of the police and stating that 'Southall is shocked, depressed and very sad. There are not many families or friends who have not had someone arrested or injured' (NCCL, 1980, p.66).

Militant rhetoric *was* adopted by the Co-ordinating Committee when it called for protests against the death of Peach, but this militancy served as a support for the Committee's desire to defuse communal feelings and head off unorganized or spontaneous protests. The Co-ordinating Committee was also acutely aware of the need to keep itself at the head of the protest movement and to undermine any potential initiatives by militant groups such as the SYM which could provide a political focus against the Committee.

The SYM had decided to establish its own Defence Fund while at the same time lending support to the proposed 'March of Sorrow' for Peach. The SYM attended a meeting held on 25 April which had been called by the local Community Relations Council, which formulated detailed plans for this march. This drew the support of the Sikh temples, the Southall Mosque, Peoples Unite, local churches and the Chamber of Commerce (NCCL, 1980, p.69). The CRC and the Co-ordinating Committee were thus able to contain the militants of the SYM and the ANL within the bounds of the main protest movement.

London's East End

The Southall case indicates the characteristic politics of the moderates and the caution displayed by even militant organizations in circumstances where large protest movements pose a threat to traditional political practices. Further evidence of this comes from an examination of events in the East End of London. Chapter 1 indicated that historically the East End has been the location of much violent political activity involving left and right. The 1970s saw a revival of extreme right-wing organizations, this time making capital from the inflow of black immigrants. Like Southall, the East End experienced a number of disturbances in 1978 and 1979, centring upon the activities of the National Front in black areas. As with Southall, the major concern here is with the character of the response of black organizations and the left.

In 1974 the Tower Hamlets Movement Against Racism and Fascism established itself as a broadly based organization committed to combating racism. In the summer of 1976 the Bangladesh Welfare Association and the

Race Today Collective joined with a number of other groups to form the Anti-Racist Committee of Asians in East London (ARCAEL) which organized a march from Brick Lane to Leman Street Police Station in Tower Hamlets to protest against National Front activities and alleged police actions against Asians. The Bangladesh Youth Association and the Bangladesh Youth Movement also emerged at this time, representing the more militant wing operating around various anti-NF protests. These youth organizations had a relationship to the moderate organizations and ARCAEL which was similar to the SYM in Southall.

In autumn 1976 the Tower Hamlets Trades Council organized the East London Conference Against Racism at a meeting which attracted some 200 representatives of a variety of political and ethnic-minority organizations. On 7 November 1976 the Trades Council, ARCAEL and others called a protest march against NF activities in the Brick Lane area. The march attracted little support and was physically attacked by the NF (Bethnal Green and Stepney Trades Council, 1978, p.55).

In October 1977, following major disturbances in Lewisham involving anti-NF demonstrators, a number of East End organizations called a march and 'Festival for Racial Harmony'. The 5,000-strong demonstration proved to be a major stimulus to the formation of the Anti-Nazi League and to further anti-NF activities in the East End. Much of the ANL's early propaganda concentrated upon East End campaigns and also upon organizing its 'Carnival Against the Nazis', which attracted around 80,000 people who were entertained by well-known popular musicians affiliated to the ANL-backed 'Rock against Racism' campaign.

Continuing racial tensions in the East End led to the Community Relations Councils in Hackney and Tower Hamlets calling together local groups to form the Hackney and Tower Hamlets Defence Committee. On 18 June 1978, after further racial violence in Brick Lane, the ANL called a protest demonstration in Brick Lane itself, which attracted about 4,000 people. More protests followed, again organized by the Defence Committee, leading to the declaration of a so-called 'Black Solidarity Day' on 17 July. This attracted wide support from trade unions and local businesses.

These events are not simply interesting in themselves. What is important to note is the similarity of the political character of the organization of the anti-racist campaigns in the East End and Southall. In both cases the campaigns were politicized and led by 'umbrella' organizing groups keen to direct communal protests towards work in conjunction with local authorities and politicians. In both cases local Community Relations Councils were involved in the formation of organizing or defence committees. There was also a point of political contact between Southall and the East End. On 29 July 1978, prior to the major Southall events, the Southall Standing Conference of Pakistani Organizations, the IWA and the Federation of Bangladeshi Organizations issued a statement supporting the formation of self-defence and vigilante groups along the lines already adopted at Brick Lane (Bethnal Green Trades Council, 1978, p.60). By 1979, 'self-defence' became another term for peaceful protest designed to discourage the NF and intended to consolidate the influence of community organizations. This strategy was endorsed, if not always explicitly, by the Trades Union Congress and the Commission for Racial Equality. According to the Bethnal Green and Stepney Trades Councils, these two organizations were keen to support local initiatives. Visits by the Trades Union Congress General Secretary, Len Murray, and the CRE's Chairman, David Lane, gave the seal of approval to the East End campaign and to the Defence Committee (Bethnal Green and Stepney Trades Council, 1978, p.60).

1980: the unorganized in action

Despite the militancy of the East End campaign, the fact that it was headed by recognizable political leaders was important. Local authorities, politicians and the police at least knew who to liaise with over questions of crowd control and they could be sure of monitoring changing attitudes within the black community by way of their contacts with black leaders and community-relations bodies. Leadership rhetoric usually disguised a practical willingness to co-operate with the authorities and return the community to a 'normal' state as soon as possible. The events of 2 April 1980 in Bristol marked a change in the situation to one in which leadership 'control' was challenged.

On that day a serious outbreak of street violence took place in the city following a police raid on a black club in the St Paul's district. St Paul's was an area with a large West Indian population, but not one which had previously been associated with communal disorder.

The disturbances initially lasted for about eight hours, during which time the police surrounded and sealed off an area around the club; 42 people were subsequently charged with offences related to disorderly conduct, criminal damage and theft. In the House of Commons the following day the Home Secretary, William Whitelaw, remarked that 'all the evidence suggests that it was not in any sense a race riot', despite the obvious involvement of large numbers of black youths. Mr Whitelaw went on to describe the events of 2 April:

The Chief Constable, who had taken personal charge of the operation, decided temporarily to withdraw his officers from the area pending the arrival of further reinforcements. As soon as reinforcements were available, the police moved in with riot shields and secured the area. Order was restored by midnight. The police are continuing to patrol the district to prevent further trouble. During the course of the evening considerable damage was done to shops and other premises. A bank was set on fire. Looting took place (Hansard, 3 April, 1980).

Mr Whitelaw made a point of informing the Commons that the local Community Relations Council was working with the police to monitor the general situation. On 28 April he detailed a number of measures which had been initiated to deal with what appeared to have been a communal disturbance in which a definable 'leadership' had been absent. Senior officials in the Home Office and the Chief Inspector of Police, together with the Commissioner of the Metropolitan Police and the Association of Chief Police Officers, were asked by the Home Secretary to re-examine arrangements for handling such public disorder. In addition, the Home Secretary welcomed the House of Commons Select Committee on Home Affairs' decision to study racial disadvantage in St Paul's (despite claims that the disturbances were not racial). Finally, the government supported a move by Avon County Council and Bristol City Council to work jointly to improve community relations in the area.

The willingness of black community leaders broadly to support a new community initiative was indicative of their concern about the controllability of the disturbances. To many, Bristol signified a new turn in inner-city community relations which threatened to challenge the established consultative mechanisms and 'helpful' group/local-authority relations. Black leaders, as in Southall and the East End, were thus keen to maintain their support for ordered consultation and participation while at the same time being concerned about defending the legal rights of participants in the disturbances.

Brixton, April 1981

More serious for government and for moderate black leaders were the disturbances in Brixton in south London in April 1981. Bristol had fired a warning shot to community leaders, but Brixton provided evidence that the temperament of the inner cities was rapidly changing to produce a situation which was potentially explosive.

The Scarman Report (1981), published after the disorders, provides the most authoritative account of the disturbances themselves and of conditions prevailing prior to April. The report shows that for some years black organizations had been closely involved with the Council for Community Relations in Lambeth (CCRL) and the London Borough of Lambeth in promoting numerous projects and programmes involving the black community. These projects served an area in which about 25% of the population was black, with West Indians forming the largest single ethnic group.[2] Not surprisingly, this statistic held implications for the policing of the area as well as for its general community development.

On appointment to the district in December 1977, Commander Adams of the Metropolitan Police decided to renew efforts to improve policing in the locality. His intention was to establish a more effective method of street patrol and a 'positive system of community relations' involving consultation between the police and community organizations and local people.

Conflicts between police and the community had, however, created intense suspicion of the Adams initiative among those at 'grass roots' level. On four occasions between 1978 and the end of 1980, Adams had initiated special operations against crime in Lambeth with the active assistance of the Metropolitan Police and the mobile Special Patrol Group (SPG). Scarman claims that these operations provoked the hostility of young blacks who felt that they were being intimidated by SPG activities. According to Scarman:

their [the young blacks] hostility infected the older members of the community, who, hearing the stories of many innocent young people who had been stopped and searched, began themselves to lose confidence in, and respect for the police. However well-intentioned, these operations precipitated a crisis of confidence between the police and certain community leaders. In particular they led to the breakdown of the formal arrangements for liaison between the ethnic minority communities, the local authority and the police (Scarman Report, 1981, para. 4.22).

In May 1978 the Principal Community Relations Officer at CCRL approached the police with draft terms for the establishment of a Police/CCRL Liaison Committee, backed by local black organizations. The first meeting of this Committee was held in October 1978, with Commander Adams in attendance. This meeting was therefore held well after the January 1978 launching of SPG operations and after black leaders had had time to be 'infected' with a degree of verbal hostility to the police. Indeed, police operations were intensified following the meeting with CCRL, although Adams did not inform community leaders of his intentions with respect to this (Scarman, 1981, para. 4.25).

According to Scarman, the failure of Adams to communicate his intentions 'encouraged CCRL members in the view that the police did not see liaison as a two-way process' (Scarman Report, 1981, para. 4.25). The problem was regarded very much as one of communication rather than in terms of SPG heavy-handedness. This applied to the final Scarman view of the situation and also to the view adopted by certain moderate community leaders who were at that time keen to maintain a 'helpful' profile. However, the attitude of black leaders was to be modified.

On 12 February 1979 three members of CCRL's own staff were arrested by Brixton police in connection with investigations into an assault on two plain clothes officers and a black barman by a group of blacks in a public house. The incident led to an emergency meeting of CCRL's Executive Committee, which decided to withdraw support from the Police Liaison Committee. However, the Committee indicated that formal relations could be re-established if the police 'made positive proposals to improve their relations within the community' (Scarman, 1981, para. 4.26).

The formal withdrawal of CCRL and local groups from the Liaison Committee was thus implemented with the possibility held open for informal contacts between community leaders and the police to continue. Scarman details a number of points of contact which enabled leaders to talk to Adams outside the more public forum provided by CCRL. He also provides evidence that 'not all community leaders agreed with the decision to withdraw from the Liaison Committee' and that efforts to re-establish the Committee were made (Scarman Report, 1981, para. 4.27). CCRL's Principal Community Relations Officer continued to meet with the police, and some community leaders who opposed the break with the police continued regular meetings with Commander Adams and senior police officers. Lord Scarman actually described these contacts as constituting an 'informal liaison group'.

The more militant leaders supported a local-authority Working Party which sought 'community control' of the police through improved mechanisms which, it was claimed, would make the police more accountable to the community. In November 1980 a new Commander was appointed and this provided both the moderates and the militants with an opportunity to reassess their attitudes to the question of police/community relations. As a result of this, CCRL established a committee to initiate direct discussions with the police and with the newly appointed Commander Fairbairn.

Shortly after these moves, at the beginning of 1981, Commander Fairbairn disappointed CCRL by failing to consult community groups about another major police operation in Lambeth. This operation became known by the police as 'Swamp 81' and was scheduled to begin on 6 April and to last for six days, to combat street crime. Prior to Swamp 81's start-date the police entered a number of premises in the so-called 'Front Line' area of Railton Road in Brixton. There were 22 arrests, made by the Brixton Crime Squad and the Robbery Squad, leading to complaints in the locality that the raids had heightened community tensions which were building up as a result of police activities (Scarman Report, 1981, para. 4.38).

Swamp 81 itself involved extensive application of police powers to 'stop and search' people on the basis of a 'reasonable suspicion' that they were in possession of unlawfully obtained property. Police squads were deployed in the Brixton area and arrests were made in and around the Railton Road area. Swamp 81 thus became a highly visible affair and consequently angered community leaders who felt that police consultation should have been initiated before such a major operation, which would inevitably impact upon the communal temperature in areas affected by poor police/community relations (Scarman Report, 1981, para. 4.42).

Lord Scarman himself concluded that the actions of the police contributed, in part, to the serious street disturbances which took place between 10 April and 12 April 1981. While the attitude of community leaders towards police liaison comes in for criticism, Scarman suggested that racial prejudice did manifest itself 'in the behaviour of a few officers on the streets' (Scarman Report, 1981, para. 8.20). Harassment also occurred and this, together with other grievances against the police, contributed to the riot situations.

Despite the initial lack of consultation, the police were quick to contact community leaders once the disturbances had assumed a widespread character. Concerned about the spread of unfounded rumours,

Chief Superintendent Nicholson decided to call in several leaders of the community to put to them the police account of the incident [involving an injured youth] and to seek their help in stilling those rumours (Scarman Report, 1981, para. 3.19).

A meeting with community representatives was arranged for 9 p.m. on the night of 10 April. The meeting was conducted by Commander Ferguson, Head of A7, the Community Relations Branch of the Metropolitan Police. Those who presented themselves at Brixton Police Station were: George Greaves, Principal Community Relations Officer in Lambeth; Tony Phillips (Greaves's deputy); the Revd Graham Kent; Mr and Mrs Ivan Madray from the Railton Road Youth and Community Centre; and Courtney Laws, Director of the Brixton Neighbourhood Association.

The police gave those attending an account of the day's events and asked for their assistance in dispelling rumours. Some of the community representatives urged the police to talk to worried relatives and friends of those arrested, while at the same time expressing concern about the number of police deployed in the Railton Road area. Despite the pleas for calm and for a defusion of the situation, the next day saw further disturbances met by the police with SPG assistance. During the night of 11 April the disorders had escalated to include looting and arson centred on the northern end of Railton Road and Leeson Road, but with serious disruption taking place over a wide area of central Brixton and involving both black and white youths.

Disorders continued on the Sunday, 12 April. Another meeting with community representatives was held, but this time in the presence of Timothy Raison MP, Minister of State at the Home Office. At precisely that time the police were under siege in parts of Brixton and sporadic looting continued. Again the SPG was brought in to clear the crowds, but they too came under pressure from intense attacks against them. Despite this intensity the rioting was in fact less severe than the day before – the strategic advantage lay firmly with the police, who not only possessed the organizational ability to mount counter-riot measures but who also could rely upon the important co-operation of moderate community leaders. Scarman underlined the importance of this kind of co-operation:

I am satisfied that police forces generally recognise the importance of good relations with the community they police. Most if not all forces express this recognition through the establishment of specialised Community Relations or Community Involvement Branches. The larger forces in particular usually also appoint Community Liaison Officers at Divisional level with special responsibility for fostering good relations with the community. The emphasis of most of these Branches is on securing good liaison with the community. A number of those who have given evidence to the [Scarman] Inquiry, however, see these Branches as a mere public relations exercise. They instance the reluctance, amounting in many cases to outright refusal, of senior police officers to discuss operational questions with leaders of local communities.

Further:

Community involvement in the police and operations of policing is perfectly feasible without undermining the independence of the police or destroying the secrecy of those operations against crime which have to be kept secret.

Also:

Consultation and accountability are mechanisms – in part administrative, and in part legal – upon which we rely to ensure that the police in their policies and operations keep in touch with, and are responsible to, the community they police (Scarman Report, 1981, paras. 5.55–5.58).

Summer 1981: moderates and militant 'co-operators'

The most serious rioting to affect Britain's inner cities was to come after Lord Scarman had accepted the Government's invitation to head the Public Inquiry into the Brixton disorders. Serious outbreaks of street violence occurred in July in many English towns and cities, beginning with Southall in London and Toxteth in Liverpool on 3 July. The re-emergence of trouble in Southall was of a different character to that which had occurred there in 1979. The disorders began after several hundred 'skinhead'-style youths arrived for a rock music concert in a public house. The concert had definite racist overtones, leading to conflict with local Asian youths. During the evening's violence, vehicles were burnt and shops damaged as police attempted to keep skinhead and Asian youths apart. The Home Secretary, William Whitelaw, in a statement to the House of Commons on 6 July, indicated that it was the skinheads who actually initiated the street violence and that the disturbances had distinctly racist connotations. The Toxteth events also had a racial character, as violence broke out on 3 July after a police patrol stopped a black motorcyclist for a routine check. The violence continued intermittently until 6 July, during which time the Merseyside police were reinforced by officers from surrounding constabularies and the use of CS gas was sanctioned to disperse the crowds.

At a press conference on 7 July, Mr Kenneth Oxford, Chief Constable of Merseyside, declared that in his opinion the Toxteth disturbances were not 'race riots' – a point which seems to be consistent with evidence provided by community leaders indicating that a significant number of 'rioters' were white. Oxford also praised the leaders of ethnic-minority communities in Toxteth who had attempted to restore order to trouble-torn areas. On 13 July Prime Minister Margaret Thatcher visited Liverpool and met with local-authority, community and church leaders. Inevitably many black (and white) political activists were unhappy with this apparent association with a Conservative Prime Minister, but opposition to this liaison was surprisingly muted since even radical organizations reckoned that they had little to gain from seriously disrupting attempts to restore communal order. There was, however, some debate within black and leftist organizations about whether or not groups should overtly co-operate with the Scarman Inquiry and with local attempts to co-ordinate groups with the police. Even here some organizations decided to take part in Lord Scarman's collection of evidence, despite their evident political objections to government and police attitudes to the disturbances.[3] A similar pattern of co-operation was evident with groups from Manchester, where the Moss Side area of the city witnessed two days of disorder on 8 and 9 July. Many black leaders in Manchester seem to have believed that Scarman provided them with an opportunity to express their concern about conditions in their communities and to voice some of the criticisms of the police emanating from the black populations there.

The Greater Manchester Council established a Panel of Inquiry into the disturbances, chaired by Brent Hytner QC. The Panel had no statutory powers to call witnesses and its proceedings were regarded as informal. Some community organizations decided to boycott the Panel's investigations despite its claims to be impartial. In the event, the Panel was critical of some police measures in Moss Side while approving of the Chief Constable's 'low profile' policing approach during the disturbances. The Panel also attempted to set the disturbances within the broader context of Moss Side's inner-city decline (Greater Manchester Council, 1981; Venner, 1981).

In Handsworth in Birmingham the Scarman Report found that community leaders emphasized social conditions rather than police actions as being the major cause of the disturbances:

The ethnic community leaders in Handsworth stressed that the recent disturbances had been neither racial nor directed against the police and the underlying reasons for the recent disturbances were considered to be essentially social and economic. The main problem lay with young people, who required jobs and facilities for recreation. Inevitably this meant more money: such funds should not be allocated only to those areas, where they were bad, but also to areas, like Handsworth, where they were good. While it was important that all groups within the community remained united, as such unity had been a foundation for the improvements in the area, additional resources were necessary if the remaining difficulties were to be readily overcome (Scarman Report, 1981, Appendix B, Handsworth, para. 7).

In Liverpool, Lord Scarman visited the Charles Wootton Centre in Toxteth, where he met members of the Liverpool 8 Defence Committee who stressed that blacks in the area were a well-established group who should not be regarded as immigrants but as good black Britons. Unlike the Handsworth groups, however, the Defence Committee complained about alleged police harassment as being the major cause of disorder, and criticized the Chief Constable for his handling of police/community relations. In calling for the Chief Constable's resignation they drew attention to the black community's resentment of the use of CS gas and what they claimed was the heavy-handedness of policing in Toxteth. The Committee also pointed out that such actions in the future would be met by opposition from the community and that the best solution was improved policing and a change in attitudes towards blacks (Scarman Report, 1981, Appendix B, Liverpool, para. 7; Liverpool 8 Defence Committee, 1981). There was actually some evidence to support the contention that the community would oppose what it saw as over-heavy policing, since a second wave of disturbances affected Toxteth between 26 and 28 July and this situation clearly raised doubts about the longer-term ability of the area to come to terms with the police and to continue support for the moderate pleas of community-relations officials and local politicians.

CRE and Scarman

Lord Scarman's findings, relating mainly to the April 1981 Brixton disorders, were presented to Parliament in November 1981. Briefly, his main findings and recommendations were as follows (in the order presented by Scarman):

(1) Social factors *had* contributed to creating the conditions for communal disturbances.

(2) The disorders had begun as a spontaneous reaction to what was seen as police harassment although, in Brixton, an 'element of leadership' did emerge (the precise nature of this 'element' is left vague in Scarman).

(3) In general the Metropolitan Police were *not* racist, but racial prejudice did occasionally become manifest in the behaviour of a few officers.

(4) Some police harassment had occurred in Brixton.

(5) The actions of both police and community leaders had contributed to the disorders.

(6) More blacks should be recruited to the police and racially prejudiced applicants should be identified.

(7) Police training should be extended and education should be given covering the cultural backgrounds of minorities and the nature of communal tensions.

(8) Police performance should be monitored by the police themselves.

(9) Racially prejudiced behaviour should be an offence in the Police Discipline Code.

(10) 'Hard policing' (e.g. use of the SPG) will be necessary in the future, although improved and extended 'community policing' was important.

(11) There should be consultation between police and community and some accountability of the police to the community (through consultation committees, for example).

(12) CS gas, plastic bullets etc. should only be used as a last resort by police during disturbances.

(13) Improved policing was not enough by itself. Better housing, education and employment opportunities were vital to meet ethnic-minority needs within the inner city.

(14) A more determined effort should be made to enforce the existing law on racial discrimination.

(15) Police powers to 'stop and search' were necessary, but the law should be

rationalized and an improved police complaints' procedure should be established.

(16) A new Riot Act was not required, since existing law was adequate.

(17) The 1936 Public Order Act should be amended so that it would be possible to enforce a selective ban on processions and demonstrations including 'racist' marches.

The Scarman approach was thus a mixture of the 'physical' approach (improved policing) with pleas for social reforms in line with those called for in the July 1981 House of Commons Home Affairs Committee Report on Racial Disadvantage. Acts of violence were to be condemned but, for Scarman, the blame should not be attributed to any single section of the community or to individual public authorities. The willingness or otherwise of black organizations and others to actually condemn the disorders and street violence thus provided some indication of group attitudes – the more militant organizations tending *not* to denounce violence directly and to point to government and the police as having created the conditions leading to social conflict.

The CRE nationally went further than local groups in condemning the violence, calling for more to be done to tackle the needs of young people in the inner cities and warning that the disturbances were 'merely the tip of the iceberg of anger, frustration and despair not just among the young but among the older blacks too' (CRE, 1981, p.2). The Commission endorsed Lord Scarman's view that racial disadvantage had to be tackled urgently and broadly supported his recommendations for changing police practices and launching new inner-city development initiatives. The CRE urged the government to give a stronger and more effective lead in implementing the necessary changes and in reducing communal tensions. CRE strongly supported the establishment of consultative committees along Scarman lines as a way of bringing community representatives together with the police. The majority of police forces also supported this approach, but the CRE doubted 'whether ethnic minority voices are being adequately represented on some committees' (CRE, 1982, p.13). So keen were the CRE to promote the Scarman Report that they joined a Home Office Working Party on police training and race and worked closely with the Metropolitan Police to promote 'human awareness training' to improve police approaches to black people. In 1982 the CRE also published a 'popular version' of the Scarman Report, in conjunction with Nottingham CRC, to make Lord Scarman's findings more widely available to the general public and to local black groups.

The militant black response: non-cooperation

Those black organizations which opposed the CRE line and the attitude of those who co-operated with the police and with Lord Scarman were never able to co-ordinate their opposition or to erode significantly the influence of the more moderate community leaders. The critical stance of many moderates towards the government, the police and local authorities effectively under-mined the militant opposition which itself failed to develop a viable alternative to the politics of co-operation.

The black militant A. Sivanandan, through the Institute of Race Relations and its journal, *Race and Class*, produced a provocative critique of the Scarman Report, based upon his conception of state 'institutionalized racism' and 'domestic neocolonialism'. According to this view, the racist state had produced the Scarman response which simply consolidated the hold of prevailing institutions, such as the CRE, which channelled black politics into support for the police, immigration controls and ineffective race-relations legislation. Sivanandan spoke of the police as an authoritarian 'army of occupation' in society and pointed to the need for black groups to organize themselves to 'rebel' against the state (Sivanandan, 1981, p.150).

Sivanandan's analysis examined the wide range of black organizations which had adopted anti-racist and anti-imperialist political positions. The message was that the growth of such organizations was to be welcomed, but that they had to adopt a more coherent concept of political action which would transform them into fighting organizations in defence of black interests. Tony Bunyan, also writing in *Race and Class*, developed the idea that the 1981 'riots' were an indication of the desire of blacks to take up the challenge of organizing resistance and joining with working-class organizations to facilitate a united struggle against capitalism. The implication was that the disturbances were in some way a portent of future *political* action which would lead to a strengthen-ing of black resistance (Bunyan, 1981, pp.153–70).

Apart from the eclectic nature of the *Race and Class* contributions, there was little in the way of practical organizational advice to existing militant black groups. The suggestion that the disturbances somehow provided political opportunities for such organizations was made, but because this view actually misinterpreted the character of the 1981 events in political terms, groups were effectively left to wait for further events to throw up organizational structures to carry on 'the struggle'. Darcus Howe, editor of the militant *Race Today* journal, even went so far as to describe the disturbances as an organized guerilla uprising against the police. It was, according to Howe, a black rebellion with whites participating. More riots were predicted as a way of opposing the Scarman Report and racism (*The Times*, 26 November 1981; Venner, 1981a). This kind of analysis, as with the *Race and Class* view, in practice led some militants to a belief in a 'false dawn' which, in turn, produced demoralization within their ranks as expected increases in group memberships failed to materialize.

The radical/militant stance led many to a boycott position on the Scarman Report. The Brixton Defence Campaign, for example, called 'for a total boycott of the state's inquiry into the Brixton Uprising of 10–13 April 1981 set up under the chairmanship of Lord Scarman'. Further:

There is no escaping the fact that the Scarman Inquiry, but particularly Phase 1, *very seriously prejudices the legal position and therefore endangers the liberty of all defendants yet to be tried.*

And:

The Brixton Defence Campaign is satisfied that Lord Scarman is disposed to be used by the state to provide it with a basis for re-writing the Riot Act and to provide justification for dramatically increasing repressiveness in policing methods which are already massively racist, lawless and brutal as well as substantially uncontrolled [italics in original] (Brixton Defence Campaign, 1981).

Despite calls for 'defence' of black communities in many other towns and cities and despite calls for boycotts, the small defence committees and radical groups were unable to provide a political programme which would take them beyond a critique of the state, government and police. These groups lacked a political perspective which could direct their energies against the moderate community leadership and recruit black working-class youth. As a consequence, the moderate leadership was not seriously challenged in its attempts to preserve the political *status quo,* to bring order to troubled communities and to persuade established white politicians to campaign more effectively on issues affecting blacks. Moderate leaders, moreover, could themselves be highly critical of the state, thus displacing the militant groups on the police question while at the same time urging blacks to co-operate to achieve reforms in police practices and procedures. The Liverpool 8 Defence Committee, mentioned above, went some way in this direction, being opposed to co-operation with Kenneth Oxford, but agreeing to meet with Lord Scarman and demanding that 'fair and proper policing' should be the responsibility of the Chief Constable (Liverpool 8 Defence Committee, 1981, p.232). The Defence Committee, therefore, straddled the line between the total boycotters and the community-relations officials. The widely circulated black paper, *West Indian World,* adopted a similarly uneasy position, originally calling for a boycott of the Scarman Report and accusing the Inquiry of 'playing for time', but essentially toning down its critique and calling for a greater effort by blacks themselves to solve their own problems (Venner, 1981b).

The nature of black responses, particularly for the police and local authorities, was of greater importance. For the police in particular, the moderate acceptance of the Scarman Report and the ability to 'sell' the report to the black community was more important than the police's own objections to it. Police and community acceptance of the general thrust of the Scarman Report provided some common ground from which future policing approaches could be agreed upon between interested parties. On questions such as police recruiting, for example, Lord Scarman called for more black youths to be encouraged to join the police and agreement on this extended widely from the police themselves to many active community workers and activists. In a questionnaire in *New Community* (Winter, 1981), 80% of Asians and 76% of Afro-Caribbeans were found to be in favour of increased black recruitment into the police and large majorities expressed a desire for changes in the law to prevent public demonstrations in racially sensitive areas. The responses, gathered in November 1981, thus reinforced the view that the characterization of the riots as politically advantageous to militant black groups was mistaken, and that the 'official' response had actually achieved its goal at the militants' expense.

Conclusion

The analysis of leadership responses to the disturbances and to the police and to the Scarman Report reveals a pattern which is consistent with the study of groups under more ordered conditions. Groups maintained their basic political appetites throughout, although events did modify and temper group responses by forcing them to respond to immediate and urgent political situations. Defence committees had to take practical decisions about co-operation or non-cooperation; established community notables were tempted to articulate their critical views of the police more explicitly in response to community anxiety over police measures; community-relations bodies sought actively to re-establish communal peace to undermine the 'rule' of spontaneity. In very general terms, black responses could be divided in three ways, with gradations within and between these categories:

(1)   The 'moderate', CRE/CRC responses, which urged communal peace through co-operation with the police and with the Scarman Report and with local authorities. This response involved an appeal to the black community as a whole to lobby for reforms, to support elected political representatives and to support measures designed to alleviate urban deprivation.

(2)   The radical/militant co-operative stance, which adopted much of the rhetoric of the militants but which generally saw an advantage in co-operating with 'official' attempts to restore order and with the Scarman Report.

(3)   The radical/militant non-cooperators, who, from an isolated position, sought to attract support to their own organizations to oppose the established moderate black leadership. Many of these groups identified political costs of co-operation in terms of a potential loss of quasi-Marxist and Black Nationalist ideology.

The precise categorization of these groups is not so important at any one time as the recognition of the ability of groups to move along the co-operation/non-cooperation spectrum according to particular circumstances. The ANL, for example, tended to shift between categories 3 and 2 above, while some smaller defence groups appear to have hardened their opposition attitudes (e.g. during the Brick Lane events). The different directional propulsions of such groupings would appear to have been related to the general character of the events in question – that politicized confrontations could initially strengthen the hand of small groups as events produced an upsurge in activity, while 'riot' situations, such as 1981, were essentially sporadic reactions which provided relatively limited opportunities for political mobilization. Under these latter circumstances many groups began to recognize greater benefits in a closer relationship with 'official' bodies, which offered them a greater opportunity to impact upon public policy.

Another reason for the adoption of moderating stances by groups such as ANL related to their general political orientation – for example, their attitude to Labour Party politicians was, locally, quite conciliatory, and their immediate interests lay in the restoration of a more ordered bargaining situation. The ANL's particular 'broad' political programme required its leadership to adopt a more pragmatic approach throughout its most intensive campaigning period, which produced a compromise between the politics of community direct action and the politics of establishing a unity which would encompass socialists, liberals, churchmen and essentially apolitical youths. To preserve this base the ANL opted for an increasingly populist form of pressure-group campaigning which, for example, encouraged many blacks to harness their energies to organizing rock concerts and carnivals.

It is *not* the purpose of this book to put forward prescriptions or to make moral comments about political strategies. In an objective spirit, therefore, it seems that the foregoing analysis presents a view which suggests that black groups in the 1970s and 1980s achieved little in terms of changing the fundamental relations between community-relations bodies, local government, the police and community leaders. Official bodies, on the other hand, did learn something about the dynamics of community relations and, as in Lord Scarman's case, came to a more informed understanding of some of the influences moulding community attitudes, based upon close liaison with many black organizations and individuals. This contrasted with comments on the disturbances by some national politicians, made without prior consideration of the facts available. Local politicians were in many ways better informed than those at national level. The government response, however, favoured the Scarman Report and, following 1981, implicitly accepted the notion that a combination of private- and public-sector initiatives was required to meet some of the most pressing problems of the inner cities. Measures were also taken to make the police more effective in riot situations and to extend community policing with the consent of community leaders. In practice, all such initiatives depended upon the kind of ordered political environment described in Chapter 5 and upon local consent.

The following chapter describes some of the major economic initiatives which themselves depended upon communal consent and the co-operation of community leaders. The decentralized nature of some of the initiatives described helped central and local governments to attract community support and, in many cases, to develop skills within communities which created the conditions for a more professional and entrepreneurial community leadership drawn from the ranks of moderates and militants alike. Given the general disposition of groups, as described in this chapter, we may speculate that this policy approach will prove to be most attractive to community activists keen to consolidate and extend their influence within particular localities.

The key to achieving a degree of success in urban-policy initiatives is, therefore, the extent to which urban initiatives provide the conditions for integrating groups into the public policy process and into a closer relationship with the private sector. The role of group leadership will be as crucial in this as it has been in controlling, or attempting to control, communal violence. Increased 'benefits' available to groups work to provide the incentive to participate and help to define the conditions under which the unorganized, the unemployed and the poor in the inner cities are attracted towards public and private community programmes. A major problem for national government, however, is that even the more innovative programmes tend to be limited in terms of their coverage, being inaccessible to wide sections of the black community and remaining relatively underfunded and poorly supported by local authorities and private-sector agencies (see Chapter 8 for comparisons with the US). On the other hand, governments may be encouraged by the disposition of many community leaders to adopt relatively 'moderate' attitudes, as evidenced in this present chapter. The degree to which even quite militant organizations tended to play a generally stabilizing and supportive role (in terms of their attitudes to community institutions) implies the existence of an important disposition amongst groups to co-operate with central and local authorities. Chapter 8 shows the political success of this co-operation for US governments which, in the 1960s and 1970s, persuaded diverse groups to integrate their activities into community development programmes, and the following chapter should thus be considered in this light and in view of the fact that for British governments 'urban renewal' has become an essential ingredient in a strategy designed to create the political conditions conducive to fostering wider consent for urban policies. This reflects an attempt to maintain communal peace without having to rely so heavily upon physical controls or police measures.

7 Urban renewal

The 1981 riots stimulated discussion within government about the direction of policy in the inner cities, not just as it affected the black community but also with regard to the general problems of urban areas. The concern with the race question, however, was marked by the designation of Sir George Young (Parliamentary Under-Secretary at the Department of the Environment) as Minister with Special Responsibility for Race-Related Matters within the DOE. Amongst other things, Young was concerned to relate Urban Programme projects more precisely to the needs of blacks and to increase the range of benefits to blacks within the Programme.

It will be seen below that the extension of 'benefits' also involved a multiplicity of other initiatives. This chapter examines some of the public and private agencies involved in such inner-city initiatives. By no means all of these initiatives date from the disturbances, but some of the recently formed agencies have been created directly out of the 1981 events. Many of the approaches viewed are associated with Britain's Urban Programme and have vaguely defined objectives which we may assume to be broadly under the heading of 'community development'. Some agencies are concerned more with specifically commercial, economic or private social objectives which to a greater or lesser extent complement central-government inner-city strategy.

The term 'community development' is hard to define precisely. In the United States during the late 1960s there emerged a clearer conception of the term, as community development programmes developed out of the 'Great Society' initiatives. Community development came to be associated with the stimulation of social, economic and sometimes political change designed to effect a general improvement in community economies, living standards, physical environments and levels of popular participation. This package of policy areas may be taken as the foundation for any community-development programme. In this respect the British experience differs from the United States, to the extent that community development has never been adequately defined in these terms, and insofar as public policy has been directed in more pragmatic and piecemeal terms. The British Urban Programme perhaps comes nearest to promoting proper community development, but even with this there is less of an emphasis on community participation than in the USA and a much more fuzzy conception of economic development. Whereas in the USA there tends to be considerable concern over local regeneration of communities through the mobilization of a variety of human and economic resources, in Britain the Urban Programme has often tended to be regarded as a means of distributing grants to 'worthy causes' and deprived groups. It may thus be more accurate not to talk of community development in Britain but to refer to various policies which together contribute to 'urban renewal'. Indeed, a recent report of the House of Commons Environment Committee (HC, 103, 1983) used this term to describe central- and local-government responses to the Merseyside disturbances. Despite the fact that the term sounds like a town planner's description of inner-city development, it does at least draw a useful distinction between the American and British approaches in the inner city.

Agencies and urban renewal

The Environment Committee Report was essentially concerned with the problems of management of urban renewal and it concentrated upon the causes of urban decay and community decline which generated 'problems of processing and achieving effective and coherent change' and the achieving of suitable approaches to decision-making and policy implementation which could satisfactorily identify existing and future problems facing inner-city communities (HC, 103, 1983, vol.2, p.1). The need for greater co-ordination of policies being promoted by agencies was of central importance to the Committee and its own survey of agencies involved in urban renewal served to underline the fragmented pattern of administration in this area. Indeed, the Report recognized that there was no single government agency or central department which could be exclusively responsible for renewal, since responsibility for policy rested with a wide range of service-delivery bodies and planning authorities. Although the DOE had acted as the 'lead' agency, the 'necessary responses extend across a wide range of different policy fields, including housing, transport, social services and economic policies' (HC, 103, 1983, vol. 2, p.2).

The question of funding is thus one which involves all of these areas of administration and so the main funding source for the inner cities has been through central- and local-government main programme areas. In this process of funding, local authorities have been involved in distributing resources quite widely across their administrative jurisdictions and not necessarily discriminating in favour of inner-urban areas where these compete with less economically deprived areas within the same authority. Traditionally authorities have been viewed as a whole by local politicians and officials as far as major programme areas are concerned and the administration of grant distribution has been carried out mainly through highly 'centralized' local-government departments.

To offset the general local provision of services, the Urban Programme (UP) was launched by the Labour government in 1968. Under the UP, local authorities could receive grants for schemes to meet areas of special need in urban areas. UP funds were thus designed to supplement main programme funds and were distributed specifically to designated areas within the existing local authorities.

Edwards and Batley (1978) have studied the historical foundations of the UP approach and have concluded that the Programme arose in response to the need to alleviate problems associated with communities in which there were high immigrant concentrations. While the UP was apparently to be of benefit to the whole community, black and white, the intention actually appeared to be to establish a flow of additional funds into communities which were likely to exhibit racial tensions. Indeed, the UP was influenced by the 1960s American anti-poverty programmes, which themselves were interrelated with the race-relations theme and which were concerned with the maintenance of social peace in the inner cities (DOE, 1980, p.1). Also, 38% of Britain's ethnic minorities live in UP-authority areas, with this figure rising to 62% in London (HC, 103, 1983, vol.2, p.3).[1]

The urban programme and the 1977 White Paper

In 1977 another Labour government published its White Paper, *Policy for the Inner Cities* (Cmnd 6845, 1977). The White Paper was important in that it marked a change in terms of the definition of what the inner-city problem was about. The problem was seen to be not one of 'congestion' but one of decline which involved the running-down of central areas economically and the relative deprivation of their inhabitants. Decline involved the decay of the infrastructure, bad physical conditions in general, high unemployment, limited job opportunities and a concentration of the socially disadvantaged.

Another important development related to the UP's administration. Up to 1977 the UP had always involved a number of government departments with the Home Office in the lead, in association with the Department of Education and Science and the then Ministry of Health. These were joined by the DOE in 1971, but in 1977 the lead passed to the DOE itself. In June 1977 the White Paper announced a recasting and enhancement of the UP which enabled the DOE to extend the Programme's coverage to include industrial, environmental and recreational provision. The size of the Programme was also substantially increased.

In November 1977 Urban Programme Circular 17 was issued. Under this

Circular Partnership Authorities were to be dealt with separately in order to strengthen the UP's intervention in the inner cities and facilitate improved co-ordination between agencies and groups involved in the UP. In Circular 18 (August 1978) the so-called Traditional Urban Programme was established to cater for projects in areas outside the inner areas covered by the newly defined UP Partnership and UP 'Programme' areas. There were seven Partnership Authorities in which central and local authorities would jointly promote programmes and initiatives which would be 75% centrally funded. The original 15 Programme Authorities were similarly able to initiate projects and draw up inner area strategies, but these were rather less ambitious and consequently rather freer from central intervention by the DOE. The funding levels covering the Partnerships, the Programme Authorities and the Traditional Urban Programme are shown in Table 7. The table includes expenditures in UP districts which fall outside the main budgetary headings and also expenditure on the more recently introduced Urban Development Grant.

For Partnership and Programme Authorities the basis for co-ordinated effort is the Inner Area Programme (IAP), which sets out an agreed strategy and a programme of action. The IAP in Partnerships is agreed by the Partnership Committee which oversees the work of the Partnership as a whole. The Committee is chaired by a DOE Minister and comprises representatives of local authorities and of other central-government departments involved in the inner city. Responsibility for preparing IAPs rests, for Partnerships, with an Official Steering Group (OSG) which shadows at official level the Partnership Committee. Some OSGs have representatives drawn from the local community and from the police. It is the task of the Steering Group formally to ensure that the programme which emerges is a co-ordinated document, but the preparatory work on the programme involves

Table 7. *Urban Programme expenditure*

Year	£m	
	Cash terms	1982–3 prices
1978–9	95.0	154.0
1979–80	165.0	229.0
1980–1	202.0	237.0
1981–2	215.0	229.0
1982–3	295.0	295.0
1983–4	317.0 (estimate)	300.0 (estimate)
1984–5	338.0 (estimate)	306.0 (estimate)
1985–6	338.0 (estimate)	302.0 (estimate)

Source: Department of the Environment, Inner Cities Directorate, 1985.
Note: Figures include Traditional UP, Partnership, Programme and Designated funding and Urban Development Grant (UDG). The 1984–5 figure is liable to downward adjustment should there be underspend in the UDG programme (as in 1983–4). The 1985–6 inflation-adjusted figure is an independent projection, although the cash estimate figure for that year is official.

much informal consultation about the balance of the programme and about the overall aims and objectives to be contained in the final programme document. Detailed work is often carried out by local-authority working groups, which in some cases involves DOE Regional Office staff. Local authorities are required to work within centrally determined guidelines which require consultation with the private sector (usually through local Chambers of Commerce). The DOE encourages consultation with community organizations and ethnic-minority groups at an early stage in the drafting of programme objectives. It is up to the local authorities to make their own arrangements for such consultations but, in some areas, the group representations are taken very much as purely advisory in nature.

Voluntary participation in the Urban Programme has been widespread because the UP is an important source of funds for organizations. Under the Traditional Urban Programme local authorities have always been keen to devote a substantial proportion of their funds to the voluntary sector, with around half of UP funds going to local groups. For the Urban Programme as a whole about £35 million went to the voluntary sector in 1981–2, including the allocations to ethnic-minority groups less able to attract funds from the main programme funds of local authorities. Many groups have traditionally not organized their activities in such a way as to link to the main programme committees, such as education and social services. The Urban Programme arrangements are specifically designed to identify areas of need which affect communities and, in a sense, actively seek out those groups which would not otherwise come forward or be confident of coming forward for financial assistance.

The UP thus encourages involvement of groups at different levels. At the lowest level groups may simply be involved because they are fund recipients and at the highest level they may be politically involved in the consultative process. The London Borough of Lambeth, for example, in 1982 used its Partnership Programme to encourage groups to become deeply involved in the implementation of Programme objectives. In Lambeth it was the needs of ethnic minorities which 'provided a focus for nearly all aspects of the work of the Lambeth Partnership' (London Borough of Lambeth, 1982, p.7). The number of black unemployed was of particular concern in the Lambeth Programme, which established a special Employment Working Group to tackle the problem. A Housing Working Group accepted that ethnic minorities were disadvantaged in terms of accommodation and set to work to examine special ethnic needs such as housing for old black people, hostels for the young and housing allocation policy. An Under-Fives Working Group identified the problems of black households through various schemes involving fostering and adoption units and language-enrichment schemes. The Adolescents at Risk Working Party considered education provision for minorities with special reference to future employment prospects and the development of multi-ethnic education for the whole community. The

Programme also involved black representatives in community/police liaison, which was a particularly sensitive area following the Brixton riots which fell within the jurisdiction of the local authority. In each of these activities the Partnership was assisted by the Council for Community Relations in Lambeth and by the Consortium of Ethnic Minorities which was formed as an umbrella group representing the interests of black organizations in Lambeth. Some 350 voluntary groups and non-statutory agencies became involved in the Lambeth Programme, many working through the Lambeth Inner City Consultative Group which, since 1978, had acted as the main organization representing community groups of diverse ethnic affiliation (London Borough of Lambeth, 1982).

Groups tend to identify with the UP because it gives them an opportunity to develop their own areas of interest in co-operation with other organizations and with the advice of professional administrators in the local authority. Even some very militant and vocal organizations which are highly critical of the system play the UP game and modify their criticisms to become more amenable to local politicians and government officials. Verbal militancy is not a particularly pressing problem for local government or Programme or Partnership Authorities. What is more important to them is that community leaders of all shades of opinion are prepared to work within 'accepted channels' rather than causing disruption elsewhere or encouraging dissent at grass roots level. For governments, the success of the UP depends upon the maintenance of this generally favourable attitude of black organizations. Governments have thus attempted effectively to increase the benefits of participation in the UP and the range of incentives available.

With the return of the Conservative government in 1979, a new statement of central government UP policy was made. The Conservatives retained the Partnership/Programme arrangements and streamlined the administration of the Partnerships. Most important was a shift in emphasis towards the encouragement of private initiatives to supplement and even replace certain public fundings. The promotion of small businesses and the backing of big business involvement in urban regeneration became an increasingly important theme of ministerial statements, particularly after the 1981 disturbances. The practical impact that this had on urban policy will be shown below. It was an emphasis which was always present in Conservative thinking, but which was given a boost when 1981 showed the apparent failure of public intervention. Social programmes and UP fundings had done nothing, it seemed, to prevent social conflict, and ethnic minorities still felt as alienated as ever from the due process of government, as urban areas continued down their path of decline despite the policies of a generation of reforming governments and socially concerned local politicians.

Discrimination within the Urban Programme?

Perhaps one reason for the feeling of alienation among some blacks relates to the past ineffectiveness of the UP in adequately meeting the needs of inner-urban black communities. This is illustrated by reference to a study carried out in 1980–1 by Birmingham Community Relations Council (BCRC, 1980/1), which showed that for 1981–2 there had been an increase of £30,000 in funds allocated to ethnic-minority voluntary organization projects under the Inner City Partnership's grant-aid scheme. This was seen to be quite a positive development, in view of a total reduction of £480,000 in UP funds allocated for voluntary groups in general. This meant that around 37% of the funds for voluntary organizations would directly benefit ethnic minorities, representing a 10% increase on the previous year. The allocation of funds for 1981–2 was as shown in Table 8.

Despite this apparent modest improvement, the Community Relations Council was disappointed that a number of projects which it had strongly supported had not, in the end, been allocated funds. It was also found that Asian organizations often did relatively badly compared to Afro-Caribbean organizations in Partnership funding assessments, and that ethnic-minority groups as a whole fared relatively poorly in the allocation of grants (BCRC, 1980/1, p.29). These allocations thus had to be viewed in the context of the total funding of Birmingham's Partnership, since the funding of voluntary organizations accounted for a mere 10% of total Partnership funds. The remaining 90% of funds hardly affected ethnic minorities. The Community Relations Council concluded its analysis with the following remarks:

Table 8. *Birmingham Inner City Partnership: forward fund allocations for voluntary organizations, 1981–2 (£ thousands)*

	Number of projects	Capital	Revenue	Total
(a) Total allocated to all voluntary organizations*	71	299,270	448,479	747,749
(b) Aimed primarily at ethnic communities	17	38,500	126,094	164,594
(c) Projects which would directly benefit ethnic communities	28	40,072	69,884	109,956
(d) Total affecting ethnic communities directly (b+c)**	45	78,572	195,978	274,550
		26.3%	43.7%	36.7%

Notes: * Includes budget for voluntary organizations, funds from Partnership main budget and £93,000 for a one-year extension of time-expired projects.
** The figures in (d) represent estimates. Where percentages are indicated, they relate to the share of funds from the totals allocated to all voluntary organizations which go to ethnic communities.
Source: Birmingham Community Relations Council, *Annual Report, 1980–81* (amended).

While many officers in the City and Council Departments have an increasing awareness of the needs of ethnic minorities, there is as yet a degree of failure on the part of the Partnership Committee to appreciate that race is a fundamental dimension in the development of policies to regenerate the inner city. The experiences of ethnic minorities in employment, housing, education, health and social services are so inequitable that the Partnership Programme is doomed to failure unless it explicitly takes the needs of ethnic minorities into consideration. It is therefore very much to be regretted that the current ICP (Partnership) Consultation Document, *Future Directions of the Partnership Programme 1982–85*, makes minimal reference to the needs of ethnic minorities. This is a challenge to ethnic minority organizations and other interested bodies to lobby for a fundamental change in direction (BCRC, 1890/1, p.29).

An indication of the Community Relations Council's own alternative set of priorities for UP allocations is shown in Table 9, where the Partnership's 1981–2 priorities are directly compared with those of the BCRC. The table refers only to projects aimed 'primarily' at ethnic minority communities – this being the same category shown in Table 8, but in terms of a total of capital plus revenue allocations. Clearly the BCRC favoured an increase in expenditure under this category and a different spread of allocations in percentage terms. The larger allocation to Afro-Caribbean groups is partly accounted for by the BCRC's support for a project for the Birmingham Rastafarian Association.

Black groups were also critical of the official Partnership priorities, but they had to maintain a relatively 'helpful' stance in order to increase their chances of successfully bidding for funds in future years. The 1982–3 Annual Report of the Birmingham Community Relations Council reflected this necessity by adopting a more conciliatory tone and by seeking to encourage black organizations to adopt a more professional approach in their quest for financial assistance.

The Birmingham situation, of course, instances only one local experience under the UP. The concern about the UP's neglect of the black community is, however, reflected in continuing studies presently being conducted in other UP-authority areas and by institutions such as the School for Advanced

Table 9. *Birmingham Community Relations Council (BCRC) priorities for Urban Partnership funding for 1981–2*

	BCRC Priorities		Partnership priorities	
	Funds	%	Funds	%
Afro-Caribbean groups	£464,193	74	89,905	55
Pakistani and Bangladeshi	47,700	8	13,210	8
Indian	18,710	3	7,210	4
Other ethnic minorities	45,132	7	–	–
Multi-cultural	50,967	8	54,269	33
Totals	626,702	100	164,594	100

Source: Birmingham Community Relations Council, *Annual Report, 1980–81* (amended).

Urban Studies at Bristol University. Research at Bristol and elsewhere, in conjunction with the DOE attempts to evaluate UP projects more effectively, and should throw further light on some of the problems faced by blacks in cities like Birmingham with regard to UP allocations.

Beyond the urban programme

The professionalization of organizations mentioned above was very much in line with government attempts, particularly after the 1981 disturbances, to create a greater degree of co-ordination between community leaders, private sector interests and national and local government. The inadequacies of the UP and the general feeling that new kinds of initiatives were required in the inner cities acted as a stimulus to change. In this environment, local businessmen and community organizations were to be encouraged to develop new approaches, both within and outside the UP, to the regeneration of their communities and the expansion of local economic activity.

In order to achieve these ends and to meet the problems caused by the 1981 riots in Liverpool, the Conservative government established a new agency – the Merseyside Task Force (MTF).[2] The MTF, in fact, was the DOE's shining light at the time of the 1981 riots. Michael Heseltine, as Minister with Special Responsibility for Merseyside, promoted the Task Force as a dynamic new innovation in British administration which would be able to cut through some of the red tape and bureaucracy of local authorities and central-government departments. The MTF was headed by civil servants drawn from several government departments, including the DOE itself, the Department of Trade and Industry, the Department of Employment and the Manpower Services Commission. The Task Force also included seconded managers from the private sector, who worked together with regional agencies and authorities. Despite this impressive structure, the Task Force was not an agency which had any specific powers as such over other agencies or authorities. It acted essentially as a facilitating or enabling agency aimed at bringing other agencies together to get projects implemented quickly and efficiently. At Ellesmere Port (on the southern bank of the Mersey), for example, the MTF provided the stimulus for the creation of a Boat Museum in conjunction with the local authority and the private sector, accelerating a scheme that, according to one MTF spokesman, 'in the past could have taken twenty years to get off the ground'.[3]

The promotion of projects involved a wide variety of activities. The MTF has, for example, been involved with the setting up of training centres using funds from the Manpower Services Commission and with the development of proposals to increase apprentice-training opportunities in the Merseyside area. Also on the MTF's list of priorities has been the improvement of housing conditions on local-authority housing estates and the encouragement of private housing development in Liverpool's inner districts. The development of tourism and leisure projects fell within the ambit of the MTF, which was consistent with the objective of stimulating small businesses and encouraging companies and people to purchase goods locally rather than from abroad. In each of the areas mentioned, other government departments provide grants where appropriate, and in some cases it has been the presence of the Task Force that has provided the initial impetus for funding projects which might not otherwise have existed.

The Task Force, it should be remembered, was initially set up as a limited experiment to tackle the problems facing one area of Britain. However, the experience of the MTF over its first year highlighted a great many benefits which could flow to government out of greater co-ordination between different authorities. It also demonstrated that government could work with the private sector in generating ideas and actions which could contribute towards urban renewal. The joint working arrangements entered into by those concerned all involved changes within existing public sector administrative processes and structures, which will probably have lasting implications for the administration of Britain's urban areas. Indeed, following the Merseyside experiment, a number of additional Task-Force-type agencies or City Action Teams were announced by the government, which were similarly charged with the job of bringing about a change in the relationship between public and private fund providers. Perhaps even more important was the expectation that the community itself would be drawn into the process of negotiation between the various agencies involved. With respect to this there seemed to be little widespread opposition to DOE thinking from community leaders. Within the black community there was, admittedly, a somewhat muted response to the MTF-type approach, but on the whole black leaders were aware of the fact that it was their supporters who were the chief beneficiaries of some of the new employment schemes being introduced and who were keen to take advantage of small business initiatives funded by central and local government and by the private sector. As with the initiatives to be described below, the immediate effect of the new programmes has been to provide community leaders with a channel into which they can, at least to some extent, guide the efforts of their supporters. They can claim that *something* is being done, however limited this may be, and that they, the representatives of the community, are 'in on the action'. Evidence suggests, therefore, that when community organizations have been given the opportunity to comment upon the activities of government agencies, comments have often been supportive rather than critical, precisely because groups regard programmes as being directly beneficial in enhancing the economic standing of their members.

The Development Corporations

This applies to a broad range of groups and not just to black organizations. One government agency, the Merseyside Development Corporation (MDC) recently recorded the response of interest groups which had taken part in a local consultation exercise with the Corporation. In the consultative meetings, groups tended to welcome the broad strategy adopted by the Development Corporation – a strategy which was wholly in line with the objectives of the MTF. Some organizations expressed their support for the Corporation, saying how impressed they were with the speed and wide-ranging proposals that the Corporation had produced for the redevelopment and regeneration of the MDC area. MDC officers were moved to comment that such remarks reflected the general support of residents and community groups for the Corporation's broad strategy and its intention to bring about the regeneration of the (MDC) designated area. Residents and voluntary groups were generally concerned to put forward very practical proposals for changes to their areas which fell within the MDC's objectives. There was some scepticism regarding the possibility of attracting large-scale private investment into the area, but this kind of attitude hardly indicated opposition to prevailing policy commitments.[4]

Bearing this attitude of the groups in mind, it is useful to briefly consider the role of the MDC to see exactly what it was that local groups were so keen to support. The MDC and the London Docklands Development Corporation were established prior to the riots, under provisions contained in Part XVI of the 1980 Local Government Planning and Land Act, with the objective of regenerating their respective dockland areas. The two Corporations were broadly modelled on the new town development corporations with the added function of development control. Each Corporation is directed by a non-executive board appointed by the Secretary of State and includes members with a wide range of experience in the private sector.

The MDC is situated close to Toxteth, the scene of Liverpool's worst riots. It caters directly for that community and also for Merseyside as a whole. Not surprisingly the local authorities and the MDC placed a high priority on the dockland regeneration following 1981. The MDC sought to supplement and assist the work of the local authorities in this task and attempted to discourage duplication or wasteful competition between agencies. To be effective in pursuing and achieving its objectives, the MDC regarded its consultation and collaboration with local groups and public authorities as essential throughout the period of implementation of its strategy. As the MDC itself stated:

apart from the planning and highways framework, such matters as environmental health, building regulation control, fire protection, public transport and public safety will require careful consideration. The support and involvement of community and voluntary organizations will also be enlisted in appropriate circumstances.[5]

On the surface, the MDC's public consultation appeared to be a very open process in which a wide range of interests was brought together with the MDC to help determine the shape of development in the area. In practice, however, we can see from the above quotation that consultation took place within a relatively narrow frame of reference. Topics for consultation were concerned with technical matters related to the implementation of the Corporation's objectives. Voluntary groups had little say over the major policy questions affecting the community. These matters of 'high policy' were left to the non-elected MDC board, which itself determined the 'appropriate circumstances' under which groups would be allowed into the consultative process. The degree to which a diversity of views as to the future pattern of development on Merseyside was excluded is illustrated by the statement in the MDC's 1981 *Initial Development Strategy* that: 'The creation of a single-minded Development Corporation backed by public funds and able to unify ownership can achieve many goals which would otherwise be denied.' The term 'single-minded' by definition reduced consultation to an essentially corporatist-type technical exercise, which raises serious questions about the nature of the MDC's role within a local-government setting which claims to be democratic. The MDC has powers which are commensurate with a large local authority, but it has the additional 'advantage' of being isolated from the kind of public accountability through the ballot box which local councils are subjected to. There can be no 'community development' through agencies like the MDC as long as it preserves its exclusive nature and privileged position as a planning authority. If community development is seen to involve a significant degree of participation which actually affects policy 'from below', then the MDC approach is conducive to blunting the effectiveness of community groups by linking them to predetermined policy objectives which emanate from the MDC board and the DOE.

Public and private initiatives

The activities of the MTF, the MDC and other public agencies were, of course, not sufficient by themselves to generate the much-sought-after private involvement in urban communities. Indeed, there was nothing particularly unique about the MTF or the Development Corporations in terms of their governmental nature. Both types of organization would seem to fit in with a long tradition of public agency involvement in the inner cities, promoted by both Conservative and Labour governments. We thus have to look further for the more specifically private/entrepreneurial aspect of government policy which is usually associated with Conservative thinking on urban renewal.

At the national level the major private initiatives were the establishment of the Financial Institutions Group (FIG) and Business in the Community. FIG marked a unique policy approach involving investment and other financial institutions in the inner cities. FIG – a group of 26 managers seconded by leading banks, building societies, insurance companies and pension funds – was charged with the task of identifying new investment opportunities to stimulate deprived areas. FIG started out with the commitment of seeking opportunities to combine private and public efforts in the inner city. It was assumed that the financial activities of the private sector in particular could have a dramatic impact on local communities, provided that resources could be released in an effective way to generate the required economic impetus for growth. It was also felt that the private sector could usefully comment upon the policies presently being conducted by central and local authorities, and, in this context, there was a strong implication that investment advice coming from the private interests represented in FIG would influence future government policies relating to urban renewal.

The FIG initiative was launched in July 1981, amidst a blaze of publicity surrounding the Secretary of State's visit to Merseyside following the riots and the establishment of the Merseyside Task Force. Representatives of the various financial institutions were invited to accompany Michael Heseltine in looking round Liverpool at prevailing conditions in the riot-torn areas. Private-sector seconded managers were invited to work closely with civil servants on inner-city problems and to develop new approaches and ideas which would lead to the launching of programmes relevant to problems faced nationwide.

During 1981 the FIG-seconded managers set to work, looking at problems under four main policy areas: development; small businesses; housing; and employment. In each of these areas a number of reports were produced for consideration at ministerial level. FIG was assisted by the civil service and by local authorities keen to develop their own solutions to the urban crisis. The local-authority involvement enabled FIG to produce reports more effectively on such topics as the development of publicly owned land, selective employment incentives, rating and rate-support-grant arrangements and inducements designed to stimulate the housing sector. Many of the FIG ideas were implemented quite quickly, such as the introduction of the Urban Development Grant and the so-called Inner City Enterprises service, which was proposed to work with institutional shareholders in order to identify investment opportunities in inner cities which would not normally attract the interest of private investment institutions. Another initiative related to encouraging building-society involvement in house repair and improvement with a pilot scheme involving two societies being launched in Birmingham. There was also a recommendation that banks should take more positive measures to assist small businesses, with major clearing banks appointing special inner-city development offices.

The FIG idea of an Urban Development Grant (UDG) was essentially an import from the United States, where the Urban Development Action Grant had been used to encourage private investment in community-based projects. Local authorities designated under the 1978 Inner Areas Act, or whose areas included Enterprise Zones, were able to bid for UDG grant schemes within the Derelict Land and Urban Programmes, where public investment would attract a significant amount of private funding. Initially £70 million was allocated under the UDG for 1983–4 and the grant was to be distributed to authorities which could show that investment levels would be substantially larger than the public-sector contribution taken alone.

Business and the community

As well as the FIG approach, the DOE was keen to persuade more companies to play an active role in local communities. One way of doing this was by following the lead of Business in the Community (BIC), which arose from an April 1980 meeting of British and American representatives of business and government held at Sunningdale Park. A working party, serviced by the DOE and chaired by Sir Alistair Pilkington of the Pilkington Glass firm of St Helens, concluded that collaboration between public and private sectors, trade unions and the voluntary sector was to be the way forward.

BIC's own publicity stressed the active aspect of the organization's objectives. In its *Newsletter* of June 1982, BIC set out 'to do something rather than just publish another pious report'. BIC described its role as helping others to establish mechanisms and projects that would reflect the local needs and resources of communities. Where effective initiatives already existed, such as local Action Resource Centres, BIC's role was to support these rather than to duplicate their work. In addition BIC sought to encourage the emergence of local leaders who would 'take credit for local initiatives'. In this respect it is interesting to note that BIC preferred to preserve its anonymity: 'We have to accept that our service should not be advertised, because any claim on our part detracts from the strength of what local people and interests have achieved' (BIC, *Newsletter*, June 1982).

This approach to community leaders meant that voluntary organizations stood to gain by co-operation with BIC-backed schemes, being able to point to some very tangible returns from co-operation with the private sector and, at the same time, taking the lion's share of the credit with the full backing of BIC. BIC's backers in the commercial, financial and industrial world were content to see this happen in view of their willingness to promote policies which were consistent with an 'enlightened self-interest.' Large companies were not too concerned with reaping the accolades of success if they could be sure that what they were promoting would contribute towards a more assured stability in localities which would enhance their own longer-term business prospects. Calm in the inner cities is more profitable in financial terms than disturbance and civil disorder (London Enterprise Agency, 1981).

Black leaders also had an interest in playing along with the private sector for their own 'enlightened self-interest', since they stood to enhance their status and position within the community. By drawing in such leaders and representatives from the trade unions and other voluntary organizations, BIC hoped to increase the potential support which these groups gave to both private and public policy strategies. The more the locality became enmeshed in the day-to-day running of programmes and the more the community came to be dependent upon external funding sources, the less likely it was to support political opposition to prevailing urban policy. However, even given this co-operation between leaders and the private sector and government, there was no absolute guarantee that the mass of unorganized inhabitants of the inner city would be drawn into new administrative and financial arrangements on any large scale or any more than they had been under the provisions of the Urban Programme. Community leaders often appeared to the unorganized to be remote and unconcerned with the problems faced at grass-roots level. Was it likely, therefore, that leadership representation in new agencies and on a wider range of committees would effect a significantly closer identification of the broader community with officially-sanctioned programmes?

More recently in the black community, a growing number of unemployed youths *have* at least begun to seek employment opportunities by linking their fate to the private sector. Many have visited local Enterprise Agencies in an attempt to join the ranks of the self-employed. The Enterprise Agencies are supported by the DOE and BIC and operate throughout the country. They satisfy the overall BIC objective by giving practical help to those wishing to start out on their own. Enterprise Agencies are often established by one or more private companies, sometimes in association with public bodies or local authorities, in order to promote business activity in the immediate locality. Most of the agencies have concentrated upon the promotion of fairly traditional small-business activity, but some have worked on environmental schemes and the alleviation of local social problems.

The enterprise-agency idea is not new and springs from action taken in the 1970s by a number of leading companies, which were concerned to develop ideas in order to tackle some of the problems associated with unemployment created by technological change in industry. Once again there was an 'enlightened self-interest' here, with companies trying to ease the direct impact upon their own employees facing redundancy. In some cases, whole local communities would be affected by factory closures which would have a severe impact on local business and the general morale of the areas concerned – thus what better way, it was argued, was there to stave off local recession than by stimulating alternative sources of demand for goods and services through the small-business sector?

In the 1980s the Enterprise Agencies have developed their conception of the role of the small business into one which sees the small firm as a centrally important force within inner-city areas. With public expenditure cuts from the centre reducing the ability of local authorities and other agencies to initiate expansive programmes themselves, it is envisaged that the small business will, in many cases, provide a restructuring of the local economy which will generate profits to be reinvested at the local level, thus stimulating a wide variety of commercial and social activities. In this way the generated 'value added' produced by the small private sector can bring about, it is argued, a multiplier effect which will raise the overall standard of life in affected areas.

On the surface this prospect may be quite appealing, if only because it is apparently logically very neat and simple. However, there are numerous practical problems facing small businesses at a time when profit levels in general are under severe pressure and when it takes a considerable time to develop the necessary entrepreneurial skills to run successful enterprises. More importantly, there are fundamental economic difficulties hindering the smooth operation of the economic multiplier at local level, particularly as, at the same time as private initiatives are established, local authorities have been forced to reduce their expenditure on education, housing and social services. These reductions themselves represent considerable withdrawals from the local economy in terms of the run-down in the level of service provision and the local level of consumer demand. While there is some indication that the private business sector has a role to play in supplementing the increasingly large reductions in public funds, there is no assurance that Britain's larger firms are willing to take on the major responsibility for inner-city funding (see Chapter 8). These larger companies are themselves under strain during a period of recession and their contributions to local development have tended to be directed to areas which have a more direct bearing on their own situations rather than to projects which, in a sense, let the government 'off the hook' as far as its own responsibilities are concerned. Private initiatives in this area will thus be seen to have limitations beyond which it will be the job of the government to make provision. In some ways there has been an implicit recognition of this problem by the Conservative government itself. The idea that the private sector cannot be expected to work miracles is reflected in the need for an agency such as the Merseyside Task Force. The MTF represents the recognition that there is still to be a significant public involvement in inner-city initiatives and that it is to be a centrally backed government agency which will be there to provide the stimulus to the public and private sectors (see also Chapter 8 for a fuller discussion of private-sector involvement).

The corporate connection

In the area of specifically black economic development, the Commission for Racial Equality was concerned to provide the stimulus referred to above. In 1982 the CRE sponsored two major conferences to discuss problems experienced by black business and to suggest actions which could stimulate black business development. One of the conferences was intended for local authorities and was organized by New World Business Consultants (a London-based advisory service for ethnic-minority businesses). The conference dealt with the problems faced by black firms and assessed local-authority policies towards the black private sector. The other conference was sponsored jointly by the UK/Caribbean Chamber of Commerce and the CRE itself. This was intended to provide a general forum for debate between interested parties and government representatives. The keynote speech was given by the then Environment Secretary, Michael Heseltine (CRE *Annual Report*, 1982, p.11). Local authorities, such as Lambeth, have followed this example in their Urban Programme submissions and with regard to their general policy approaches to the voluntary sector. For instance, Lambeth's Inner City Partnership established a Working Party on Private Sector Investment which prepared a report, between November 1981 and May 1982, emphasizing that it had been of central importance to seek ways of encouraging the growth of flourishing, profitable businesses rather than finding ways in which the public sector could 'prop up' businesses which were not really viable. In addition it was stressed that if private-sector investment was to be attracted to Lambeth, this had to be done by using market criteria and to develop contacts between public and private agencies in this process. The desire to 'privatize' development in the inner city was seen to be particularly relevant to ethnic minorities:

We are firmly of the opinion that inner city businesses, particularly where the ethnic minority is concerned, experience great difficulty in obtaining finance, especially in a start-up situation.

Moreover:

The [Lambeth] Business Advisory Service should be encouraged to approach the Head Offices of the clearing banks with the request that loan policies in the Lambeth and Brixton area should be examined to see if any disadvantage of applicants can be substantiated, particularly where the ethnic minority is concerned.[6]

The Partnership was also keen to involve Business in the Community and the London Enterprise Agency (LEntA) in the implementation of its strategy.

LEnTA was established in 1979 by nine of Britain's major firms, to help and encourage the creation and expansion of the small-business sector in London. To UP Partnerships and local authorities LEntA represents a significant corporate connection – a mechanism whereby large private organizations may become involved in local-authority community development activity. LEntA speaks for itself in *The Private Sector and the Inner City:*

Those companies actively implementing community involvement policies are most commonly the largest of the indigenous companies or the subsidiaries of multinationals following the parent company's policy. In the UK they include ICI, BP, BOC, GEC, IBM, BSC, Marks and Spencer, Shell, ESSO, Pilkingtons, ICFC and the clearing banks. These companies accept that they have a social responsibility for the well-being of their communities and that they have resources which can be of assistance to those communities. The companies active in corporate responsibility have also perceived an element of enlightened self-interest, believing that in the long term business must flow with the tide of community prosperity (LEntA, 1981, p.2).

Lord Byers, a member of LEntA's Advisory Council, writes, in the same place, that the basic philosophy behind this version of 'enlightened self-interest' is:

(1)   That a business cannot progress in isolation from the community in which it works and trades.
(2)   That the mixed economy is probably the best milieu for the economic health of the country.
(3)   That in the mixed economy the private sector has responsibilities as well as benefits.
(4)   That helping wherever possible to restore a healthy and prosperous environment is a responsibility which is not only good citizenship, but is good for business (LEntA, 1981, p.5).

Much of this has been imported from the United States and from Europe. Indeed, a paper by Leslie Slote, Vice President of Corporate Communications (RCA Corporation, USA), follows in the LEntA document. Slote states bluntly:

In the US, the social force that pushed business involvement in urban affairs was the new wave of civil rights demands which swept through American life, beginning with the Supreme Court School desegregation decision in 1954. By the Fall of 1963, agitation against segregation and discrimination was being pursued across the nation. . . . Then came the riots (LEntA, 1981, p.34).

Further, according to Slote:

General Motors executives who had never done so before came down from their office towers and walked through burned-out ghetto streets, expressing a shock that was genuine. When anti-Vietnam activists burned a small branch bank owned by the Bank of America in California, the President sat down with the students and listened, for the first time, he admitted (LEntA, 1981, p.35).

That this should be written only months before the summer 1981 disturbances in Britain was timely, to say the least.

Local initiatives American style?

Apart from corporate initiatives involving strong big agency inputs, there are many other local private enterprises and voluntary activities involving members of local communities, black and white. One organization, Local Initiative Support (LIS) (UK), inspired by American experience, has sought to develop a greater understanding of the non-governmental sector in communities and to devise new arrangements for funding private initiatives.

In this context LIS (UK) sees local initiatives as private-sector associations which generally have a loyalty to a particular locality. Many will be non-profit community organizations which, despite their independence, will almost inevitably strike up working relationships with local authorities (LIS *Report*, 1983, p.6). Such organizations will frequently be situated in areas of decline and will thus, according to LIS, provide potential for localized economic development.

LIS (UK) itself was established following the example of the American

Local Initiatives Support Corporation (described in Chapter 8), which is a Ford Foundation community development agency. Like the American corporation, LIS (UK) intends to produce private-sector investment funds, acting as a broker between investors and the local projects. In essence this will place LIS (UK) in the position of a specialized merchant bank for local communities (LIS *Report,* 1983, p.12).

For such an approach to be successful LIS (UK) recognizes that local initiatives have to operate in a broader economic environment which must be conducive to the growth of smaller enterprises and which must be sufficiently healthy to provide investment funds from larger private-sector backers. Such initiatives have borne fruit in the United States, but in Britain the philosophy of corporate provision for community development has still to be fully developed and corporate funding still has to be committed to significant amounts before it is seen to make an impact.

One indication, however, of the potential inherent in an LIS (UK)-type of strategy is the fact that many community leaders have apparently accepted the increasingly evident corporate connection in localities and the integration of leaders into governmental agencies is often an important prerequisite for the gradual assimilation of leaders into private-sector-backed programmes. This development follows American experience and signifies a shift in the political spectrum of black and community politics away from the collectivist reformism of the 1970s towards a form of integration involving a more direct identification with the values and ethos of the private sector (Friedland, 1982).

The full implications of a more 'privatized' approach to community development are examined in the following chapter. It will be suggested that recent initiatives have produced certain decentralizing developments in urban policy which run counter to the more traditional pattern of government intervention and centralization. The attempt to extend the role of the private sector in urban renewal has thus produced at least a degree of 'localization' in community development which provides the potential for the development of a new strategic policy perspective for government and the private sector in their approach to black and other community leaders.

8 Policies considered

This chapter provides an assessment of the policies considered in the previous chapter and relates the developments described to the process of integration. Chapter 7 indicated that an important change in emphasis has become evident in policy towards ethnic minorities and community regeneration. This change has been expressed in terms of a greater concentration upon private sector and voluntary involvement in urban renewal which has effected a limited degree of privatization in funding and organizing urban policy in Britain (as opposed to main government funding). The full long-term impact of this still remains uncertain, but to date the major political outcome would seem to be the further gradual propulsion of moderate blacks towards co-operation with the private sector and government-backed initiatives. In some respects this is in line with experience in the United States, where decentralist urban policies were quite successful in integrating a layer of black leaders into private-sector agencies designed to encourage broad community uptake of locally run projects. This chapter will look at British policy approaches against the background of this American experience. The argument here is that the present British approach to urban policy outlined in the previous chapter may be regarded as fairly unambitious when set against US experience and that, as a consequence, the 'benefits' available to groups are more limited and less attractive. The US situation also raises the issue of group integration through a relatively decentralized community development strategy which concentrates heavily upon *local* effort and *local* control which again tends to produce important benefits and incentives for groups. It is crucial, therefore, to assess the *extent* and nature of decentralization in the context of the developments in the last chapter.

It is thus important to define the nature of decentralization prior to embarking upon a comparative analysis of policy. In Britain, the Thatcher Conservative government's policy approach, outlined in Chapter 7, produced an alternative to more 'traditional' post-war government interventionism. In terms of urban policy this implied a shift away from a heavily public interventionist strategy to one in which intervention was mixed with a substantially greater degree of local initiative. During the 1960s and 1970s intervention almost inevitably spelled a combination of the DOE, local authorities and quasi-governmental agencies (such as the Commission for Racial Equality) in the promotion and implementation of programmes. Decentralization implied the adoption of a greater variety of approaches through less direct reliance upon the public sector and the promotion of local voluntarism.

Despite this development, there has been no conscious policy of decentralization as such in Britain and the concept has never been coherently defined in policy terms by government. What exists is the gradual emergence, in an uncoordinated and piecemeal fashion, of the diverse approaches covered in Chapter 7, which mark a change in relations between the public and private sectors in terms of their share in the funding and administration of community initiatives. Many programmes are thus becoming 'localized' through the infusion of private financing and local voluntary participation, although for this process to be translated into a clearly conceived strategic alternative to public interventionism it would be necessary for government and private sectors to develop clearly a conception of decentralization as an integral aspect of an 'arm's length' approach to community development. While decentralization and private initiative are therefore present-day realities in Britain, their full realization in strategic policy terms would probably require significant additional commitments of funding and organizational effort by governments, private agencies and by voluntary groups.

It is useful to identify four main areas which constitute something of a general perspective on a more 'localized' community policy. These help to highlight the difference between a more traditional government intervention-ist approach and a more 'privatized' approach and, if taken together, the areas define the basis for a more clearly conceived view of the decentralist aspects of urban policy. The areas are:

(1) A changed emphasis with respect to central government intervention in urban policy and in funding community initiatives. This does *not* necessarily require a real reduction in government funding of programmes, but it does imply some change in favour of private-sector and voluntary funding in terms of their share of total expenditure.

(2) We would expect, as a result of the above, a greater degree of involvement of the larger private companies in community initiatives, and this development was observed in Chapter 7. This was seen to be part of a move toward the generation of 'corporate responsibility' in community involvement.

(3) The small-business sector is also being encouraged, despite the enormous difficulties currently faced by new businesses and existing small firms. For black minorities these difficulties have hindered the uptake of

business opportunities and have raised doubts about the potential success of private initiatives in this area of urban policy. This, however, still constitutes an important aspect of national and local government policies towards urban renewal.

(4) A concerted decentralist strategy would also involve the devolvement of a degree of 'responsibility' and control to the local level. This was a centrally important aspect of American community development in the 1960s and 1970s, but it has proved to be difficult to realize in Britain where organizational and political obstacles have been placed in the way of 'community control'.[1]

In general the political environment itself has not always been conducive to decentralization, since much of central government policy has actually developed centralizing strategies for handling local affairs. Central attempts to keep local-authority expenditure under control and to restrict local authority powers to raise local rates have had the effect of concentrating *more* controls and sanctions at the centre. This represents an important apparent contradiction between centralizing and decentralizing aspects of government policy, but it should not detract from the significance of changed relationships between centre and locality *specifically* in the area of community development and urban renewal. It is the decentralist elements of policy which often have the greater immediate political impact upon the pattern and nature of participation in community programmes and even though a local authority may be subject to tighter central scrutiny, this often has a delayed impact upon groups because of, for example, the local assurance of the sustained provision of public or private funds to community programmes or projects. On another level, greater central control of local-authority finances may actually come to be perfectly *consistent* with the promotion of privatization of community effort as the longer-term withdrawal of government funding produces (at least in theory) the right environment for increased private provision.

The emergence of a new urban policy

It is important to gain some impression of the *extent* of the movement towards decentralization and private initiative in order to gauge more precisely the degree to which such developments may be regarded as broadly constituting a new urban policy in Britain. *How far*, then, has the process advanced in Britain and how does this compare with the extent of such approaches in the USA? These questions may be answered by reference to the four areas of decentralization just mentioned above and to the evidence produced in Chapter 7.

So, with reference to the first main area, relating to the changed role of government, it was seen in Chapter 7 (Table 7) how expenditure on the Urban Programme was expected to fall in real terms between 1985 and 1986. In addition, local-authority spending restraint is constraining the overall growth of local government and this consequently restricts the amount of expenditure by local authorities on community services and other programmes (see Introduction to this book and Steather, 1984). As far as the 'race industry' is concerned, it was shown in Chapter 4 that the Commission for Racial Equality was unexceptional in terms of constraints upon expenditure. The Commission's expenditure between 1982 and 1983 rose by only £411,868 and £8,718, 454, which represented a small real-expenditure reduction.

While the evidence points to the general drawing back of government from funding interventions in areas directly affecting urban communities and minorities, one offsetting factor in this situation has been the actual increase in government expenditure on grants to charities. The August 1984 edition of *Charity*, published by the Charities Aid Foundation, showed a large increase in central funding of charities during 1983–4 (increasing from £2,256,750 to £4,399,972 for surveyed charities). This increase, however, has to be treated with caution, since it covered a sample of only 30 charities and probably concealed the withdrawal of government in other areas. For example, increasing grants to educational and welfare organizations may cover reductions in local spending on these very services under main spending programmes. There is a need for greater research in this area and also for an improvement in the quality of charitable statistics, which at present make accurate assessments very difficult. However, these increases to charities would still appear to provide little in the way of compensation for reductions in traditional public-funded programmes.

The question relating to the magnitude of private sector supplementation of government fundings and the general increase in private involvement in community development may be examined by looking at the second major aspect of decentralization – namely the increasing role of large companies. Chapter 7 indicated the willingness of companies to become involved through direct financial support and through the Business in the Community initiative, enterprise agencies and quasi-governmental bodies such as the Merseyside Development Corporation, but as with the charitable statistics, precise estimations of corporate giving are very difficult to assess accurately. The Charities Aid Foundation has attempted to compare corporate charitable giving in the USA and Britain and has pointed to a gradual increase in British giving, but on a less extensive scale than in America. Given the long tradition of philanthropic giving by the large corporations in the USA, this finding is hardly surprising, but it does help to underline the embryonic stage of British corporate involvement in communities compared to America.

The Charities Aid Foundation survey found that UK charities received a total income of around £4.7 billion in 1980 (the most recent year assessed to date). The amount given for charitable purposes by the top 200 corporate donors for that year was £25 million or 0.53% of the total. Taking the total number of registered British companies and the total of their charitable donations (£46 million), this produced an average charitable donation of around £30 per company. In the USA the comparable average figure worked out at $1,300 per company for 1980 (Charities Aid Foundation, 1983, p.79).

These figures, of course, do not give the whole picture of corporate involvement in communities, since companies devote resources to activities and projects in localities which do not necessarily carry charitable status. Corporate involvement in the enterprise agencies, for example, requires the allocation of substantial administrative resources, the provision of staff and other direct financial contributions. Also, so-called 'in kind' contributions may be made to community groups or to individuals participating in voluntary work. In the USA, such corporate contributions have stimulated a large and expanding 'non-profit' sector of the US economy, which provides local organizations with benefits which extend into the spheres of education, human services (health and welfare), cultural and ethnic affairs, and community economic development. Within the non-profit sector are usually included professional associations, religious organizations (churches and other religious congregations), charitable private foundations providing funds to other non-profits (fund providers) and those serving primarily a public or charitable purpose, which provide actual services for the community.

In the USA, the Reagan administration's policy Initiative on Voluntarism, announced in 1981, was partly intended to stimulate the non-profit sector. The initiative involved the appointment of a Presidential Task Force and the establishment of a special Cabinet Council on Private Sector Initiatives and served to emphasize the already strong commitment of corporate interests to voluntarism and to private non-profit effort in communities. The private foundations are examples of this, providing finance in a variety of ways through trusts, endowments and other funds. The Ford Foundation is the largest of these enterprises, distributing over $103 million in 1979.

Also in the USA, company-sponsored foundations obtain their funds from the profit-making corporate sector, but still operate with a wide degree of autonomy. Large corporations frequently use these foundations to channel funds into projects which are intended to improve local communities and which also benefit the provider corporations themselves in terms of commercial 'spin-offs' and improved public relations. Such foundations also serve company employees and the communities where the company operates, but in practice there is no geographical limitation on the extent of this kind of corporate involvement.

Many US corporations do not use the foundation form of provision, but simply channel money directly into community projects. This is facilitated through corporate contributions programmes, which are operated by companies and which provide those companies with opportunities for involving their employees directly in community activities. The tax climate, as for the foundations, is favourable, since there are quite generous tax reliefs to be gained which make corporate giving worthwhile, even for companies concerned about their overall profitability (The Foundation Center, 1981; Pierson, 1982; Stewart, 1982).

If Britain compares unfavourably in terms of the level of large-company involvement in communities, then it may also be argued that this is the case with the third aspect of decentralization, relating to the creation of small businesses. This may be illustrated by direct reference to the experience of ethnic-minority businesses, although the problems associated with the small-business sector are generally applicable to all small enterprises. In 1984, for example, there was a record level of small-business failures in Britain, despite an increase in the level of business starts.

The autumn/winter 1983 edition of the Commission for Racial Equality's journal, *New Community*, brought together a number of contributions covering the most recent research into the nature and problems of ethnic-minority businesses. Robin Ward introduced the contributions by pointing to the problems of access faced by minorities to the wider labour market. Clark and Rughani alluded to problems faced by blacks in accommodating to the native British business community, while Brooks studied the obstacles to the expansion of black businesses in Lambeth. Sawyer also covered the problems facing blacks and called for improved government incentives to help minority businesses by way of central government intervention and the assistance of Britain's major business schools. The implication of this collection, therefore, is that blacks face particularly difficult problems within the wider business sector because of cultural and racial factors which traditionally inhibit the development of the black private sector. Efforts have consequently been directed at eliminating these disadvantages. Central government policies and the policies of local authorities have therefore been designed to foster more favourable conditions for small-business development and this has effectively broadened the range of opportunities for blacks in the private sector. (This may be viewed in terms of the extension of the range of benefits to black leaders and voluntary organizations, which in turn induces a greater propensity to take part in community projects – see Chapter 7.)[2]

With respect to these opportunities, we may point to programmes run by the Manpower Services Commission which assist the unemployed to start their own businesses, to assistance given through the Department of Trade and Industry's Small Firms Service and to the local authority encouragement of worker co-operatives and non-profit community initiatives. The Greater London Enterprise Board (GLEB), for example, has given a considerable amount of assistance to co-operatives and has laid heavy emphasis upon the value of such enterprises within the black community (GLEB, 1984). These initiatives represent a move in the direction of a growth in private entrepreneurialism within the black community which marks a significant progression along the road to community involvement in the private sector. As indicated above, however, this kind of activity must be viewed within the context of a difficult economic environment, where large companies still provide comparatively little assistance and where the increasing level of unemployment and business insolvencies adversely affects the expansion of small companies.

It is possible, moreover, to envisage a reversal in the limited decentralization described. This could happen if, for example, the private sector's ability to
intervene in local programmes was hampered by worsening economic circumstances or by a change of government. Nevertheless, in some fields of urban
policy even the intent to move in a decentralist direction may be lacking. This
certainly applies to the fourth aspect of a decentralist policy: the extension of
'community responsibility' or 'control'. This question again may best be
illustrated by comparison with the USA, where the early process of political
integration of groups was facilitated most effectively in programmes which
afforded local organizations a direct role in management and, in some cases,
in the election of representatives to community agencies and boards. Perhaps
the nearest British equivalent to this kind of local participation existed in the
neighbourhood councils and the Community Relations Councils, but in these
bodies the absence of elective arrangements limited their representativeness
and generally served to indicate their close relationships with government and
their heavy dependence upon central support.

Community development, US style

In contrast, in the USA it was government which assumed a major role in
promoting community development and greater autonomy at local level.
'Participation' at local level became a crucially important aspect of government policy, particularly during President Johnson's so-called War on Poverty
in the mid 1960s. The federal-supported Community Action Agencies
(CAAs) were instrumental in bringing large numbers of local activists together
to exercise community 'control' with the support of public and private funds.
Indeed, federal government often officially recognized the bureaucratism
inherent in its own administration of urban policy and openly encouraged
local agencies to act as pressure groups against over-centralization and
government officialdom (Jacobs, 1983).

This officially sanctioned version of pressure-group politics proved to be
enormously attractive at local level, even to many of the most militant and
political activists. The liberal notion of community 'control' seemed to satisfy
many of the objectives of the radical community 'power' advocates, who
shared with the liberals a rather ill-defined notion of the efficacy of local self-
determination and independence from big government. Within the black
community the appeal was particularly strong, as black groups were seeking
practical alternatives to street violence and the apparently objectiveless
politics of the Black Panthers and Black Nationalism. This political turn by
many radicals and militants created the conditions for a marriage between
themselves and the advocates of community control within the Democratic
Party and the supporters of community development within the corporate
private sector.

The development of 'black capitalism' was conducive to the political integration of leading blacks and to the generation of jobs within community agencies which brought blacks into closer contact with private-sector interests. The fact that such contacts developed on a wide scale was partly due to the range of public and private points of intersection with black leaders and black organizations. Localization and privatization thus produced different kinds of linkages between the parties involved, which provided community activists with a broad range of opportunities for participation in programmes offering different incentives and outlets for the expression of group demands. By the late 1970s and early 1980s the professionalization of black leaders within these programmes had produced a distinct managerial group within the black community. Official US government statistics showed that, by 1981, the proportion of blacks in the civilian labour force in managerial and professional occupations had increased to 13% of the black workforce and that 23% of blacks were employed in service occupations and 27% in technical, sales and administrative positions (US Department of Commerce, Bureau of the Census, 1983, p.9).

Professionalization and entrepreneurialism developed, broadly, in the following environments:

(1)   Through the CAAs or anti-poverty agencies.
(2)   Through the Community Development Corporations (CDCs).
(3)   Through private-sector initiatives and government/private-sector partnerships.

In each general area, community programmes provided blacks with mechanisms through which they could advance socially and economically, often by adapting agencies to the particular needs of local black groups or to the distinctive cultural or racial backgrounds of those communities. Such adaptation was an important element in providing a practical measure of local autonomy and control over local programmes. To illustrate this, each of the three types of approach mentioned above will be examined, taking the CAAs first.

US community action agencies

Although the CAAs originally catered for the needs of the black community they were never envisaged as being exclusively black-orientated and they did not develop a specifically 'black image' in the way that British Community Relations Councils did. The 'universalistic' nature of the CAAs thus had a wide appeal to black leaders who could enter them without being branded as 'Uncle Toms' entering paternalistic 'black' agencies. There was also the added appeal to the militants of the prospect of joining together in the CAAs with representatives of the white urban poor and unemployed as part of a 'class'-based approach to community development. Such 'unity' could be justified as consolidating the bargaining strength of the inner-city poor in the general struggle for economic resources. In this respect the CAAs, in the mid

1960s, possessed a certain liberal idealism which was never really evident in the 'race' bodies in Britain.

This early idealism, however, was dissipated as a result of later attempts to control community funding. The 1967 amendments to the Economic Opportunity Act threatened the autonomy of the CAAs, by seeking to bring them more effectively under public control (Levitan, 1980, p.87). The Nixon administration went even further along this road, abolishing the Office of Economic Opportunity, which had represented much of the idealism of the original community-action approach.

More recently many CAAs seem to have re-established a greater degree of freedom from public control (Jacobs, 1982) and have maintained their commitments to employment and training programmes, educational programmes and projects catering for a range of ethnic minority needs. There has also been an increase in public funding for the CAAs which marks a firmer commitment to their general objectives and role in localities (Levitan, 1980, p.87). This public funding has not produced undue governmental interference in CAA administrations and many local governments have been keen to respect the independent nature of the agencies. In many ways, however, central interference became much less of an issue for participating groups as the CAAs established themselves as self-motivated agencies led by highly qualified professionals who were quite good at combating the encroachments of public agencies and quite capable of generating private sources of funding for CAA programmes. That initial 'burst' of autonomy in the 1960s was the most crucial test for the CAAs in terms of the integration of black activists and others who, by the late 1970s, had become very much at home within the CAA career and employment structures. There is little evidence of such a well-developed career community service in Britain, even within the CRE and CRCs. It is, of course, possible that the various initiatives described in the previous chapter could create the conditions for a greater range of opportunities, but limited financing of local projects in Britain restricts the development of professionalization and the provision of salary levels equivalent to those in the US.

Community Development Corporations

The degree to which groups in the US stand to obtain benefits in an integrative environment is further emphasized by reference to the Community Development Corporations (CDCs). The CDCs were first established under the mid 1960s 'Great Society' programmes as federally funded agencies under the Office of Economic Opportunity, the Small Business Administration and the Department of Housing and Urban Development (HUD). The CDCs increasingly became involved in entrepreneurial-type activities and attracted an increasingly important private-sector input of funds and support. In many instances during the 1970s the CDCs competed with small-business programmes, but despite this they were able to develop a strong community focus which attracted groups which may not have been drawn to the more traditional small-business sector.[3]

There is evidence to suggest that the CDCs have been responsible for involving a substantial number of blacks in private commercial and trading activities and it is possible that as many as one third of the CDCs are black-dominated (Jacobs, 1983, p.18). A Report produced by the US Ford Foundation's Local Initiatives Support Corporation (LISC, 1982) provides a very clear picture of the nature and extent of black involvement in the CDCs and similar kinds of community-development agencies funded by LISC. The Lower Roxbury Community Corporation and the Community Development Corporation of Boston, for example, received LISC funding and, in the case of the Corporation of Boston, minority groups have been active in developing a large industrial park in the city with LISC assistance. In other cities LISC has promoted small businesses, non-profit activities and other community initiatives. Much CDC and LISC activity has been concerned with housing improvement and support for housing co-operatives involving ethnic minorities and the inner-city poor. LISC's Report provides one example of its involvement, which gives a very clear picture of local entrepreneurialism in action:

A joint effort of three civil groups and the city government has so far raised $906,000 from 21 businesses and foundations to launch a major program in Philadelphia emphasizing economic development. Four groups already being assisted are: The Franklin Foundation, the Southwest Germantown Development Corporation, the Spanish Merchants Association, and Kensington Action Now. The Franklin Foundation, already active in housing rehabilitation and employment training, has received $51,694 for staff, technical assistance and a financial development program. LISC is partially financing the acquisition and rehabilitation of abandoned houses being undertaken by the Germantown group for use by low income families. The Spanish Merchants Association has received $60,000 to expand its commercial and economic development programs serving the City's Hispanic community. A loan of $50,000 for housing rehabilitation has been approved for Kensington Action Now. A LISC loan for a small business investment company is being negotiated (LISC, 1982, p.21).

Public–private partnerships

Inevitably such initiatives require the support of the public sector. Partnerships have developed to meet the requirements of various projects which depend upon the co-ordination of public and private agencies. A Report on Private Sector Initiatives produced by a special Governor's Task Force in Massachusetts defined the nature and rationale of such partnerships:

Public–private partnership is collaboration between businesses, non-profit organizations (including foundations) and government agencies in which risks, resources and skills are shared in projects which benefit both the partners and the broader community. In essence, partnership is a mechanism through which two or more organizations can each bring to bear their unique skills and resources in the planning or pursuit of a goal of mutual public interest. Each partner contributes the knowledge and expertise of individuals, facilities, equipment, and funds not normally available to the other partner but essential to the achievement of the common goal.

Partnership is distinguished from philanthropy and volunteerism (though both are frequently present) by the elements of self-interest, organizational identification with the project, and personal cooperation in planning, operation or oversight. Partnership as defined here, then, should include:

the active involvement of personnel from each of the participating partners,
clear identification of the partner organizations with the project, and
relatively direct and identifiable benefits to the partners as well as to the community as a whole (Commonwealth of Massachusetts, 1983, p.9).

Within this broad framework partnerships take on a variety of forms. Partnerships may be between business and government, business and non-profit organizations, non-profit organizations and government or between all three groups (Levy, 1982).

The rationale of partnerships is to produce benefits for the community *and for the partners* and to make the most effective use of available economic and other resources. The business community stands to gain through this version of corporate responsibility in a more positive way than in situations where corporations and foundations simply act as fund providers, since the partnership generates incentives for the providers in very immediate and practical terms and provides a mechanism for corporate interests to become intimately involved in the pursuance of community goals and stated community interests. In this context the Massachusetts approach to partnership covered five broad areas:

(1)   public education
(2)   employment and training
(3)   economic and community development
(4)   public safety and criminal justice
(5)   health and human services.

Under each heading initiatives may take many forms, covering CDCs, non-profits and businesses and catering for all racial groups. Importantly, these initiatives require the active participation of groups and the improvement of their technical and managerial capabilities for the effective implementation of partnership objectives (see also the Greater Boston Chamber of Commerce 1983–4, 1984).

One outcome of the connection between the public and private sectors over a whole range of forms of co-ordination, including partnerships, has been the heavy reliance of non-profits upon government funding for their activities and services provided through community programmes. As in Britain with charitable funding, US central government has seen fit to financially assist the voluntary sector in order to strengthen it and to extend its scope of activities. In 1980, 35 per cent of the US $114 billion worth of non-profit expenditure was provided by the federal government, although by the mid 1980s the impact of budget cuts, particularly in community development, was forcing non-profits to seek ways of raising extra funds from private sources. Even so, government funding of whatever magnitude may again be seen in terms of centralization and this is certainly a view which is justified to some extent when the sums involved are so large. The fact remains, however, that substantial public funding has helped to consolidate the private sector in many areas of community activity and has encouraged many larger corporate interests to develop their corporate responsibility in the inner cities beyond the levels which might otherwise have been attained.

Evaluation: a threat to group independence and integration?

From this brief survey the American approach may be characterized by its diversified approach towards communities and by its concern with community involvement. The catchment of programmes, therefore, tends to be relatively wide, drawing in minority leaders, voluntary organizations and corporate interests. British 'corporate responsibility' has only made tentative steps in this direction. Indeed, it may be questioned whether the American enthusiasm for corporate responsibility could ever be matched in Britain, given the different expectations of companies and groups about the role of the private sector in Britain and the comparative lack of resources available for community development. The environment in Britain is significantly different, providing less of an impetus for community involvement and corporate intervention than the American 'enterprise economy' and its adherence to the 'American way' of corporate and philanthropic giving.

British companies and government agencies have, it is true, become aware of American practice and have been keen to adapt American-style approaches to the different economic, social and legal conditions in Britain. Increased corporate involvement, the encouragement of minority and community co-operation have been widely examined, together with an indication of the things to be gained from across the Atlantic. However, many of the US approaches have been deemed inappropriate and innovations have had to take account of Britain's own peculiarities and long experience in implementing urban policies of its own. The British corporate sector, in any case, tends to be defensive of its own commitments and often suspicious of foreign innovations and the same may be said of the public sector, which remains cautious in a period when public expenditure constraints are being increasingly felt and when various approaches to community involvement are required to be tested over time with respect to their 'productiveness' and performance.

Concentration upon productiveness and performance raises discussion of a further important area affecting local groups, integration and the implementation of urban policy. The monitoring of programme performance has long been a feature of administrative practice in the USA and is becoming increasingly important as a method of evaluating the effectiveness of programmes in Britain. In the USA most programme evaluations have been concerned with inputs and the management process, rather than with how programmes directly affect clients or the general public and so evaluation has tended to be regarded very much as a managerial tool for monitoring programme performance in terms of management objectives and financial goals (Hatry, Winnie and Fisk, 1981). Because of this, programme evaluations have not necessarily produced 'better' policies or administrative practices for governments, although they have produced guidelines for administrators seeking to examine the viability of programme expansion and the elimination of particular programmes and evaluation has also been important in helping to assess programmes in their early stages before further resource allocations are made to them.

American practice has placed considerable stress upon programme goals which specify criteria for measuring progress, or otherwise, in meeting objectives and for measuring the effects of programmes which have been implemented. Federal and local governments and private-sector agencies have all employed evaluations to help in the monitoring of programmes which receive external funding and there seems to have been a general acceptance of this approach by fund recipients. Research conducted in the USA by this author in 1984 indicated a willingness by voluntary agencies to participate in the evaluation process and to report back to funding agencies requiring information on programme performance and the meeting of objectives. There was, however, a feeling amongst some fund recipients that evaluation had become little more than a financial accounting exercise which had little in common with evaluation of overall programme performance. In many human-service (health and welfare) agencies, it was found that agency managers often complained about the bureaucratic burden of financial evaluation and the lack of any real attempt to relate such evaluation to the improvement of agency efficiency or to the betterment of services to the public.[4]

Evaluation can also be a costly business and can be disruptive to agencies which perhaps possess only limited administrative resources and staff time to devote to evaluation. Research and agency experience in the USA suggest that evaluations can be inaccurate, poorly reported and poorly understood by managers and government officials (United Community Planning Corporation, 1982, p.1). In response to this situation many evaluations in the early 1980s adopted so-called 'naturalistic' methodologies which were mainly concerned with describing the operation of programmes and the intended and apparent benefits *to clients*. Such evaluations were relatively informal in approach, but still failed to address directly the issue of the actual impact of programmes *upon clients*. With this in view a larger number of evaluations began to stress the client response in programmes, particularly in areas such as the human services where client assessments were of central importance.

Concern with client responses indicates that there is a definite political side to evaluation. Evaluation usually involves a degree of accountability insofar as agencies or groups receiving funds from governments or the private sector are required to report back to their sponsors. As Hatry *et al.* have indicated, governments regard it as crucial that there should be clearly defined lines of responsibility in evaluation exercises, although the actual task of evaluation should, in the majority of cases, be carried out by the staff that actually operate the programmes involved. It is argued that 'whenever possible' a central staff unit should have overall responsibility for evaluation within the government' (Hatry *et al.*, 1981, p.88), despite delegation to local agencies. This therefore envisages a degree of centralized monitoring in urban programmes which creates linkages between local agencies and the centre and which to some extent compromises local autonomy in measuring agency performance.

This compromising of agency autonomy should not be over-emphasized, because few American agency managers see top-down monitoring as a fundamental issue hindering their ability to set objectives or locally operate programmes. The situation varies according to the degree of funding going into recipient agencies and according to the degree of monitoring involved, but it can be argued that all relationships between providers and recipients involve *some* loss of independence (see Chapter 3) and that evaluation and reporting back simply confirm this rather than themselves creating particularly burdensome degrees of centralization.[5]

How far this becomes an important political issue in Britain remains to be seen, as evaluation of urban programmes is becoming more widespread and more important in the practical monitoring of local initiatives. It is possible that political tensions will emerge as evaluation extends to a wider variety of voluntary organizations, since in Britain monitoring could become rather more closely associated with some of the centralizing tendencies within local and national government. This, of course, would run counter to the objectives of those programmes tending towards a degree of localization, but it may arise as an unintended consequence of central scrutiny.

An example of central scrutiny is provided by the DOE. The DOE has been particularly keen to monitor its Urban Programme (UP) more effectively and since 1983 has operated a computerized information system used by the DOE Inner Cities Directorate and DOE regional offices. The system currently covers about 5,000 projects, detailing information about the nature of the projects and their funding. The Inner Cities Directorate also annually reviews UP expenditure and, from 1983, has undertaken annual monitoring of UP projects to ensure that they conform to ministerial guidelines. The DOE has also recently embarked upon the evaluation of UP-funded projects by looking at the effects of projects upon levels of employment, and by assessing environmental projects and the impact of the UP upon the young unemployed (covering the effectiveness of projects in meeting the needs of young unemployed people). Such evaluations have concentrated upon project effectiveness, value for money and project management (including problems of implementation and their resolution).

A DOE review of community projects was undertaken in 1983. The review lasted three months, during which time a small team visited 40 UP-funded voluntary-sector projects in London and Birmingham. The team sought to provide an assessment of how projects actually spent the money allocated to them and what resulted from this expenditure in the community. The team recommended a more comprehensive approach to evaluation of voluntary-sector projects and the development of strategies by local authorities which would achieve local coverage and efficient use of resources.

The DOE has complained that most of the Partnership and Programme authorities within the UP have neglected their own formal assessment of the overall performance or effectiveness of local programmes (DOE, 1984, p.5). Some programme authorities have reviewed their yearly activities, but such efforts, according to the DOE, have often been superficial and lacking any formal appraisal. The DOE have, therefore, supported local efforts to improve programme monitoring and appraisal and have encouraged UP authorities to study the impact of projects in local communities. Lambeth, for example, has undertaken a review of its economic projects and has examined selected projects to assess their impact on the black community. Leicester has also been quick to initiate some quite sophisticated project-performance exercises.

The DOE has also encouraged self-monitoring, particularly in voluntary-sector projects. The Birmingham Partnership has been regarded as a leader in this area, in attempting to ensure that all new projects identify 'key elements' which can be monitored in order to provide a justification for grant funding. Nottingham has also introduced self-evaluation as a requirement for some voluntary groups, which have to produce quarterly monitoring reports to the Inner Area Team.

The DOE intends to encourage further developments towards more effective monitoring and to support research and studies which will develop guidelines for monitoring in the future. It has been suggested that requirements for self-monitoring could be written into agreements between sponsors and project managers which lay down clear obligations on both sides (DOE, 1984, p.9). Project managers could then be required to make annual reports on standardized DOE forms which would give an indication of how project objectives were being met, together with an assessment of project performance.

The responses of voluntary groups to such monitoring would be crucial to the future success of the DOE's plans. The experience so far in Lambeth and elsewhere would suggest that many group leaderships are prepared to co-operate if they see benefits in doing so, but some groups have remained highly suspicious of any attempts to implement government scrutiny of community activities. In previous chapters it has been shown how black groups have long maintained such suspicions in Britain and this poses problems for governments and private-sector agencies attempting to extend the coverage of community programmes. That this is not exclusively confined to black groups is evidenced by the National Council for Voluntary Organizations' (NCVO's) March 1984 *Code for Voluntary Organizations,* which laid down 16 guidelines for voluntary groups receiving funding from government sources. The NCVO *Code* stressed the importance of groups guarding their basic objectives and independence where financial dependence on government increasingly threatened group freedom over their own affairs and decisions relating to financial allocations. The *Code* went beyond the monitoring issue by drawing attention to the whole issue of group/government relations and the need for groups to maintain control over their own policies and programmes. This issue would therefore seem to be of importance in determining the success or otherwise of urban initiatives and in obtaining broad consent for those initiatives in local communities.

Consent or dissent: some concluding remarks

The NCVO attitude is indicative of the often uneasy relations between groups and governments seen throughout this study. The policy initiatives described may be effective in attracting many more blacks into co-operative relationships with governments and private agencies but, as seen in this chapter, such initiatives have not been provided on such an extensive scale as in the USA and have not achieved the same degree of group 'advancement'. In this respect, British community initiatives cannot be regarded as having provided the fundamental solutions to the problems covered by the 'urban crisis'. Local initiatives may provide some relief from economic and social problems, but relatively little in the way of major solutions to the structural problems of unemployment, urban decline and the manifestation of underlying racial and class antagonisms. The distress of Britain's cities is too deep-seated to be 'cured' by the promotion of often economically marginal projects, although the political impact of such initiatives may be more important in the short term if such initiatives encourage the integration of black community leaders (and others) into community programmes, race-relations agencies and local-authority policy processes. The initiatives described here thus help governments to extend certain important political 'benefits' to black leaders, which strengthen their ties with public and private agencies and which enable community leaders to promote those agencies within the broader communities which they represent.

The success or failure of present initiatives can also be measured in terms of the degree to which the unorganized and the unemployed can be persuaded to identify more closely with the objectives of those who are co-operating within 'the system'. The gulf between community leaders and the unorganized, which became so apparent during the 1981 disturbances, can be partially bridged through extending the coverage of local programmes, although as the level of unemployment continues to grow (early 1985) the fundamental problem of disaffection remains and even deepens.

In addition to such problems, social conditions continue to foster numerous responses to the urban crisis and the urban condition. Racial attacks against blacks in London's East End have increased; many black youths remain politically apathetic while a minority respond by looking towards more radical political solutions. For the moderate black leaders the radical politicization of many young blacks serves to widen the gap between the leaders and the 'disaffected'. In effect this implies a demarcation between black leaders and militant blacks which is defined in terms of the perception of the costs and benefits of participation in the political system and the identification of quite distinct interests between these contending groups. The divergence of these interests in Britain contrasts with the *convergence* of political radicalism and liberal community politics in the America of the 1960s and marks an important difference between the political environments prevailing during periods of communal disturbance and government reassessment of public policy. In practical terms, however, this may not seriously hinder the implementation of urban policy as long as the 'traditional' community leaderships are able to maintain their political authority as representatives within local government, within the political parties and within race relations and other agencies.

The ability of moderate community leaders to maintain sufficient communal consent for their politics in this situation is conditioned in part by the ability of national and local governments and private agencies to provide groups with economic and political benefits and also by government responses to the crucially important race question itself. The use of 'physical' approaches to race relations and immigration, as seen in Chapter 1, has historically assumed political significance, insofar as blacks have been regarded as special in terms of their treatment within public policy. The continued criticisms of governments which have attempted to control immigration more rigorously have effected a certain distancing of black leaders of all shades of opinion from 'centralized' British political institutions, politicians and even race-relations agencies. Public and private inner-city initiatives may help to overcome this distancing by fostering the identification of blacks with local economic and political structures, but just how far these initiatives can reduce the general suspicion of blacks towards a public policy associated with racially discriminatory assumptions will depend upon the practical impact of measures upon the black community. There is also the 'physical' impact of community policing and the responses of government to communal disturbance which affect the perceptions of black communities. Again, blacks tend to react in an adverse manner to measures which appear to identify their communities as 'special' and thereby problematic (Chapter 1).

Chapter 5 indicated that local-authority approaches to the black community and its problems often fail to meet adequately the demands of even moderate black organizations. The development of new policy strategies, objectives and organizational arrangements by local government is constrained by economic adversity and by the very magnitude of urban problems in the inner cities. Many prominent politicians locally and nationally have recognized the extent of the problems faced and have called for substantial increases in infrastructural investment in Britain's decaying urban cores. These calls have come from within the Conservative Party as well as from Labour and other Opposition leaders. Such calls implicitly draw attention to the restricted economic impact of the Urban Programme and small-business and other community initiatives. They also thereby underline the delicate growth of decentralization as described in this chapter, since without a viable economic expansion in the economy as a whole, community development must inevitably lose the impetus which can effectively be sustained by the infusion of resources from government and a profit-making private sector. America's success in the 1960s in promoting community development relied heavily upon the growth potential of an expanding capitalism – a condition which, in Britain in the 1980s, has not been reproduced.

Postscript, October 1985
Disturbances in Handsworth, Brixton, Toxteth and Tottenham

The night of 6–7 October 1985 produced the most violent scenes in a British mainland disturbance yet recorded. The violence resulted in the death of a policeman and the use by rioters of shotguns and a revolver against the police. The disorders followed the events of 9 and 10 September in the Handsworth district of Birmingham, the 28 and 29 September disorders in Brixton and the disturbances of 1 October in Toxteth in Liverpool. Inevitably, the disorders stimulated renewed controversy about the nature of government measures to deal with rising unemployment, about the state of inner-city areas and about the place of blacks in British society.

Enoch Powell MP again raised the theme contained in so many of his speeches since 1968, for repatriation of black immigrants (and now also of British-born blacks as well). For Mr Powell, it was Handsworth which presented an opportunity to remind the British public again that the return of blacks to their 'homelands' would be an effective way of preventing future social disorder. Mr Powell's speech on this subject coincided with statements by Labour politicians which implicitly, and often quite explicitly, laid the blame for the disturbances on sections of the black community who were allegedly influenced either by drug traders or hooligan elements. In this 'debate' the root causes of social disorder were often ignored and the 'unorganized' black (and white) youth – first of Handsworth, then of Brixton, Toxteth and Tottenham – left to carry responsibility for fundamental ills within the inner cities.

The acts of violence were, it is true, committed by rioters, many of whom were no doubt hooligans in the strict sense of the term, but while such actions were not politically or socially productive it could be argued that they should not have been used as an opportunity for politicians to deny important causal factors at the expense of the very people affected by social deprivation and racial discrimination in employment, housing, education and welfare. Many of the government's Urban Programme and local-authority urban initiatives, particularly those launched since the Scarman Report, had themselves initially been designed to address some of the problems officially recognized as being related to deprivation, urban decay and racism. They had even achieved a degree of political co-operation from black community leaders and had encouraged blacks to establish small businesses, join community projects and develop various cultural and artistic programmes. The disturbances, however, were an indication of the inadequacy of local programmes with respect to the recruitment of the 'unorganized' and the unemployed. It was also evident that suspicions about such initiatives still ran deep in Handsworth, Brixton and Toxteth, and that these were reinforced by a wide disrespect for the police in these areas – which apparently had intensified since 1981. This was the case despite attempts to implement effective 'community policing' strategies which, in Handsworth, dated back as far as 1977 when the Superintendent of Police, David Webb, introduced his officers 'on the beat' to local streets. The close contact of these officers with the local community was intended to improve police/community relations and it provided a model for Lord Scarman and for future policing strategies in other areas. In Birmingham, it seems that by 1985 Mr Geoffrey Dear, the Chief Constable of the West Midlands, had decided to implement a rather more traditional policing approach, in response to an increasing crime rate and general shortage of police manpower. The 'hard' policing in Handsworth inevitably caused resentment within the black community and seems to have contributed to the increasing tensions which led to the outbreak of the 1985 disorders. A similar 'hard' policing approach also seems to have been adopted in Brixton.

Handsworth 1985

It is expected that the precise pattern of events leading up to the disturbances will be revealed following future Public Inquiries, but at the time of writing a fairly clear picture has already emerged about the Handsworth events. On Sunday 8 September an Afro-Caribbean carnival took place without any problems, but on the following day two incidents occurred which proved to be potentially explosive. The first saw the stabbing in the arm of an Asian shopkeeper by a West Indian at 11:30 am. At about 5:30 pm a policeman attempted to arrest a West Indian, suspected of driving a stolen car, near the Villa Cross public house at the end of Lozells Road. West Indian youths threatened the policeman, punching him and facilitating the escape of the suspect. Police reinforcements arrived, only to be met with a barrage of abuse and physical violence from black youths.

According to police reports it was about three hours before further trouble occurred. At approximately 8:00 pm the fire brigade was called to a fire at an old bingo hall opposite the Villa Cross public house. Violence erupted as black youths threw stones at the firemen and minutes later the first petrol bombs were thrown. The firemen retreated as a crowd of some 400 youths gathered at the scene and police equipped with protective helmets and riot shields were drafted into the area.

The strong police presence caused the crowd to retreat down Lozells Road towards a shopping area where there was a large number of ethnic-minority-owned shops and businesses. The retreat was accompanied by firebombing and looting which resulted in the destruction of shops and business premises. Rioters also constructed barricades and overturned cars as police slowly moved in, eventually sealing off the whole Lozells area. By 10:00 pm the police had advanced over the barricades in an attempt to contain the disturbances. During the early hours of Tuesday the disorders had subsided and the police had control of the streets.

In the morning it was evident that the devastation was extensive, having resulted in the destruction of properties which had formed part of one of the major commercial areas of the Handsworth district. Angry Asian and West Indian businessmen were quick to complain about what they regarded as open hooliganism; but they also complained that the police response to the situation had been inadequate and had paid little attention to the very urgent plight of Asian businesses which had come under attack. Gradually the traders began to articulate an essentially conservative view, centring upon criticisms of both the police and the chairman of the Birmingham Community Relations Council. The attitude of the traders, also adopted by various Asian groups, thus became an important feature of the Handsworth events, which also involved a serious open split between some Asian leaders and the CRC.

The marked conservative response was a by-product of the character of local CRC politics which tended to foster political moderation and 'responsible' leadership. To some extent this created the conditions for the increasing 'visibility' of conservative groupings and community notables. These groups and individuals had consolidated their position in Birmingham during the 1980s as their economic, commercial and business base expanded and at a time when the activist and militant left had been weakened locally and nationally by political conditions which were generally unfavourable to them.

Despite the differences within the CRC, the call for community calm was not confined simply to local traders or to the more 'moderate' or conservative groups. Communal peace was an objective that was common to other organized political groups concerned to influence community affairs and to prevent a repetition of the street violence which had served to disrupt the social fabric of Handsworth. Leaders of many shades of opinion, both within and outside the CRC and within the local Labour Party, were concerned about community tensions and many were also worried about the reaction to the visit of the Home Secretary, Mr Douglas Hurd, who came to the area on 10 September. Mr Hurd was pelted with stones, jeered by a crowd and forced to leave the area hurriedly, after expressing his own concern about the situation and about the discovery that two Asians had been killed during the height of the disorders, when a small sub-post-office which they were in burnt down (subsequently a white man was charged with their murder). Mr Hurd's hostile reception and the news of the deaths led to intensified demands for a full government inquiry.

The Hurd visit did nothing to alter the government's decision not to mount another Scarman-type inquiry. Instead, a police inquiry was to be initiated, but its announcement was met with condemnation from black groups, both Asian and Afro-Caribbean, who preferred to support Birmingham City Council's proposed inquiry which, it was claimed, would be more impartial and more likely to take note of black representations. Jeff Rooker, the local Labour Member of Parliament, lent his support to the idea of a city council inquiry by pointing to what he called 'different reasons' for not relying upon a police investigation. In a quote in *The Times* of 14 September it was clear that by this Rooker was taking into account opposition to a police inquiry from those who were critical of alleged police inaction and 'softness' towards the rioters, as well as opposition expressed by more militant and leftist organizations who were complaining about the 'harshness' of police tactics.

Rooker's comments followed the announcement that Asian representatives on the CRC had drafted a joint letter of resignation in protest against the CRC's own 'soft' attitude towards the rioters. The protest was reportedly supported by 20 members of the CRC representing the Indian, Pakistani and Bangladeshi communities and centred upon the demand for the resignation of James Hunte, Chairman of the CRC and a black Handsworth Labour county councillor. There were also demands for the resignation of the CRC's Principal Community Relations Officer.

At the time of writing, however, no resignations have been submitted to the CRC formally, despite the generation of much heated argument. Indeed, the revolt within the CRC seems to have taken a rather less dramatic course than that suggested in the newspapers. The resignations threat itself, according to one reliable source, was confined to only seven Asian members of the CRC, plus two who were publicly threatening to 'resign' but who were not in fact CRC members.

One reason for the controversy focusing upon personalities was the peculiar nature of Birmingham CRC's way of achieving community representation. Unlike other CRCs there were no ethnic-minority organizations affiliated to the CRC. Instead, only individuals were represented, on the basis of ethnic identity. Many of these individuals could be selected by the ethnic groups themselves, a practice which tended to favour moderate or conservative religious leaders and moderate community notables. At the end of September 1985, CRC membership included three Pakistanis, ten Indians (including East African Indians), five Pakistanis (including East African Pakistanis) and sixteen Afro-Caribbeans, although Afro-Caribbeans were proportionately better represented on the CRC's Executive than the Asians. This disproportionate representation added fuel to the 'resignations' controversy and helped to stimulate interest in the possibility of the dissident Asians tending to support more strongly an organization to rival the CRC.

The core of this organization was forming around the so-called Community Advisory Liaison Committee (CALC). CALC had been formed following an initiative by Birmingham City Council and the Ethnic-minority Liaison Committee (EMLC) of the Birmingham District Labour Party. CALC was not, however, officially recognized by the city council. This was related to CALC's lack of Afro-Caribbean representation and the fact that CALC had been formed only after the council's initiative had clearly failed to produce a broadly based Asian and Afro-Caribbean organization which could have acted in an advisory capacity in local-authority consultations relating to race issues.

In a letter in *The Guardian* of 20 September 1985, an EMLC representative indicated that EMLC was 'deeply concerned' about some of the divisive statements being made, especially within the Asian community and by CALC. The day before, in the same newspaper, Bilhu Singh, a member of the Asian Youth Movement in Handsworth, also expressed opposition to the political stance adopted by what were described as 'Asian shopkeepers', who were 'very much organized as Conservatives in alliance with the police'. Although this claim was not substantiated it did highlight the tone of the essentially left/right political character of the differences between groups in Handsworth.

While the strength of these differences seems to have increased since 1981, it should be recalled that this book has shown that the diversity of the political responses of black organizations has always been a characteristic feature of local political situations, and that this diversity affects post-disorder political alignments and relationships among ethnic-minority groups, local authorities and the police. Handsworth in 1985 proved to be unexceptional when it came to the manifestation of moderate-versus-militant demands, the expression of rhetorical demands by radicals (and conservatives), and the use of tactical boycotts and resignation threats. In Handsworth, however, the political basis of inter-group differences was to some extent expressed in terms of differences between Asians and Afro-Caribbeans on the CRC.

As stated in Chapter 6, different local circumstances and immediate practical political considerations influence the nature of specific local reactions following disorders. In general, however, the attractions of compromise, order and consent are powerful amongst black leaders. While there is no 'iron law' compelling leaders to orientate towards existing processes and institutions, there is a strong tendency for them to want to maximise their political resources and reduce the costs of political isolation. The wide support for Birmingham's Public Inquiry into the Handsworth events was an indication of this, as was the willingness of Asian leaders to maintain their positions on the CRC (even though reluctantly). Similarly, for many more radical leaders there was little mileage to be gained from absentionism, although many were forced to be highly critical of the police in response to 'rank-and-file' pressure (this was especially so following the 1985 events in Brixton and Tottenham, where community feelings prompted a critical response from many black leaders). In Birmingham, as elsewhere, the local CRC also provided one way of campaigning for reforms, and, even outside the CRC, the local Urban Programme initiatives and projects could still offer the prospect of increasing group resources, however limited the 'benefit' may have been. Clearly such programmes had not eliminated basic economic and social problems, but they had helped to maintain a climate in which political incentives associated with co-operation had remained attractive to black leaders with reformist political ambitions.

Brixton 1985

The disorders in Brixton stemmed directly from an incident on Saturday 28 September involving the police and a black woman, Mrs Cherry Groce. Mrs Groce was shot in her home when armed police called during a search for her son in connection with an arms charge. Shortly after the 7:00 am shooting, Mrs Groce was reported to have a wound in her back, and remained seriously injured. The police stated that the shooting had been a mistake and issued an early apology. During the morning a crowd of about 50 people gathered outside Mrs Groce's home in Normandy Road, Brixton, chanting various terms of abuse at the police and unsuccessfully attempted to advance on the house. Later, protesters gathered outside Brixton police station as tension increased and the mood of the crowd became more volatile.

By 6:00 pm several hundred people, many wearing face masks, had assembled outside the police station. Bricks and bottles were thrown and then petrol bombs were aimed at the building. The petrol bombs fell on target, landing in an upper floor of the police station. Fire engines arrived on the scene, only to be met with more bottles and stones. Then, from inside the police station, police in riot gear emerged to disperse the crowd. While retreating, the crowd of both whites and blacks overturned cars and burned buildings. Widespread disorder had thus been sparked off, which involved Brixton and eventually other areas of south London as well. The disturbances lasted throughout the night, to be brought under control only in the early hours of the Sunday morning.

The police shooting of Mrs Groce had come at the worst possible time for those involved in community-relations work. The Handsworth events had provided a 'model' for the unorganized youths of Brixton, and the Groce shooting had provoked a deep-seated ill-feeling towards the police throughout the black community. For moderate black leaders this inevitably produced political pressures from 'below' which, in turn, meant that protest was widely expressed. However, if moderate leadership responses were critical, they were also quite guarded, given the situation and the strength of feeling in the community. One reason for this may have been related to the record of the local Police Consultative Committee, which had established close contacts between police and community representatives. The committee was established following the Scarman Report, as a Home Office-supported body. In the 1 October 1985 edition of *The Times*, Canon Charles Walker, a Roman Catholic priest and former committee chairman, claimed that the police committee included tenant and neighbourhood associations and 'the main community organizations' in Brixton. This was despite the withdrawal of support for the committee by the Labour-controlled Lambeth Borough Council which, in opposition to the claims of the Canon, regarded the committee as not properly representing the community. Mr Richard Allen, a council officer working for the committee, claimed that the committee was nevertheless taking steps to consult more effectively with local people, but admitted that the 45 organizations associated with the committee were 'establishment' (*The Times*, 1 October 1985) and that only about 20 per cent of those attending meetings were black. Clarence Thompson, treasurer of the Railton Road Youth Centre and general secretary of the West Indian Standing Conference, was also quoted as having declined to sit on the police committee because of suspicions in the community. However, according to the newspaper report he did not support those who had rioted and 'he did not represent them when they were attacking the police'.

If the responses of many moderate leaders were guarded, then the same could be said of the comments of the Home Secretary. Douglas Hurd's response to the Brixton disorders was interesting in its admission that the troubles were part of a larger problem afflicting the inner cities. Mr Hurd, in a *World at One* national radio interview on 29 September, stated that a police officer had made what he called 'a terrible mistake' in shooting the innocent Mrs Groce. This, according to Mr Hurd, was a good reason for a police inquiry into the incident although not an excuse for violence. Mr Hurd, however, admitted that 'there are hideous social and economic problems in many of our inner cities, as there are indeed throughout the United States and throughout Europe as well'. He went on to say that even after investment in urban initiatives 'you still have the risk of disorder, and in those circumstances it is the job of the police to keep order and the job of everybody in the community, including community leaders, to help them to do that'. In this context Mr Hurd added that 'we still haven't got a proper sense of community in all parts of our country, and I think there are many reasons for this'. What the Home Secretary called the need for 'building the community' thus involved the concept of involvement in political, economic and other programmes which would supplement police control and integrate leaders more effectively into 'legitimate' processes, with the consent of the wider community. This view of urban renewal and political alignment is illustrated clearly in Chapters 7 and 8, where it is shown that the government has placed great stress upon the need for 'corporate responsibility' in its bid to reduce communal tensions. Handsworth and Brixton served to underscore the government's commitment to that broad strategy.

Toxteth 1985

The outbreak of disturbances in the streets of Toxteth during the evening of 1 October 1985 seemed to confirm the Home Secretary's view that disturbances were still possible even after government investment in urban initiatives. In some respects Liverpool initiatives had been the model for those elsewhere. But in Liverpool, left-led Labour councillors were facing disqualification from office over their defiance of central government expenditure penalties and conditions within the inner city were adversely affected by the additional factor of impending local-authority financial crisis.

Rather ironically, the disturbances took place on the evening following the historic condemnation of Liverpool's Labour council by Party Leader Neil Kinnock at the 1985 Party Conference. Mr Kinnock's views were intended to strengthen the hand of political moderates and therefore contrasted strongly with the militancy of local protest groups. Seen in this light, the moderate Labour politics of Mr Kinnock appeared to have rather more in common with Mr Douglas Hurd's plea for a 'sense of community' than with the philosophy of community activism propounded by the Liverpool Labour left.

Tottenham 1985

There was, however, a very obvious lack of 'sense of community' in Tottenham on the night of 6–7 October, when violence erupted following an incident in which Mrs Cynthia Jarrett, a black Tottenham woman, was reported to have collapsed and died during a police search of her home. Relatives of Mrs Jarrett led a march to Tottenham police station on 6 October and major violence began after community leaders had spoken to a public meeting on the predominantly black Broadwater Farm council housing estate.

A crowd began to throw petrol bombs in Willan Road, close to the estate, at around 7:00 pm, and the disturbances quickly spread to nearby streets. Police sealed off the area but this failed to control the escalation of the riot. As police moved into the area in greater force, the rioters resorted to burning cars and properties and launched a concentrated series of attacks on the massed police lines. The Broadwater Farm housing complex gradually came to assume the character of a 'base' for the rioters, who found that their strategic advantage lay there, since many of the overhead ramps and walkways on the estate could be used to hail missiles down on the police. The intensity of the attack on the police became very clear as petrol bombs, bricks and concrete blocks rained upon police riot shields and helmets. In addition, shotgun and revolver reports could be heard mingled with the frightening din. A policeman died from knife wounds and two policemen and three journalists were treated in hospital for gunshot wounds. Police on the scene of the riot were reported to have been prepared to use plastic bullets and tear gas in response to the situation, but the decision to use such tactics was withheld, apparently, in favour of an eventual advance into the housing complex using more 'traditional' methods.

Sir Kenneth Newman, Commissioner of the Metropolitan Police was on the scene to direct the advance into the complex at 4:00 am on the morning of 7 October. Sir Kenneth, at a press conference later, promised that plastic bullets and CS gas would be used, if necessary, in future instances when the scale of violence reached seriously high levels. There is little doubt, therefore, that the police and the Home Office had become actively concerned by the intensity of the disturbances and the implications of the possibility of the police losing control in riot situations. There was also concern amongst community leaders that they too had lost control at the crucial time of the build-up to violence in Tottenham on 6 October. Sir Kenneth Newman, like many of these community leaders, claimed to be concerned about the consequences of the alienation felt in many communities (Channel 4 television interview, 7 October) but was also critical of many community leaders and politicians who were, according to the Commissioner, over-critical of the police and unhelpful in co-operating with local police initiatives.

Indeed, community leaders in Tottenham remained highly critical of the police. The intensity of the riot was therefore reflected in the sharpness of the reactions to it, and for community leaders this meant responding to and, to some extent adapting to, the 'demands' of the community insofar as they expressed dissatisfaction and hostility towards police tactics. Sir Kenneth Newman's allegation that the riot had been influenced by agitators and political activists did nothing to quell the criticisms voiced by community leaders and certainly failed to convince the rioters that they had been wrong to take to the streets. Mr Bernie Grant, black Labour Leader of the local Haringey Council, was prominent in criticizing the initial police action at Mrs Jarrett's home and this led to further criticism of police action during the riot itself and threats to withdraw Haringey's financial contribution to the police. Grant's intervention helped him, as an important community representative, to maintain his authority within the broader black community and enabled him to articulate a radical-sounding political response, while at the same time working to restore communal order. In that respect Grant's view and his general response quite effectively met the immediate practical political needs of the moment, particularly as far as established local leaders were concerned. Indeed, as with the 1981 disorders and the events in 1985 in Handsworth, Brixton and Toxteth, it was these established leaders who quickly returned to the centre of the political stage once the flames of riot had burned out. This was as crucial to maintaining order as the view of Sir Kenneth Newman that order depended upon 'physical' measures and the effective deployment of police resources. Should the moderates' position be undermined by political radicalism or be modified by other circumstances, this could seriously threaten the chances of political compromise during times of social unrest. In 1985, however, the unorganized nature of the disturbances failed to create the conditions for an end to the politics of political reform. The call for greater police accountability from moderate leaders and also from more militant groups served as an indication of the desire to remain within the prevailing participatory processes existing at local level, despite the opposition to community accountability from the police and despite the proposed adoption of tougher police measures to deal with riot situations. The political rift between Haringey Council and the police thus represented a dispute over the style and tactics of policing, rather than over the fundamental role of the police in relation to the black community and in the context of the powers of the state.

Appendix: Sources

Representatives of the following organizations were interviewed during the course of research for this book:

Britain

Barrow and Geraldine S. Cadbury Trust – 1982
Birmingham Community Relations Council – 1985
Birmingham University Institute of Local Government Studies – 1978
Black Country Co-operative Development Agency – 1982
British-American Tobacco – 1982
British Petroleum, Government and Public Affairs Department – 1984
Business Initiative, Stoke-on-Trent Enterprise Agency – 1984
Business in the Community – 1982
Cannock Road Sikh Temple (Wolverhampton) – 1977
Centre for Employment Initiatives – 1984
Charities Aid Foundation – 1984
Commission for Racial Equality (London) – 1985
Federation of Afro-Caribbean Associations – 1977
Harambee Association – 1977
Home Office Voluntary Services Unit – 1985
Indian Workers' Association (IWA/GB) – 1977
Local Initiative Support (UK) – 1982, 1984, 1985
Manpower Services Commission (Liverpool) – 1982
Manpower Services Commission (Wolverhampton) – 1982
Merseyside Development Corporation – 1982
Merseyside Task Force – 1982
National Council for Voluntary Organizations – 1985
Peat, Marwick, Mitchell and Co. – 1984, 1985
Policy Studies Institute (London) – 1984, 1985
Sikh Association of Great Britain (Wolverhampton) – 1977

Staffordshire County Council, Planning Department – 1980
Staffordshire Development Association – 1984
West Midlands Caribbean Association – 1977
Wolverhampton Anti-Racism Committee – 1977
Wolverhampton Borough Council:
   Education Department – 1977
   Housing Department – 1977, 1978
   Inner Cities Unit – 1982
Wolverhampton Census Survey – 1977
Wolverhampton Council for Community Relations – eight interviews between 1977
   and 1982
Wolverhampton Enterprise Ltd (Enterprise Agency) – 1982, 1983
Wolverhampton Labour Party:
   SW Constituency – 1976
   St Peter's Ward – 1977
Wolverhampton Voluntary Sector Council – 1982

USA

Action for Boston Community Development (Boston, Mass.) – 1984
American Cancer Society (Boston, Mass.) – 1984
Associated Grantmakers of Massachusetts Inc. – 1984
Boston Children's Service Association – 1984
Boston City Council – 1981
Brookline Association for Mental Health (Mass.) – 1984
Executive Office of Communities and Development (Mass. State) – 1984
Family Service Association of Greater Boston – 1984
Jamaica Plain Area Planning Action Council (Boston, Mass.) – 1981
Massachusetts Department of Social Services – 1984
The Medical Foundation (Boston, Mass.) – 1984
State of Massachusetts Office of Community Action – 1984
United Community Planning Corporation (Boston, Mass.) – 1984
United Way of Massachusetts Bay – 1984
Visiting Nurse Association of Boston – 1984
Vocations for Social Change (Boston, Mass.) – 1981

Research resources and additional contacts

Apart from the above-mentioned interviews, between 1977 and 1985 less formal
contacts were maintained with numerous organizations, community workers and
local politicians in both Britain and the United States. In addition, some 200
public and private organizations supplied documentary material relating to their
activities, aims, objectives and finances. An extensive survey of newspaper and
other media sources was initiated in 1980, covering the urban policy field relating
to ethnic-minority issues.

Notes

Introduction: Black politics and urban crisis

1. While population decline in Britain's cities is a generalized problem, there is an important exception. Bradford, in West Yorkshire, actually faces a substantial increase in its total population. With a high fertility rate, coupled with continuing immigration, Bradford expects a 'natural' increase in its net population of some 20,000 between 1982 and 1992 (see Bradford Metropolitan Council's *Bradford's Community Programme, 1982–83*). This will place added strains on social services, community provisions and the educational system in a city which has a large multi-ethnic population.

2. Legislation introduced in 1984 effectively limited the right of local authorities to determine their own rate levels. Limitation, or rate 'capping', could be imposed upon selected local authorities by central government in cases where local councils were regarded by the government as 'overspending'. Central limitation of rate levels implies significant reductions in expenditure on local services which are dependent upon revenue support funded by rates and so it is hardly surprising that many rate-capped authorities, particularly those under Labour Party control, have strongly opposed the introduction of a measure widely regarded as a threat to local autonomy.

3. In July 1985 the government abandoned the system based on expenditure 'targets' and associated penalties for over-running targets. Under this system, 'overspending' above the target resulted in loss of the grant paid by central government to the local authority. In place of this system a different form of penalty was introduced, based upon local block grant mechanisms which allocated money in relation to calculations of local 'needs'. Under the new approach, authorities exceeding government assessments face a reduction in grant or even a 'negative grant' according to their spending record over the previous financial year. In theory the new approach gives central government more effective control, since the old targets frequently worked to favour high spenders following years of increasing expenditure, thus effectively discriminating against many Conservative authorities (and others) which had effected financial restraint.

1.   Race and policy

1. Colin Crouch (1983), in a rejoinder to an article by Ross Martin (1983), points to a continuum of membership discipline and representation which contrasts pluralism and corporatism and which has poles that place opposed weights on the two aspects of intermediation: discipline of members in favour of a general interest; and representation of their interests. At one end, the interested organizations carry out no representative functions and simply discipline their members (authoritarian corporatism). At the other extreme, there are organizations which prosecute the demands of members without compromise. Pluralism is seen to fall 'somewhat short' of the second pole. This may involve groups asking their members for restraint at the conclusion of a bargain, or order to maintain the group's credibility as a bargaining partner (Crouch, 1983, pp.452–60).

   Miller (1983) provides an interesting analysis of pluralism and its contribution to stability in society. This raises the question as to whether pluralism or corporate forms of group/government co-ordination are equally conducive to social stability.

2.   The black constituency

1. Constitution of the IWA (GB), Central Executive Committee, Bradford. For criticisms of the IWA's politics from a radical standpoint see, for example, *Liberation Mukti*, No. 1, Dec. 1977; *Teachers Action*, No. 9, Dec. 1977 (journal of the All-London Teachers Against Racism and Fascism); *On the Lap-Dogs of Indian Fascism*, Indian Workers' Front, 1976 (an attack on the leadership of the Southall IWA).
2. Interviews with IWA (GB) representatives, 3 May 1977 and 30 May 1977.
3. Interviews with Wolverhampton community worker, 1984. The point about moderation is illustrated by reference to the general desire of community leaders in the West Midlands at this time to maintain order. In November 1984 police and community leaders met in Birmingham's Handsworth district to maintain communal calm. Councillor Sardul Marwa, Chairman of Birmingham City Council's Race Relations and Equal Opportunities Committee, condemned street demonstrations by Sikhs (*The Birmingham Post*, 2 November 1984) and was critical of those who celebrated at the time of Mrs Gandhi's assassination. Piara Singh Uppal, National President of the Indian Overseas Congress Party, was also quoted as appealing for calm and communal harmony. Also, Hindus, Sikhs and Moslems were reported as visiting the Indian High Commission in Birmingham to sign the book of condolences for Mrs Gandhi.
4. Some of these ethnic-minority groups were not included in the 1978 survey of groups in Table 3.

3.   Black political action

1. An early detailed study of American community leadership was produced by M. Aiken and P. E. Mott (eds.), *The Structure of Community Power*, in 1970. The collection deals with questions relating to defining 'power', factors influencing configurations of power and interaction among centres of power in communities. The papers relate to the important place of community leaderships and their roles in mobilizing support in communities. Generally leaders develop their own interests through acquisition of political power and control of local economic

resources. Black leaders are seen to be no exception, despite the relative disadvantage of their communities. Reference shoud be made to the paper by L. M. Killian and C. U. Smith, 'Negro Protest Leaders in a Southern Community' (in Aiken and Mott, 1970). This defines the attitudes of younger black leaders and their relatively radical attitudes. It shows the strategies adopted by these leaders in negotiating with local politicians and their desire to locate their politics within already-established black political organizations. See J. B. McKee, 'Community Power and Strategies in Race Relations: Some Critical Observations' (in the same collection). The McKee paper examines theoretical approaches to examining race relations within prevailing community power structures.

2. See *Financial Times*, 17 July 1981; *The Guardian*, 24 July 1981; 4 August 1981. See also *Keesing's Contemporary Archives*, 18 September 1981, pp.31077–81.

3. During 1982–3, 107 organizations were funded by the Ethnic Minorities Committee, 31 of which had a London-wide focus and 76 of which were more locally based. The Committee's grant-aid created or sustained a total of 70 full-time and 26 part-time jobs (although not all were supported during the entire year). To date, in 1983–4 (mid October) 175 grants have been awarded, totalling nearly £2,000,000 (of these grants 75 were originally approved in 1982–3 but included payments for 1983–4).

   Many of the organizations funded provide a variety of social, counselling, welfare and community functions. Such groups include: the Acton Asian Association, Afro-Caribbean Voluntary Self-Help Associations, Afro-Caribbean Community Association, Agudas Israel, Anjuman-E-Islamia, Asian Community Action Group, Bangladesh Centre, Bangladesh Welfare Association, Bengali Community Association, Black Insight Community Organization, Caribbean Progressive Association, Colebrook Social, Cultural and Welfare Association, Dachwng Parents' Association, Family Welfare Association, Hackney CRE Family Centre, Haringey Task Force, Indian Muslim Federation, Indian Workers' Association, Islington Asian Centre, Muslim Welfare Centre, Mixi-Fren, Muslim Parents' Association, Newham Community Renewal Programme, North London Bangladesh Welfare Association, Redbridge Asian Women's Association, St Anthony's Caribbean Association, Shiloh United Church of Christ Apostolic, South London Islamic Centre, Tabernacle Community Association, Tottenham Community Project, Wandsworth Latchkey Development Project, Waltham Forest Caribbean Council, and the West Indian and African Community Association in Deptford (GLC, 1984, section 24–5, p.8).

4.   The race industry

1. Interviews with CRE officials, March 1985.
2. Interviews with CRE officials, March 1985.
3. Interviews with CRE officials, March 1985.
4. See particularly CRE (1985) – a Report which called for a change in the approach to immigration controls by government to achieve equality of treatment in the application of immigration-control procedures. The Report marked the adoption by the CRE of a highly critical stand on a major issue affecting immigrants and blacks in general. It is not clear at the time of writing whether this kind of approach to the immigration issue will be repeated – the investigation having placed considerable demands upon the CRE in terms of time and resources and having drawn attention to the CRE's often controversial role.

5. Housing and education: compromise and consent

1. The greater part of this chapter is based upon research contained in the author's doctoral thesis, *Public Policy and Local Interest Groups in Britain: Three Case-Studies*, University of Keele, 1979.
2. The eight areas were: Ealing, Hackney, Haringey, Slough, Bristol, Leicester, Manchester and Bradford.
3. Interview with Councillor K. Purchase, Chairman of Wolverhampton Housing Management Committee, February 1977. Also interview with representative of the Sikh Association of Great Britain (Wolverhampton), April 1977.
4. Interview with E. C. Le Maitre, then Chief Community Relations Officer, WCCR, November, 1976.
5. See Race Relations Board (1977). These proposals were in line with the recommendations first put forward in 1968 by the Cullingworth Committee (Central Housing Advisory Committee to Ministry of Housing and Local Government).
6. The need to make special provision for black children without harming the interests of the rest of the community was stated by D. Grayson, Director of Education, in evidence submitted to the House of Commons Select Committee on Race Relations and Immigration (1975–6), paras. 565–7.
7. See request from Home Secretary in 'Urban Deprivation' (Home Office and CRC, 1977), p.v. The various policy statements were: Education and Community Relations (CRC, 1973); Educational Needs of Children from Minority Groups (CRC, 1974); In-Service Education of Teachers in Multi-Racial Areas (CRC, 1974); Unemployment and Homelessness: A Report (CRC, 1974); Language Teaching and Community Relations (CRC, 1974); Who Minds? (CRC, 1975).
8. Minutes of Education and Race Conference, October 1975. Quotes were not attributed to particular individuals. More moderate papers were presented by G. Barnsby (Wolverhampton Communist Party), *Problems of Working Class, Multi-Racial Education in Wolverhampton* and G. S. Sanghera (General Secretary of IWA (GB)), *Unfair Education*.
9. Minutes of IWA (GB) conference. The dissatisfaction of the West Midlands Caribbean Association with the MRE led to moves to establish their own 'black school' in Wolverhampton.
10. Letter from N. S. Noor (President of the IWA (GB), Wolverhampton) in *Express and Star*, 21 April 1977. There were indications that Noor had the support of others outside the black community. The President of the Wolverhampton Association of Teachers expressed similar sentiments in the local press (*Express and Star*, 25 February 1977).
11. Letter from D. Grayson (Director of Education) in *Express and Star*, 27 April 1977.
12. For example, interview with F. Carter (Deputy Director of Education), August 1977.
13. Interview with D. Grayson (Director of Education), August 1977.
14. At the time of writing, local authority reorganization in Wolverhampton had been initiated in the early part of 1985 and was still at the implementation stage. The town's Inner Areas Unit has been renamed 'Special Programmes' and made responsible to a new Policy Unit, which was also to be in charge of race-relations matters. A new Race Relations and Equal Opportunities Officer has been appointed to head a small support team concerned with local-authority policy both

internally (i.e. conditions of service, etc., in the local authority) and externally. 'Equal opportunities' was to be seen in terms of assistance and advice to ethnic minorities, women and other disadvantaged groups, such as the disabled.

6.   Riot and dissent

1. The membership of the unofficial Committee of Inquiry was as follows: Michael Dummett, Wykeham Professor of Philosophy and Logic, University of Oxford (Chairman); Roger Butler, Southall District Secretary, Amalgamated Union of Engineering Workers; Stuart Hall, Professor of Sociology, Open University; Patricia Hewitt, General Secretary, National Council for Civil Liberties; Bill Keys, General Secretary, Society of Graphical and Allied Trades and Member, General Council of the TUC; Joan Lestor, Member of Parliament for Eton and Slough; Dick North, member of the Executive Commitee, National Union of Teachers; Paul O'Higgins, Reader in Law, University of Cambridge; Ranjit Songhi, Director, Asian Resources Centre, Birmingham; the Rt Revd Hewlett Thompson, Bishop of Willesden; Pauline Webb, Methodist Church. The Committee had the following terms of reference:
to establish a full and accurate account of events in Southall on Monday 23 April 1979 and the night of 23/24 April relating to the National Front meeting in the Town Hall, and the background to those events, and to consider:
   (1) The decision to allow the National Front to hold an election meeting in the Southall Town Hall; the responsibilities of local authorities under the Representation of the People Act and the Race Relations Act; and the procedures used for taking such decisions.
   (2) The response of the community in Southall to that decision.
   (3) The presence of people from other areas, and their part in the original protest and subsequent events.
   (4) The reaction of the police to the decision to allow the meeting, and their response to representations from local community groups; the powers and responsibilities of the police under the Public Order Act and common law.
   (5) The development of confrontation on 23 April between the police and members of the public, including the use of police from outside the division and the role of the Special Patrol Group; the nature and extent of injuries suffered by police and public; the circumstances leading to the death of Blair Peach; and the procedures used by the police for the arrest and detention of suspects.
   (6) The treatment of these events by the press, radio and television.
   (7) Subsequent events in Southall.
And to make recommendations for the consideration of the relevant agencies.
2. 12.5% of Lambeth Borough's population was West Indian with Indians, Pakistanis and Bangladeshis accounting for 2.4% and Africans and other non-white and mixed minorities making up 6.5% (see Scarman Report, 1981, para. 2.15).
3. Among those diverse groups which submitted written evidence to Lord Scarman were: All Faiths for One Race; Battersea Community Action Group; Brixton Advice Centre; Brixton Community Arts Centre; the Friends of Blair Peach Committee; Lambeth Youth Committee; Legalize Cannabis Campaign; National Association for Asian Youth; National Council for Civil Liberties; Railton-Mayall

Residents' Action Group; Rasta International HQ; South London Islamic Centre; Stoke Newington Community Association; and the West Indian Standing Conference. In all, nine parties were represented before the Inquiry throughout the hearing of all the evidence: the Commissioner of the Metropolitan Police; Concern; the Council for Community Relations in Lambeth (CCRL); the London Borough of Lambeth; the Brixton Neighbourhood Community Association (BNCA); the Brixton Domino and Social Club; the Melting-Pot Foundation; the Railton Road Youth and Community Centre; and the Rastafarian Collective.

7. Urban renewal

1. The London figure covers UP Partnership, Programme and UP-designated districts.
2. Three interviews were conducted with representatives of the Merseyside Task Force (one civil servant, one from the Manpower Services Commission and one MTF secondee from the private sector) in June 1982. Reference has also been made to a draft paper by P. Lindley of the Civil Service College (1983), presented at a Political Studies Association (UK) Workshop at Oxford Polytechnic.
3. Interview with MTF representative, June 1982.
4. Interviews with MTF and MDC representatives, June 1982.
5. Merseyside Development Corporation, *Initial Development Strategy*, August 1981 and interviews which supported this view.
6. Lambeth Inner-City Partnership (1982) *Working Group on Private Sector Investment, Final Report*, pp.2–6. The Working Group was chaired by Sir John Prideaux, Director of Arbuthnot Latham Holding Ltd and included representatives from private-sector firms, community organizations (Lambeth Co-operative Development Agency and the South Bank Centre for Employment Initiatives – incorporating New World Business Services Ltd) and from the DOE and local authorities involved in the Partnership (Lambeth and the Greater London Council).

8. Policies considered

1. These aspects of decentralization were first dealt with by the present author in a paper entitled 'Private Initiative and Community Responsibility: A Strategy for the Black Community?' at the Race and Politics Conference held at St Hugh's College, Oxford, September 1984. The conference was organized by the Centre for Research in Ethnic Relations at the University of Warwick and supported by the Economic and Social Research Council.
2. See also CRE, Employment Report Supplement (1984) and CRE/Royal Town Planning Institute (1983).
3. See Ford Foundation (US) (1973, 1980). For a broader perspective on corporate involvement at local level see Verity (1982).
4. Research conducted in Boston, USA, September 1984, findings to be published. See also, United Way of Massachusetts Bay (1983) and United Community Planning Corporation (1982, 1983).
5. Interviews conducted with human-service agencies and community-programme managers and government agencies in Boston, USA, September 1984. For the corporate view see Johnson (1982). For a radical critique of corporate involvement in general in the community see Boston Urban Study Group (1984).

Bibliography

Aiken, M. and Mott, P. E. (eds.) (1970), *The Structure of Community Power* (New York, Random House).

Aurora, G. S. (1967), *The New Frontiersmen* (Bombay, Popular Prakashan).

Bains, H. (1984), *Multi-Racist Britain* (London, Macmillan).

Banton, M. (1972), *Racial Minorities* (London, Fontana/Collins).

Beetham, D. (1970), *Transport and Turbans* (London, Oxford University Press, for Institute of Race Relations).

Behrens, R. and Edmonds, J. (1981), 'Kippers, Kittens and Kipper Boxes: Conservative Populists and Race Relations', *Political Quarterly*, vol.52, 1981, pp.342–7.

Ben-Tovim, G. and Gabriel, T. (1979), 'The Politics of Race in Britain 1962–79: A Review of the Major Trends and of Recent Debates', in Husband (1982), pp.145–71.

Benyon, J. (ed.), *Scarman and After* (Oxford, Pergamon Press).

Berger, J. and Mohr, J. (1975), *A Seventh Man* (Harmondsworth, Penguin).

Bethnal Green and Stepney Trades Council (1978), *Blood in the Streets: A Report by Bethnal Green and Stepney Trades Council on Racial Attacks in East London*.

Birmingham Community Relations Council (BCRC) (1980–1), *Annual Report*.

Birmingham Inner City Partnership (BICP) (1982a), *Birmingham Inner City Profile, 1982*.

Birmingham Inner City Partnership (BICP) (1982b), *Inner City Partnership Programme 1983–86*.

Boston Urban Study Group (1984), *Who Rules Boston? A Citizen's Guide to Reclaiming the City* (Boston, Mass., The Institute of Democratic Socialism).

Boutelle, P. (ed.) (1969), *The Black Uprisings: Newark, Detroit 1967* (New York, Merit Publishers).

Bradford Metropolitan Council (1982), *Bradford's Community Programme 1982–83*.

Bridges, L. (1981), 'Keeping the Lid on: British Urban Social Policy 1975–81', *Race and Class*, vol.23, nos.2–3, Autumn/Winter, pp.171–85.

Brixton Defence Campaign (1981), 'The Brixton Defence Campaign says Boycott the Scarman Inquiry', *Race and Class*, vol.23, nos.2–3, Autumn/Winter, p.223.

Brooks, A. (1983), 'Black Business in Lambeth: Obstacles to Expansion', *New Community*, vol.11, nos. 1–2, pp.42–54.

Brown, C. (1983), 'Ethnic Pluralism in Britain: Demographic and Legal Background', in Glazer, N. and Young, K. (eds.) (1983), pp.32–54.

Bunyan, T. (1981), 'The Police against the People', *Race and Class*, vol.23, nos.2–3, Autumn/Winter, pp.153–70.

Business in the Community (BIC) (1982), *Newsletter*, June.

Cameron, G. C. (1980), *The Future of the British Conurbations: Policies and Prescription for Change* (London, Longman).

Cashmore, E. and Troyna, B. (eds.) (1982), *Black Youth in Crisis* (London, George Allen and Unwin).

Castells, M. (1975), 'Advanced Capitalism, Collective Consumption and Urban Contradictions', in Lindberg, Alford, Crouch and Offe (1975).

Centre for Contemporary Cultural Studies (1982), *The Empire Strikes Back: Race and Racism in 70s Britain* (London, Hutchinson).

Charities Aid Foundation (1983), *Charity Statistics 1982–83* (CAF, London).

Claiborne, L. (1983), with material by Friedman, J. R., Cooke, B., Menon, K. and Stephen, D., *Race Law in Britain and the United States*, Minority Rights Group Report no.22, 3rd edition.

Clark, D. (1973), 'Urban Blacks and Irishmen: Brothers in Prejudice', in Ershkowitz and Zikmund (1973), pp.15–30.

Clark, P. and Rughani, M. (1983), 'Asian Entrepreneurs from Leicester in Wholesaling and Manufacturing', *New Community*, vol.11, nos.1–2, pp.23–33.

Clarke, S. and Ginsburg, N. (1975), 'The Political Economy of Housing', *Political Economy of Housing Workshop: Political Economy and the Housing Question*, Conference of Socialist Economists, London.

Cockburn, C. (1977), *The Local State* (London, Pluto).

Coleman, M. and McLemore, L. B. (1982), 'Black Independent Politics in Mississippi: Constants and Challenges', in Preston, Henderson and Puryear (1982), pp.131–56.

Commission for Racial Equality (CRE), *Annual Report* (1981a) (HMSO).

Commission for Racial Equality (CRE), *Local Authorities and the Education Implications of Section 71 of the Race Relations Act 1976* (HMSO).

Commission for Racial Equality (1982), *Annual Report*.

Commission for Racial Equality (1983), *Annual Report*.

Commission for Racial Equality (1984a), Employment Report Supplement, *Local Authorities and Black Business Development*.

Commission for Racial Equality (1984b), *Race and Council Housing in Hackney: Report of a Formal Investigation, conducted by the CRE into the Allocation of Housing in the London Borough of Hackney*.

Commission for Racial Equality (1985), *Immigration Control Procedures: Report of a Formal Investigation*.

Commission for Racial Equality/Royal Town Planning Institute (1983), *Working Party on the Role of Planners*.

Commonwealth of Massachusetts (1983), *The Report of the Governor's Task Force on Private Sector Initiatives*.

Community Relations Commission (1975), *Participation of Ethnic Minorities in the General Election, October 1974*.

Community Relations Commission (1976), *Housing in Multi-Racial Areas* (Working Party of Housing Directors).

Council on Foundations (1982), *Corporate Philanthropy, Philosophy, Management, Trends, Future Background* (Washington, DC).

Cross, C. (1961), *The Fascists in Britain* (London, Barrie and Rockliff).

Crouch, C. (1983), 'Pluralism and the New Corporatism: A Rejoinder', *Political Studies*, vol. 31, no. 3, September, pp.452–60.

Cushmore, E. and Troyna, B. (eds.) (1982), *Black Youth in Crisis* (London, George Allen and Unwin).

Dahl, R. A. and Lindblom, C. E. (1976), *Politics, Economics and Welfare* (Chicago, Chicago University Press).

Deakin, N. (ed.) (1965), *Colour and the British Electorate 1964* (London, Pall Mall Press).

Dearlove, J. (1973), *Politics and Policy in Local Government* (Cambridge, Cambridge University Press).

Department of the Environment (DOE) (1980), *Review of the Traditional Urban Programme Consultative Document* (Inner Cities Directorate).

Department of the Environment (1984), *Monitoring the Urban Programme.*

Desai, R. (1963), *Indian Immigrants in Britain* (London, Oxford University Press, for Institute of Race Relations).

Dettmar, R. P. (1981), 'Grants Management by State and Local Governments: A Systematic Approach'. *GAO Review* (Washington DC, General Accounting Office), Spring, pp.58–63.

DeWitt, J. (1969), *Indian Workers' Associations in Britain* (London, Oxford University Press, for Institute of Race Relations).

Downs, A. (1967), *Inside Bureaucracy* (New York, Little, Brown).

Dummett, M. and A. (1969), 'The Role of Government in Britain's Racial Crisis', in Husband (1982), pp.97–127.

Dunleavy, P. (1980), *Urban Political Analysis: The Politics of Collective Consumption* (London, Macmillan).

Edwards, J. E. and Batley, R. (1978), *The Politics of Positive Discrimination* (London, Tavistock Publications).

Ershkowitz, M. and Zikmund II, J. (eds.) (1973), *Black Politics in Philadelphia* (New York, Basic Books).

Fitzgerald, M. (1984), *Political Parties and Black People: Participation, Representation and Exploitation* (London, The Runnymede Trust).

Flett, H. (1979), *Black Council Tenants in Birmingham*, ESRC Research Unit on Ethnic Relations Working Paper (University of Warwick).

Foot, P. (1965), *Immigration and Race in British Politics* (Harmondsworth, Penguin).

Ford Foundation (US) (1973), *Community Development Corporations: A Strategy for Depressed Urban and Rural Areas*, Ford Foundation Policy Paper, May (New York).

Ford Foundation (US) (1980), *The Local Initiatives Support Corporation*, Ford Foundation Background Paper, May (New York).

The Foundation Center (1981), *The Foundation Directory*, 8th edition (New York).

Freeman, R. B. (1983), 'Public Policy and Employment Discrimination in the United States', in Glazer, and Young (1983), pp.124–44.

Friedland, R. (1982), *Power and Crisis in the City: Corporations, Unions and Urban Policy* (London, Macmillan).

Gilliam, R. E. (1975), *Black Political Development: An Advocacy Analysis* (Port Washington, N.Y., Dunellen).

Glazer, N. and Young, K. (eds.) (1983), *Ethnic Pluralism and Public Policy: Achieving Equality in the United States and Britain* (American Academy of Arts and Sciences, Commission for Racial Equality, Policy Studies Institute: London, Heinemann).

Gosnell, H. F. (1967), *Negro Politics: The Rise of Negro Politics in Chicago* (Chicago, University of Chicago Press).

Greater Boston Chamber of Commerce (1983–4), *Annual Report* (Boston, Mass.).

Greater Boston Chamber of Commerce (1984), *Boston Report*, vol.1, no.2, January.

Greater London Council (GLC) (1976), *Colour and the Allocation of GLC Housing*, Research Report 21.

Greater London Council (1984), *Responses by GLC Committees to the Government's White Paper, 'Streamlining the Cities'*.

Greater London Enterprise Board (1984), *A Strategy for Co-operation: Worker Co-ops in London*.

Greater Manchester Council (1981), *Report of the Moss Side Enquiry Panel to the Leader of Greater Manchester Council*, 30 September.

Gutch, R. (1985), *Learning from LA: Report of a Visit to Los Angeles to Study Black Community Projects and Race Relations Initiatives* (London Borough of Brent Project Report, Chief Executive's Office).

Hatry, H. P., Winnie, R. E. and Fisk, D. M. (1981), *Practical Program Evaluation for State and Local Governments* (Washington DC, The Urban Institute).

Heclo, H. (1978), 'Issue Networks and the Executive Establishment', in King (1978), pp.87–124.

Hill, M. J. and Issacharoff, R. M. (1971), *Community Action and Race Relations* (London, Oxford University Press for Institute of Race Relations).

Hillson, J. (1977), *The Battle of Boston* (New York, Pathfinder).

Hiro, D. (1973), *Black British, White British* (Harmondsworth, Penguin).

HM Treasury (1984), *Economic Progress Report*. November–December.

Home Office and Community Relations Commission (1977), *Urban Deprivation, Racial Inequality and Social Policy* (HMSO).

House of Commons, Environment Committee (1983), *The Problems of Management of Urban Renewal. Appraisal of the Recent Initiatives in Merseyside*, HC 18 i–iii (HMSO).

House of Commons, Home Affairs Committee (1981), Session 1980–1, *Racial Disadvantage*, HC 424–1, 20 July (HMSO).

House of Commons, Home Affairs Committee (1981), Session 1981–82, *Commission for Racial Equality*, HC 46–1, 23 November (HMSO).

HMSO (1975), *Race Relations and Housing* (Cmnd 6232).

HMSO (1977), *Policy for the Inner Cities,* (Cmnd 6845).

HMSO (1982), *The Government Reply to the First Report from the Home Affairs Committee, Session 1981–82, HC46–1: Commission for Racial Equality* (Cmnd 8547).

Humphry, D. and Ward, M. (1974), *Passports and Politics* (Harmondsworth, Penguin).

Husband, C. (ed.) (1982), *Race in Britain: Continuity and Change* (London, Hutchinson).

Indian Workers' Front (1976). *On the Lap-Dogs of Indian Fascism.*

Jacobs, B. (1979), *Public Policy and Local Interest Groups in Britain: Three Case-Studies*, University of Keele, Ph.D. thesis.

Jacobs, B. (1980), 'Wolverhampton Council for Community Relations: The Pattern of Participation', *Policy and Politics*, vol.8, no.4, pp.401–21.

Jacobs, B. (1982), 'Black Minority Participation in the USA and Britain', *Journal of Public Policy*, vol.2, pt.3, August, pp.237–62.

Jacobs, B. (1983), 'Coming to Terms with the System: Black Politics in the USA', *Politics*, vol.3, no.1, pp.14–21.

Jacobs, B. (1984a), 'Labour against the Centre – the Clay Cross Syndrome', *Local Government Studies*, vol.10, no.2, March/April, pp.75–87.

Jacobs, B. (1984b), 'Why Britain is slow to grasp Ethnic Needs', *Charity*, vol.1, issue 12, October, p.6.

Johnson, R. R. (1982), *Monitoring and Evaluation in a Corporate Philanthropy Program*, in Council on Foundations (1982), pp.62–4.

Jordan, A. G. (1981), 'Iron Triangles. Woolly Corporatism and Elastic Nets: Images of the Policy Process', *Journal of Public Policy*, vol.1, pt.1, February, pp.95–123.

Joshua, H., Wallace, T. and Booth, H. (1983), *To Ride the Storm. The 1980 Bristol 'Riot' and the State* (London, Heinemann).

Karn, V. (1983), 'Race and Housing in Britain: The Role of the Major Institutions', in Glazer and Young (1983), pp.162–83.

Katznelson, I. (1970), 'The Politics of Racial Buffering in Nottingham, 1954–68', *Race*, vol.11, no.4, April, pp.400–2.

Katznelson, I. (1973), *Black Men, White Cities* (London, Oxford University Press).

Keesing's Contemporary Archives (1981).

King, A. (ed.) (1978), *The New American Political System* (Washington DC, American Enterprise Institute).

Kirp, D. (1983), 'Elusive Equality: Race, Ethnicity and Education in the American Experience', in Glazer and Young (1983), pp.85–107.

Lambeth Inner-City Partnership (1982), *Working Group in Private Sector Investment, Final Report*.

Law, I. and Henfrey, J. (eds.) (1981), *A History of Race and Racism in Liverpool 1660–1950* (Merseyside Community Relations Council).

Lawless, P. (1981), *Britain's Inner Cities: Problems and Policies* (London, Harper and Row).

Lawrence, D. (1974), *Black Migrants: White Natives* (Cambridge, Cambridge University Press).

Layton-Henry, Z. (1980), *Immigration in Conservative Party Politics* (London, Macmillan).

Le Lohe, M. J. (1984), *Ethnic Minority Participation in Local Elections*, University of Bradford, School of Social Sciences Paper.

Levitan, S. A. (1980), *Programs in Aid of the Poor for the 1980s* (Baltimore, The Johns Hopkins University Press).

Levy, M. W. (1982), *Co-operation with the Public Sector*, in Council on Foundations (1982), pp.97–9.

Liebman, L. (1983), 'Anti-discrimination Law: Groups and the Modern State', in Glazer and Young (1983), pp.11–31.

Lindberg, L., Alford, R., Crouch, C. and Offe, C. (1975), *Stress and Contradiction in Modern Capitalism* (Lexington, Lexington Books).

Lindley, P. D. (1983), *The Merseyside Task Force* (Draft paper for Political Studies Association Workshop, Oxford Polytechnic).

Liverpool 8 Defence Committee (1981), 'Why Oxford Must Go', *Race and Class*, vol. 23, nos. 2–3, Autumn/Winter, p.223.

Local Initiatives Support Corporation (1982), *A Two-Year Report*, September 1 (New York).

Local Initiative Support (UK) (1983), *Local Initiative Support in the UK*.

London Borough of Islington (1977), *Allocation of Islington Housing to Ethnic Minorities*, Research Report 12, Directorate of Housing.

London Borough of Lambeth (1982), *A Guide to the Lambeth Inner City Partnership*.

London Borough of Lewisham (1980), *Black People and Housing in Lewisham*, Report to Housing Committee.

London Borough of Wandsworth (1979), *Report by the Director of Housing on Housing Department Ethnic Monitoring*, Report to Housing Committee.

London Enterprise Agency (LEntA) (1981), *The Private Sector and the Inner City*, June.

McCrudden, C. (1983), 'Anti-discrimination Goals and the Legal Process', in Glazer and Young (1983), pp.55–74.

Manley, J. F. (1983), 'Neo-Pluralism: A Class Analysis of Pluralism 1 and Pluralism 2', *The American Political Science Review*, vol. 77, no. 1, June, pp. 368–83.

Martin, R. (1983), 'Pluralism and the New Corporatism', *Political Studies*, vol. 31, no. 1, March, pp.86–102.

Mason, D. (1982), 'After Scarman, a Note on the Concept of "Institutional Racism"', *New Community*, vol. 10, no. 1, Summer, pp.38–45.

Matney, W. C. and Johnson, D. L. (1983), *America's Black Population: 1970 to 1982: A Statistical View*, US Department of Commerce, Bureau of the Census (US Government Printing Office, Washington, D.C.).

Merseyside Development Corporation (1981), *Initial Development Strategy*.

Midwinter, A. (1985), 'Liverpool – Analysing the City's Victory', *Local Government Chronicle*, 4 January, pp.18–19.

Miles, R. (1982), *Racism and Migrant Labour* (London, Routledge and Kegan Paul).

Miles, R. and Phizacklea, A. (1977), 'Class, Race, Ethnicity and Political Action', *Political Studies*, vol. 25, no. 4, December, pp.491–507.

Miles, R. and Phizacklea, A. (eds.) (1979), *Racism and Political Action in Britain* (London, Routledge and Kegan Paul).

Miles, R. and Phizacklea, A. (1984), *White Man's Country: Racism in British Politics* (London and Sydney, Pluto Press).

Miller, N. R. (1983), 'Pluralism and Social Choice', *The American Political Science Review*, vol.77, no.3, September, pp.734–47.

Mingione, E. (1977), 'Sociological Approach to Regional and Urban Development', *Comparative Urban Research*, vol.4, pp.21–38.

National Council for Civil Liberties (NCCL) (1980), *Southall, 23 April 1979: The Report of the Unofficial Committee of Enquiry* (published for the Committee by the NCCL).

National Council for Voluntary Organizations (NCVO) (1984), *Relations between the Voluntary Sector and Government: A Code for Voluntary Organizations*.

Newton, K. (1976), *Second City Politics* (Oxford, Clarendon Press).

O'Brien, D. J. (1975), *Neighbourhood Organization and Interest Group Processes* (Princeton, N. J., Princeton University Press).

Ollerearnshaw, S. (1983), 'The Promotion of Employment Equality in Britain', in Glazer and Young (1983), pp.145–61.

Olsen, J. P. (1976), *Organisational Participation in Government*. University of Bergen Paper.

Palmer, J. L. and Sawhill, V. I. (eds.) (1984), *The Reagan Record: An Assessment of America's Changing Domestic Priorities* (Cambridge, Mass., Ballinger Publishing Company). An Urban Institute study.

Parekh, B. (1983), 'Educational Opportunity in Multi-ethnic Britain', in Glazer and Young (1983), pp.108–23.

Pearson, D. G. (1981), *Race, Class and Political Activism: A Study of West Indians in Britain* (Westmead, Gower).

Pearson, G. (1983), *Hooligan: A History of Respectable Fears* (London, Macmillan).

Perkins, E. (1975), *Home is a Dirty Street: The Social Oppression of Black Children* (Chicago, Third World Press).

Pierson, J. (1982), *Options for the Level of Giving*, in Council on Foundations (1982), pp.111–14.

Piven, F. and Cloward, R. A. (1972), *Regulating the Poor* (New York, Vintage).

Political and Economic Planning (PEP) (1975), *Racial Minorities and Public Housing* (by D. Smith and A. Whalley).

Preston, M. B. (1982), 'Black Politics and Public Policy in Chicago: Self-Interest Versus Constituent Representation', in Preston *et al.* (1982), pp.159–86.

Preston, M. B., Henderson Jr, L. J. and Puryear, P. (eds.) (1982), *The New Black Politics: The Search for Political Power* (New York, Longman).

Race Relations Board (1977), *Comment on the Government's Consultation Paper on Records and Information Relating to the Housing of Members of Ethnic Groups*.

Rampton Report (1981), *Committee of Inquiry into the Education of Children from Ethnic Minority Groups: West Indian Children in our Society* (Cmnd 8273, HMSO).

Rees, T. (1979), 'Immigration Policies in the United Kingdom', in Husband, C. (ed.) (1982), pp.75–9.

Reeves, F. (1983), *British Racial Discourse* (Cambridge, Cambridge University Press).

Rex, J. (1970), *Race Relations in Sociological Theory* (London, Weidenfeld and Nicolson).

Rex, J. (1979), 'Black Militancy and Class Conflict', in Miles and Phizacklea (1979), pp.72–92.

Rex, J. and Moore, R. (1967), *Race Community and Conflict* (Oxford University Press, for Institute of Race Relations).

Rex, J. and Tomlinson, S. (1979), *Colonial Immigrants in a British City: A Class Analysis* (London, Routledge).

Richardson, J. J. and Jordan, A. G. (1979), *Governing under Pressure: The Policy Process in a Post-Parliamentary Democracy* (Oxford, Martin Robertson).

Runnymede Trust (1971), *A Runnymede Trust Summary of Census, 1971*.

Runnymede Trust (1975), *Race and Council Housing in London*.

Saunders, P. (1979), *Urban Politics: A Sociological Interpretation* (Harmondsworth, Penguin).

Sawyer, A. (1983), 'Black Controlled Business in Britain', *New Community*, vol.11, nos. 1–2, pp.55–62.

Scarman Report (1981), *The Brixton Disorders 10–12 April 1981. Report of an Inquiry by the Rt Hon. Lord Scarman OBE* (Cmnd 8427, HMSO).

Schmitter, P. C. (1974), 'Still the Century of Corporatism?', *Review of Politics*, vol.36, pp.85–131.

Scott, W. G. (1967), *Organisation Theory* (Homewood, Illinois, Richard D. Irwin, Inc.).

Sears, D. O. and McConahay, J. B. (1973), *The Politics of Violence: The New Urban Blacks and the Watts Riot* (Boston, Houghton Mifflin).

Simpson, A. (1981), *Stacking the Decks – A Study of Race, Inequality and Council Housing in Nottingham*, Nottingham and District Community Relations Council.

Sivanandan, A. (1981), 'From Resistance to Rebellion: Asian and Afro-Caribbean Struggles in Britain', *Race and Class*, vol. 23, nos. 2–3, Autumn 1981/Winter 1983, pp.111–52.

Skellington, R. (1980), *The Housing of Minority Groups in Bedford*, Open University Research Group.

Solomos, J. (1984), 'Black Youth and the 1980–81 Riots: Official Interpretations and Political Responses', *Politics*, vol. 4, no. 2, October, pp.21–7.

Steather, J. (1984), 'The Rate Cap fits Tight on the Voluntary Sector', *Charity*, vol. 1, issue 12, October, p.8.

Stewart, J. A. (1982), *The Value of Noncash Contributions*, in Council on Foundations (1982), pp.87–90 (Washington, D.C.).

Strange, J. H. (1973), 'Blacks and Philadelphia Politics: 1963–1966', in Ershkowitz and Zikmund (1973), pp.109–44.

Travers, T. (1984a), 'Ranking Local Authorities: the Lilley League Tables', *Public Money*, vol.3, no.4, March, pp.47–53.

Travers, T. (1984b), 'Assessing this year's RSG', *Local Government Chronicle*, 21–28 December, p.1429.

United Community Planning Corporation (Boston, Mass.) (1982), *Evaluation in Human Service Programs: A Practical Guide to Agency Costs and Benefits in Evaluation Research* (prepared by K. J. Paterson).

United Community Planning Corporation (Boston, Mass.) (1983), *Resource Management Diagnostic Tool*.

United Way of Massachusetts Bay (1983), *Allocations' 84*, 20 December.

Venner, M. (1981a), 'The Disturbances in Moss Side, Manchester', *New Community*, vol. 9, no. 3, Winter, pp.374–7.

Venner, M. (1981b), 'What the Papers said about Scarman', *New Community*, vol. 9, no. 3, Winter, pp.354–63.

Verity, Jr., C. W. (1982), *The Role of Business in Community Affairs*, in Council on Foundations (1982), pp.32–4.

Walker, J. (1982), 'The Origins and Maintenance of Interest Groups in America', *The American Political Science Review*, vol. 77, no. 2, June, pp. 390–406.

Walvin, J. (1973), *Black and White. The Negro and English Society 1555–1945* (London, Alan Lane, The Penguin Press).

Watkins, A. J. (1980), *The Practice of Urban Economics* (Beverly Hills and London, SAGE).

Williams, O. P. (1971), *Metropolitan Political Analysis* (New York, Free Press).

Wolverhampton Borough Council (1977a), *Consultation Paper on the Housing of Ethnic Minorities*, Housing Management Committee.

Wolverhampton Borough Council (1977b), *Report of Housing Manager to Housing Management Committee*, May.

Wolverhampton Council for Community Relations (WCCR) (1976), *Observations on a Fair Housing Policy for Wolverhampton*.

Wolverhampton Council for Community Relations (1977a), *Annual Report*.

Wolverhampton Council for Community Relations (1977b), *Minutes of Housing Seminar (Report to Housing Management Committee)*, April.

Wolverhampton Council for Community Relations (1980–1), *Annual Report*.

Wolverhampton Council for Community Relations (1982–3), *Annual Report*.

Young, K. (1983a), 'An Agenda for Sir George: Local Authorities and the Promotion of Racial Equality', *Policy Studies*, vol. 3, pt. 1, July, pp.54–70.

Young, K. (1983b), 'Ethnic Pluralism and the Policy Agenda in Britain', in Glazer and Young (1983).

Young, K. (1984), 'Local Authority Operations in Multi-Racial Areas: Providing for Organizational Development', *Local Government Studies*, vol.10, no.5, September/October, pp.12–21.

Young, K. and Connelly, N. (1981), *Policy and Practice in the Multi-Racial City* (Policy Studies Institute, Report no. 598).

Index

Tower Hamlets (London) – *cont.*
  Trades Council, 138; East London
    Conference against Racism (1976), 138
Toxteth (Liverpool), 9, 66, 87, 163
  1981 (July) disturbances, 136, 144
  1985 (October) disturbances, 190, 197,
    198
  Charles Wootton Centre, 145
  see also police; racial disturbances
Trade Unions, 29, 30, 86, 94, 166
  and the 'realities of power', 78
  and the representation of black interests,
    46, 48, 49, 94
  TUC, 139, 206, n.1
Transport and General Workers' Union,
  135
Travers, T., 14, 15
HM Treasury, 13, 14
Troyna, B., 131
Tyler, Gerald, 92
Tyneside, 11

Unemployment, 1, 9, 10, 16, 40, 94, 95,
    119, 157, 167, 177
  in Britain's major cities, 11, 155, 190; *see
    also* Birmingham, Liverpool,
    Manchester
  as a source of unrest, 11, 27–8, 32, 86,
    145
  youth, 10, 11, 12, 94, 127, 145, 167, 185,
    187
United Community Planning Corporation
  (US), 184, 207, n.4
United Kingdom Islamic Mission, 59
United Way of Massachusetts Bay (US),
  207, n.4
Uppal, Piara Singh, 203, n.3
Urban Development Grant, 156, 165
  Derelict Land and Urban Programmes,
    165
Urban League (US), 45
Urban Programme, 37, 73, 91, 101, 102,
    153–61, 167, 185
  administration, 155
  comparison with US community
    development, 153–4
  expenditure, 156, 157, 174, 185
  failings, 159, 160, 189
  group participation incentives, 158
  Inner Area Programme (IAP), 156;
    Official Steering Group (OSG), 156–7;
    Partnership Committee, 156
  and the needs of blacks, 37, 153, 155,
    160, 191
  objectives, 37, 155, 157
  Partnership Areas, 207, n.1
  Partnership Authorities, 156, 158, 169,
    186

Programme Areas, 156
Programme Authorities, 156, 158, 186
Traditional Urban Programme, 156, 157
  see also Birmingham; Lambeth; Liverpool;
    Merseyside; Wolverhampton

Venner, M., 145, 148, 149

Walker, Canon Charles, 196
Walker, J., 13
Wallace, T., 130
Waltham Forest (London), 106
  Waltham Forest Caribbean Council, 204,
    n.3
Walvin, J., 28, 29, 30
Wandsworth (London), 106, 125
  Wandsworth Latchkey Development
    Project, 204, n.3
Ward, M., 8
Ward, Robin, 177
Warwick, University of, Centre for Ethnic
  Relations, 207, n.1
Washington DC, 44
Watkins, A. J., 16
Webb, David, 191
Webb, Pauline, 206, n.1
West Indian and African Community
  Association in Deptford, 204, n.3
West Indian Family Agency, 53
West Indian Standing Conference, 35, 196,
  206, n.3
West Indian World, 149
West Midlands, 11, 12, 43, 75
  Caribbean Association, 61, 123, 205, n.9
  County Council, 12
Westminster (London), 106
White Papers
  *The Government Reply to the First Report
    from the Home Affairs Committee, Session
    1981–82: Commission for Racial
    Equality*, 90–1
  Immigration from the Commonwealth, 1965,
    35–6, 84
  Policy for the Inner Cities, 1977, 155
  Race Relations and Housing, 108
Whitelaw William, 39, 139, 144
Willesden, 206, n.1
Williams, O. P., 5
Wilson, Harold, 35
Winnie, R. E., 184
Wolverhampton, 17, 50–62 *passim*, 77, 99,
    100, 103–29 *passim*
  Anti-Racism Committee (WARC), 56, 57,
    60, 78, 124
  Asian Youth Project, 60
  Black Arrow Group, 60
  Borough Council, 111, 116, 128
  Corporation and the 'turban' issue, 47